Adorno's Poetics of Form

SUNY Series in Contemporary Continental Philosophy

Dennis J. Schmidt, editor

Adorno's Poetics of Form

JOSH ROBINSON

Published by State University of New York Press, Albany

© 2018 State University of New York

All rights reserved

No part of this book may be used or reproduced in any manner whatsoever without written permission. No part of this book may be stored in a retrieval system or transmitted in any form or by any means including electronic, electrostatic, magnetic tape, mechanical, photocopying, recording, or otherwise without the prior permission in writing of the publisher.

For information, contact State University of New York Press, Albany, NY
www.sunypress.edu

Library of Congress Cataloging-in-Publication Data

Names: Robinson, Josh (Lecturer in English Literature), author.
Title: Adorno's poetics of form / Josh Robinson.
Description: Albany, NY : State University of New York, 2018. | Series: SUNY series in contemporary Continental philosophy | Includes bibliographical references and index.
Identifiers: LCCN 2017030300 | ISBN 9781438469836 (hardcover) | ISBN 9781438469843 (pbk.) | ISBN 9781438469850 (ebook) Subjects: LCSH: Adorno, Theodor W., 1903–1969. | Form (Aesthetics) Classification: LCC B3199.A34 R63 2018 | DDC 193—dc23
LC record available at https://lccn.loc.gov/2017030300

10 9 8 7 6 5 4 3 2 1

Contents

Abbreviations of Works by Adorno	vii
Acknowledgments	xi
Introduction	1
Form	1
Adorno	8
Poetics	12
Philology	19
Constellation	24
1. Form and Content	27
Adorno and Heidegger: The Form of the Thing	28
'Parataxis'	33
Parataxis and Linguistic Form	39
Form as Sedimented Content	43
Parataxis in Adorno's reading of 'Der Einzige'	49
Consequences for Form and Content	56
2. Form and Expression	63
The Mediation of Form and Expression	67
Literary and Musical Expressionism	70
Expressionism and Surrealism	74
Kafka	81
Mimesis	85
Consequences for the Theory of Form	89

3. Form and Genre ... 95
   The Fraying of Borders ... 97
   The Genesis of the Forms ... 102
   Universal and Particular ... 107
   Nominalism and its Discontents ... 111
   Bourgeois Art and the Culture Industry ... 115
   The Novel as Form ... 121
   Theory of the Essay ... 127

4. Form and Material ... 133
   Material and Content ... 135
   Technique and the Mastery of Material ... 142
   Language and Poetry ... 149
   The Literary Manifestation of Form and Material ... 155
   Consequences for the Theory of Form ... 160

5. Artistic Form and the Commodity Form ... 163
   Social and Abstract Labor ... 166
   Abstraction and Exchange ... 170
   Mediation and Form ... 175
   Purposiveness, Communication, Language ... 180
   Poetry and Reconciliation ... 184
   Art Beauty and Natural Beauty ... 189
   Priority of the Object ... 194

Coda ... 201
   Lyric ... 201
   Engaging Form ... 207
   Beyond the New Formalism ... 212
   Conclusion ... 216

Notes ... 223

Works Cited ... 251

Index ... 263

Abbreviations of Works by Adorno

References to the *Gesammelte Schriften*, the *Nachgelassene Schriften*, and the English edition of the *Notes to Literature* consist of the relevant abbreviation followed by a volume number, a colon, and then the page number; references to other works consist of the abbreviation followed by the page number. Unless otherwise stated, all translations are my own; where possible I have also provided references to the corresponding pages of the English translations.

GS	*Gesammelte Schriften*, ed. by Rolf Tiedemann et al., 20 vols (Frankfurt am Main: Suhrkamp, 1972–86)
NS	*Nachgelassene Schriften*, ed. by Theodor W. Adorno Archiv (Frankfurt am Main: Suhrkamp, 1993–)
3SH	*Drei Studien zu Hegel*, *Gesammelte Schriften* 5 (Frankfurt am Main: Suhrkamp, 1971), 247–381
ÄT	*Ästhetische Theorie*, *Gesammelte Schriften* 7 (Frankfurt am Main: Suhrkamp, 1970)
B	*Berg. Der Meister des kleinsten Übergangs*, *Gesammelte Schriften* 13 (Frankfurt am Main: Suhrkamp, 1977), pp. 321–494
BPdM	*Beethoven. Philosophie der Musik. Fragmente und Texte*, ed. by Rolf Tiedemann, *Nachgelassene Schriften* 1.1 (Frankfurt/Main: Suhrkamp, 1993)
D	*Dissonanzen. Musik in der verwalteten Welt*, *Gesammelte Schriften* 14 (Frankfurt am Main: Suhrkamp, 1973), pp. 7–167
DA	(with Max Horkheimer) *Dialektik der Aufklärung. Philosophische Fragmente*, *Gesammelte Schriften* 3 (Frankfurt am Main: Suhrkamp, 1981)

	Abbreviations of Works by Adorno
E	*Eingriffe. Neun kritische Modelle, Gesammelte Schriften* 10.2 (Frankfurt am Main: Suhrkamp, 1977), pp. 455–594
EM	*Einleitung in die Musiksoziologie. Zwölf theoretische Vorlesungen, Gesammelte Schriften* 14 (Frankfurt am Main: Suhrkamp, 1973), pp. 169–433
M	*Mahler. Eine musikalische Physiognomik, Gesammelte Schriften* 13 (Frankfurt am Main: Suhrkamp, 1977), pp. 149–319
ME	*Zur Metakritik der Erkenntnistheorie, Gesammelte Schriften* 5 (Frankfurt am Main: Suhrkamp, 1971), pp. 7–245
MM	*Minima Moralia. Reflexionen aus dem beschädigten Leben, Gesammelte Schriften* 4 (Frankfurt am Main: Suhrkamp, 1980)
ND	*Negative Dialektik* (Frankfurt am Main: Suhrkamp, 1967)
NzL	*Noten zur Literatur, Gesammelte Schriften* 11 (Frankfurt am Main: Suhrkamp, 1974)
OL	*Ohne Leitbild, Gesammelte Schriften* 10.1 (Frankfurt am Main: Suhrkamp, 1977), pp. 289–453
P	*Prismen, Gesammelte Schriften* 10.1 (Frankfurt am Main: Suhrkamp, 1977), pp. 9–287
PnM	*Philosophie der neuen Musik, Gesammelte Schriften* 12 (Frankfurt am Main: Suhrkamp, 1975)
QF	*Quasi una fantasia, Gesammelte Schriften* 16 (Frankfurt am Main: Suhrkamp, 1978), pp. 249–540
S	*Stichworte. Kritische Modelle 2, Gesammelte Schriften* 10.2 (Frankfurt am Main: Suhrkamp, 1977), pp. 595–798
VW	*Versuch über Wagner, Gesammelte Schriften* 13 (Frankfurt am Main: Suhrkamp, 1977), pp. 7–148

Translations

AB	*Alban Berg: Master of the Smallest Link*, trans. by Christopher Hailey and Juliane Brand (Cambridge: Cambridge University Press, 1994)

Abbreviations of Works by Adorno

AE	*Against Epistemology: A Metacritique*, trans. by Willis Domingo (Cambridge: Polity, 2013)
Ashton	*Negative Dialectics*, trans. by E. B. Ashton (London; New York: Routledge, 1973)
AT	*Aesthetic Theory*, trans. by Robert Hullot-Kentor (London: Continuum, 1997)
BTPoM	*Beethoven: The Philosophy of Music*, trans. by Edmund Jephcott (Cambridge, UK: Polity, 2002)
CF	(with Hans Eisler), *Composing for the Films* (London and New York: Continuum, 2005)
CI	*The Culture Industry: Selected Essays on Mass Culture*, ed. by J. M. Bernstein (London: Routledge, 1973)
CM	*Critical Models: Interventions and Catchwords*, trans. by Henry W. Pickford (New York: Columbia University Press, 2005)
COL	*Can One Live after Auschwitz? A Philosophical Reader*, ed. by Rolf Tiedemann, trans. by Rodney Livingstone et al. (Stanford, CA: Stanford University Press, 2003)
DE	(with Max Horkheimer) *Dialectic of Enlightenment: Philosophical Fragments*, ed. by Gunzelin Schmid Noerr, trans. by Edmund Jephcott (Stanford, CA: Stanford University Press, 2002)
EoM	*Essays on Music*, ed. by Richard Leppert, trans. by Susan H. Gillespie et al. (Berkeley; Los Angeles; London: University of California Press, 2002)
H3S	*Hegel: Three Studies*, trans. by Shierry Weber Nicholsen (Cambridge, MA; London: MIT Press, 1993)
ISM	*Introduction to the Sociology of Music*, trans. by E. B. Ashton (New York: Seabury, 1976)
Jephcott	*Minima Moralia: Reflections from Damaged Life*, trans. by E. F. N. Jephcott (London: Verso, 1978)
Livingstone	*Quasi una Fantasia: Essays on Modern Music*, trans. by Rodney Livingstone (London; New York: Verso, 1998)
MMP	*Mahler: A Musical Physiognomy*, trans. by Edmund Jephcott (Chicago; London: University of Chicago Press, 1992)

NM	*Night Music: Essays on Music, 1928–1962*, ed. by Rolf Tiedemann, trans. by Wieland Hoban (London; New York; Calcutta: Seagull, 2009)
NtL	*Notes to Literature*, ed. by Rolf Tiedemann, trans. by Shierry Weber Nicholsen, 2 vols. (New York; Chichester, UK: Columbia University Press, 1991)
PMM	*Philosophy of Modern Music*, trans. by Anne G. Mitchell and Wesley V. Blomster (New York; London: Continuum: 2004)
SW	*In Search of Wagner*, trans. by Rodney Livingstone (London: New Left Books, 1981)
WWN	*Prisms*, trans. by Samuel and Shierry Weber [Samuel Weber and Shierry Weber Nicholsen] (Cambridge, MA: MIT Press, 1983)

Acknowledgments

For support institutional and material I am grateful to the School of English, Communication and Philosophy, Cardiff University; the President and Fellows of Queens' College, Cambridge; the Faculty of English, University of Cambridge; and the Peter Szondi–Institut für allgemeine und vergleichende Literaturwissenschaft and the Institut für deutsche und niederländische Philologie of the Freie Universität Berlin. Funding was provided by the Arts and Humanities Research Council and the Deutscher Akademischer Austauschdienst.

Claudia Albert, Sabine Mainberger, and Winfried Menninghaus enabled my visiting research at the FU Berlin and provided me with institutional homes. While there my research benefited immeasurably from the help of the staff at the Walter Benjamin Archive in Berlin: my particular thanks go to Michael Schwarz, Ursula Marx, and Gudrun Schwarz for their patience, advice and warm hospitality.

The development of this book during its long period of gestation has been greatly enhanced by the contribution of a great many friends, colleagues, and students, and I am profoundly grateful to all those, in Cambridge, Berlin, Cardiff, and elsewhere, whose critical insight has helped make those homes places of intense and warm-spirited discussion and debate. I should particularly like to thank Theodora Becker, Harry Gilonis, George Oppitz-Trotman, and Karen Robertson. The project has been shaped by many opportunities to present and discuss parts of it with a diverse range of audiences, and I am delighted to be able to thank the following, who enabled these exchanges to take place: Jonna Bornemark, Pete de Bolla, Tom Eyers, David Hillman, Jen Gaffney, Ted George, Aaron Hodges, Mary Jacobus, Anna Kornbluh, Rob Lehman, Mary Mullen, Liz Pender, Sara Upstone, Audrey Wasser, and John Wilkinson.

For his intellectual advice, guidance, and criticism through a large portion of the conception, writing, and revision of what became this book, I remain unspeakably and immeasurably grateful to Simon Jarvis.

Ian Patterson's mentorship, support, and encouragement long predate our discussions of this project during my time as a Research Fellow at Queens' College, Cambridge; for these I can hardly begin to apprehend the extent of my gratitude.

Several people at SUNY Press have eased the transition from manuscript to book, and I am particularly grateful to Andrew Kenyon, Chelsea Miller, and Denny Schmidt for their patience, advice, and insight. The two anonymous reviewers appointed by the Press offered exceptionally generous and incisive suggestions, and I should like to express my gratitude for the depth and subtlety of their engagement with the project, and their dedication to its improvement on its own terms. The responsibility for all errors remains of course my own.

In love and profound gratitude I dedicate this book to Eef.

Introduction

> An aesthetics of form is only possible as an act of breaking through aesthetics as the totality of that which stands under the spell of form. Whether art is even possible any more depends on this. The concept of form denotes the abrupt antithesis of art to empirical life, in which art's right to exist became uncertain. Art has as much chance as form, and no more.
>
> —ÄT 213/AT 141

Form

The resurgence of interest in form and formalism within literary criticism over the last two decades has brought with it a rethinking of the concept of literary form, and of the broader intellectual and social implications of formalism. This rethinking manifests itself in a distinct shift in the way in which the category of form has been deployed, the argumentative purposes to which it has been put, the kinds of question it has been used to address. This shift has two principal components. First, literary form has increasingly come to be thought in conjunction with rather than in opposition to social, historical, and political concerns. And second, critics have begun to turn to form in literature in order better to theorize and to intervene into the social, the historical, and the political. In this respect the renewed concern with form represents a counter-strategy to the New Historicist attempt to combat what its proponents viewed as the 'empty formalism' of the New Criticism 'by pulling historical considerations to the center stage of literary analysis'.[1] Form has come to be thought not in opposition to history but as itself historical—and, indeed, in some versions as a key to historical thinking.

In her 1997 *Formal Charges* Susan Wolfson develops a schema according to which form is inseparable from social and political concerns. She takes issue with Terry Eagleton's claim that literary form involves the recasting of 'historical contradictions into ideologically resolvable form',[2] arguing that literary form is not merely an epiphenomenon of social contradictions that are to be understood as wholly separate from it, but is rather 'always, inescapably implicated in practices that systematically form: tradition, convention'.[3] This explicit relationship of form to processes of forming sees form as a phenomenon that is shaped by historical and social dynamics, and in doing so insists on the possibility of an examination of form that is attentive to its historical and social implications, rather than taking place at the expense of their occlusion, an examination taken forward by Verena Theile and Linda Tredennick in their synthesizing project of 'uniformly reading for form, embracing cultural theory, and actively drawing on New Historicist methodologies'.[4]

Wolfson's book, along with her 2000 special issue of *Modern Language Quarterly* published under the rubric of 'Reading for Form', represents the founding moment of what has subsequently come to be known as the New Formalism in literary studies.[5] In her 2007 review essay on this emergent phenomenon, Marjorie Levinson distinguishes between an 'activist' and a 'normative' formalism: the former, which 'makes a continuum with new historicism', sees the return to form as a way of reinvigorating a historical and materialist approach to literature, while the latter, a 'backlash new formalism', seeks to restore through a return to form a strong demarcation between art and history.[6] Both strands thus share the common aim 'to recover for scholarship and teaching in English some version of their traditional address to aesthetic form', and 'to reinstate close reading both at the curricular center of our discipline and as the opening move, preliminary to any kind of critical consideration'.[7] As both Wolfson and Levinson observe, the two strands both respond, in different ways, to the situation that obtained in the wake of what George Levine identifies as 'the radical transformation of literary study' that took place in the 1980s and early 1990s—a situation in which literature is viewed as 'indistinguishable from other forms of language', and in which literary studies displayed 'a virtually total rejection of, even contempt for, "formalism"'.[8] It is a significant achievement of the New Formalism is that it is unproblematic for Carolyn Lesjak, herself critical of both the activist and the normative versions of New Formalism, to acknowledge that formalism need not 'be dispassionate nor eschew the political and the world outside the text'.[9]

This rethought formalism, then, differs from that which Wolfson rejects in that it does not involve the kind of privileging of form with respect to other concerns and sites of investigation of which she is wary. In particular, the recent developments that trade under the name of formalism are predicated on a reconfiguration of the relationships between form and history, formalism and historicism. Stephen Cohen sites his 'historical formalism' within the context of New Historicism and its legacies, not only charting the unpredictable interaction of literary forms 'with each other and with other cultural discourses', but also seeking 'to explore the variety of these interactions, mutually implicating literature's formal individuation and its historical situation in order to illuminate at once text, form, and history'.[10] For scholars such as Cohen, formalism consists not in an attention to form at the expense of concerns with history and society, but as a means of deepening our understanding of the latter, and of their relationship to form. In this version of formalism form is thus conceived not in opposition to history, but as itself deeply historical: 'the historicity of form emphasizes the particularity of literary discourse, insisting not only that literary texts have historical routes and functions, but that they do so by virtue of their discourse-specific forms and conventions as well as their extratextual or interdiscursive ideological content'.[11] Form here is conceived as enabling historicism to do its work more rigorously: a historicism that is not informed by formalism fails when measured against its own aspirations.

If the new formalism appears to be directed against formalism itself, this is in part because there are two different and in many respects incompatible concepts at stake, both referred to by the term formalism: one the investigation of forms and formal properties, the other the focus on form to the exclusion of almost everything else. This is perhaps clearest in Fredric V. Bogel's observation that 'formalism as a technique of textual analysis—"close reading," as it is often called—has never disappeared but continues to function in a variety of modes and contexts even apart from those we might term formalism'.[12] This new formalism does not consist in a dedication to form as an end in itself, but is rather a means pursued for the sake of investigating what form can tell us: in Anna Kornbluh's terms it is 'a kind of "social close reading" blending deconstructive techniques and the best historicist impulses to explore the intellectual and political force of literary forms'.[13] If the old formalism left itself open to the criticism that its dedication to form came at the expense of a concern with the social and the political, the new frequently describes itself as willing to subordinate its investigation of form to these social and political concerns.

This new formalism, then, is a formalism understood as technique or investigative procedure, which explicitly rejects the self-imposed limits of the introspective old formalism—limits which were themselves never applied entirely consistency. The rise of the new formalism is thus in a sense a reversal of W. J. T. Mitchell's observation that formalism 'continues to rear its head, even when most fervently disavowed':[14] the new formalism asserts itself most strongly when it denies or seeks to transcend the limits of the old. In many respects what has emerged is a version, expressed in different terms, of Geoffrey Hartman's skepticism as to whether the mind can ever 'get beyond formalism without going through the study of forms'.[15] What is new about the new formalism is in many respects less its attempt to revive an attention to form as a set of analytical procedures than the readiness with which it characterizes itself as a formalism.

Perhaps the most ambitious and extensively formulated account of a formalism that is oriented toward society, and toward the rôle of literature in both understanding and attempting to reshape society for the better, is Caroline Levine's 'strategic formalism', a project developed over the course of a decade, starting with her 2006 programmatic call for a new method in cultural studies, and finding its most complete expression so far in her 2015 *Forms*.[16] Indeed, to describe Levine's as a society-oriented formalism runs the risk of understating the distinctiveness of her contribution, since its orientation toward society is by no means merely an as it were incidental attribute of her formalism; form is rather the category through which she retheorizes the relationship between the work of literature and the transformation of society. Acknowledging that she deploys 'the terms "form" and "formalism" in unusually capacious ways', her strategic formalism both acknowledges and draws on 'the very heterogeneity at the heart of form's conceptual history', and seeks to extend 'formalist insights to make the case that social hierarchies and institutions can themselves be understood as *forms*', at which point they lend themselves to investigation by means of formalist analytical techniques.[17] In this sense formalism is a means not only of investigating aspects of literature, culture, and society in a manner that considers their mutual implication, but also of theorizing the relationship between them: treating both literary work and social hierarchy as form allows them to be viewed through the same investigative lens.

If this maneuver seems to conflate under a single investigative concept heterogeneous objects of investigation that are fundamentally different in kind or even incompatible, then this is a risk that Levine is willing to take for the sake of what can be revealed by bringing literary, cultural, and social forms together. Indeed, she explicitly praises the benefits of 'formalist abstraction', arguing that it is precisely '*because* they have been formalized, disciplined into recognizable, repeatable oppositions' that invidious social hierarchies, can be identified, generalized, and criticized.[18] In this respect the subsequent development of her formalism seeks to account for her claim that it is 'time to think about culture in terms of its forms'.[19] At the heart of her conviction that form represents a new way of 'connecting large and small, social flows and artistic objects' is a commitment to a conception of form that is sufficiently adaptable and scalable that it enables the urgent reconfiguration of the relationship between the literary and the social.[20]

Forms represents Levine's most thoroughly formulated attempt both to make and to account for such connections. She focuses on four particular kinds of form (the whole, rhythm, hierarchy, and network of the book's subtitle), and theorizes them as at once plural (such that they are both distinct from and able to contain one another), overlapping and intersecting, portable across both space and time, and historically and politically situated.[21] In doing so she not only charts the interactions between literary and cultural forms across changing social and political situations, but also offers an account of a way in which a conception of literary and cultural forms might enable both a more sophisticated theorization of and an emancipatory intervention into particular social forms. In order to do so she breaks with the conception of poetic meter as something akin to 'imprisonment and containment', arguing instead that we should 'consider meter as another of these social rhythms, not an epiphenomenal effect of social realities, but capable itself of exerting or transmitting power'.[22]

I agree with Levine that something goes missing when we conceive of what we think of as poetic and literary form—the sonorous, material, non- (or not only) linguistic, and non- (again, or not only) signifying elements of literature—as incidental or merely epiphenomenal of social reality, and that this form (and these forms) have themselves the capacity to exert and transmit power. As a result I also share her conviction that theorizing form has the potential to identify means of intervening into the social world. Where my project differs from hers is in my focus on the question of why it is that we think of all these apparently heterogeneous things as form, and on the implications of doing so, in particular for our understanding of the relationships between what we think of as literary, cultural, social, and economic forms. That is, I do not start from the presupposition that form is the best way to make connections between social flows and artistic objects, or that poetic meter is necessarily best thought of as 'another of these social rhythms'—that the aesthetic, or the formal, are subsets of the social. Rather, I seek to attend to form with an eye not only to exploring the analytical potential offered by the concept, but also to considering what it can efface as well as what it can illuminate. I do so by means of close analysis, explication, and critique of one of the most sustained and resonant engagements with form: the writings on literature and art of Theodor W. Adorno.

In evaluating the analytical and socio-political potential of form my approach thus aspires to formulate a critique not only of the social conditions into which form might enable an intervention, but also of the category of form and both the range and the limitation of the resources it offers. I am concerned, that is, not only with the social and political agency of form, as well as its intellectual implications, but also with how the way in which the concept of form is constituted relates to, encapsulates and expresses different philosophical and social problems. In examining, elucidating, and evaluating Adorno's deployment of form in his writings on literature, I thus attend not only to the agency of form both within a single work and within the frameworks with which we approach its analysis, but also to the questions of what characterizes form as such, how form is formed, why we think of it as form—of why it is that we think of such things as wholes, rhythms, hierarchies, networks as forms, and of the implications of doing so. In doing so I offer not only a particular theory of form, but a theory of form of a particular kind. This study aspires to be a poetics of form in the dual sense not only that it analyzes the contribution of form to a poetics, but that it also seeks to account for the particular conceptual work it carries out—for how the concept of form functions within the analysis of literary art and artworks.

In doing so I address—and seek to rectify—a situation that has been identified on multiple occasions since the recent renewal of interest in form. Reflecting on the new formalism in 2007, Levinson observed that 'despite the proliferation in these essays of synonyms for form (e.g., genre, style, reading, literature, significant literature, the aesthetic, coherence, autonomy), none of the essays puts redefinition front and center'.[23] A year earlier Simon Jarvis had noted that the philosophy of literary form 'is still in its infancy—so much so that it is even unclear whether "form" is the right word for what is to be discussed'.[24] This extended infancy, out of which we have not yet developed—possibly one of the longest on record, depending on exactly which moment is identified as that of its birth[25]—consists in the fact that for all the renewed interest in poetic and literary form, there exist only the earliest signs of a tendency to reflect on precisely what constitutes the formal aspects of a literary work, and why these should be termed form rather than anything else.

It is striking that even those works that recognize the need for this kind of reflection on concerns of definition and terminology frequently avoid doing just that. Levine's deliberately capacious expansion of the category of form to incorporate phenomena from literature, culture, and society is a methodological presupposition rather than a consequence of conceptual reflection. Angela Leighton begins her 2007 study of the implications and legacy of the term form with the three-word question 'What is form?', but while she offers several persuasive accounts of the significance or agency of what she identifies as form within particular poems, there is no reflection on whether and why it is appropriate to consider these phenomena under the rubric of form, or on the implications of doing so. This is perhaps best illustrated by her tantalizingly aporetic conclusion that form 'is the sense of nothing', a persuasive contention that form exists within a particular kind of subjective experience of or in response to a poem, but one which leaves unaddressed the question as to whether and to what extent it is appropriate to identify particular aspects of poems as form or formal.[26]

Verena Theile's prologue to her and Linda Tredennick's *New Formalisms and Literary Theory* conceives itself as a response to Levinson's diagnosis that 'new formalism is better described as a movement rather than a theory or a method', a response which seeks 'to provide the kind of theorizing that [Levinson] claims New Formalism is lacking'.[27] Theile sees the kind of theorizing, redefining work that Levinson observes is missing from the new formalism as precisely 'what we attempt to do here', and offers a further determination of that aspiration:

> Reading form as ideologically charged, as anything but 'innocent,' *New Formalisms and Literary Theory* suggests that a text's formal features, its aesthetics, in close conjunction with cultural context, convey a politically and historically significant literary experience that is both intentional and affective.[28]

This gloss reveals that rather than being the promised retheorization, *New Formalisms and Literary Theory* in fact proceeds on the basis of the assumption that we know, unproblematically, as if self-evidently, what a text's formal features are, and that they are identifiable with its aesthetics—and, for that matter, that we know what a text is. Nor does it consider the implications of bringing together these features under this particular concept (or indeed under any single concept), or imagine any potential disadvantages of doing so, such as expressed in Ewan James Jones's acknowledgment that conceiving of the evident components of verse technique as formal 'brings with it some of the obvious objections that arrive with "organic unity", and deflects attention from the manner in which such expressive features are constituted'.[29] It is precisely with questions such as these that this book is concerned. By critically examining Adorno's wide-ranging and fecund writings on form in literature, it asks whether so many manifoldly different phenomena can be brought together under a coherent concept of form, and evaluates the investigative potential of doing so.

Adorno

The recent revival of interest in form within literary and cultural studies is in many respects a testament to the legacy of Adorno's writings on art and literature, but their influence is neither self-evidently apparent nor straightforward. Levinson has drawn attention to the somewhat uneasy influence of Adorno on the new formalism, observing that 'Adorno is the prototype' for the 'reinvigorated formalism', the emergence of which is charted by Ellen Rooney (an essay in which Adorno's name is not mentioned).[30] And yet there has not been a fully developed account of Adorno's own deployment of the concept of form, or of his writings on literature, or of the implications for the study of literature of his interrogation of the concepts of aesthetics: as Jarvis observes, the engagement with Adorno in Anglophone writings on poetry 'has too often been limited to a short radio talk he once gave about lyric poetry'.[31] W. J. T. Mitchell attributes to Adorno 'a kind of formalism in the autonomous work of art as a salutary negation of the empirical reality it wants to contest': this formalism has little to do with Adorno's writings on literary or poetic form, and is instead derived from his account of the committed work of art.[32] Similarly, Robert Kaufman's account of 'negatively capable dialectics' is less an account of what an engagement with Adorno could offer to the rethinking of poetics, and more an exploration of some of the relationships and compatibilities between poetics as practiced by Helen Vendler and the 'foundational aspects of the Marxian critical aesthetics most frequently identified with Adorno'.[33] In the diverse essays that constitute the new formalism, Adorno seems to serve as a figure who enables a certain kind of formalism or aestheticism to be bolstered with sufficient Marxist credentials to inoculate it against historicist objections or to subordinate it to a politically inflected historicism. As Levinson recognizes, there is a whiff of revisionism about this: she observes how Adorno 'surfaces over and over again in these essays as the lost leader of new historicism linked with variously Louis Althusser, Pierre Macherey, Fredric Jameson, and T. J. Clark and as the bridge to a *new* (activist) formalism'.[34]

The significance—or at least, the potential significance—of Adorno's writings to the understanding of literary and aesthetic form has been evident for some time. Discussing form in her introduction to Adorno's thought, Gillian Rose draws attention to the ambiguity of the 'notion of form', a result of its ability to refer, on the one hand, 'to musical genres' (such that 'the analysis of form would examine their relation to kinds of societies and their relation to social life, such as liturgical and secular music, or opera and chamber music'), and, on the other hand, 'to the internal organisation of music, to melody, harmony, and even the tonic system itself'.[35] Moreover, as she acknowledges, these two apparently incompatible 'notions of form are not always distinct'.[36] Fredric Jameson's 1971 study of form within primarily German-language Hegelian Marxism recognizes the importance of Adorno within this tradition. However, what Jameson presents as an account of Adorno's contribution to what he terms 'the specifically Marxist form of literary analysis' is in fact not primarily a discussion of literature, let alone of literary form: indeed, the nature of Jameson's concern with form becomes clear within the opening pages of the first chapter on Adorno, in which he argues that the 'sociology of culture is [. . .] first and foremost [. . .] a *form*'.[37] In the few concrete analyses of manifestations of aesthetic form Jameson is concerned with musical rather than literary form, and discusses neither the suitability of applying a concept of musical form in discussions of literature, nor the details of this concept of musical form itself.

However, Adorno's deployment of the concept of form in relation to music has been examined considerably more thoroughly. Form is a central and recurring theme of Max Paddison's 1993 study of Adorno's aesthetics of music, itself a reworked version of his earlier doctoral thesis on the concepts of musical form and material.[38] Paddison discusses musical form primarily through its opposition to material, focusing in his 'material theory of form' on 'form at the level of the pre-formed musical material, and form at the level of the individual musical work'.[39] In doing so he insists on the wider social implications of musical form: for example, in his analysis of the concept of 'social function' he notes that Adorno 'tends to stress the *origins* of genres and forms like the symphony and sonata in the *divertisse-*

ments, serenades and operatic overtures of the *style galant*, and offers an account of Adorno's argument that 'it was through its *form* that art opposed coercion, not through direct intervention'.[40] Paddison's use of form to refer at once to generic and stylistic attributes of music on the one hand, and to Adorno's insistence on the artwork's radical distinction from what is not on the other, begins to reflect the plurality of the uses to which Adorno puts the term. Major concerns of mine in this book are to account for the relationship between these distinct and often apparently contradictory senses of form and to draw attention to and theorize ways in which they underlie some of the tensions (whether explicit or unspoken) with respect to form and formalism within many recent discussions.

Paddison's study was among the first written in English—and remains among the most detailed—to attend to the specifics of Adorno's writings on artworks. At the same time, the extent to which engagement with the posthumously published *Aesthetic Theory* might require some of Adorno's earlier writings on music to be rethought has not been fully investigated. Indeed, Gerald L. Bruns has observed something like the opposite tendency in his criticism of what he has termed the 'common practice among Adorno scholars to fold *Aesthetic Theory* back into his earlier writings on modern music'.[41] This is perhaps symptomatic of a broader neglect of the implications of his interrogation and critique of the concepts of aesthetics (and, albeit to a lesser extent, of those of metaphysics) within certain strands of the English-language reception of his thought: these include the presentation of his writings on art and artworks as a consequence or even application of his social and political thought in those works in which he is presented primarily as a critical social theorist, and the marginalization of *Aesthetic Theory* in some of the works in which he is situated within the traditions of German idealism and its Hegelian–Marxist legacy.[42]

Adorno's writings on literature have been subjected to considerably less attention than his aesthetics of music. This is in part because his contribution to an aesthetics of literature consists for the most part in a collection of often enigmatic sketches, fragments, and essays, in part because of the ways in which his work stubbornly refuses to comply with the division of intellectual labor within academic departments that are concerned with the interpretation and analysis of literature. This is a tendency to which I therefore seek to provide something of a corrective in this book, and in doing so to address ways in which the consideration of literary artworks further complicates some of the theories that underlie Adorno's aesthetics of music—these complications frequently arise in consideration of the conjunction between art and language within the work of literature, including with respect to the distinction between literary and nonliterary uses of language, and the way in which the linguistic work of art further complicates Adorno's theory of the resemblance to language of artworks, and of music in particular. Adorno's œuvre sits uneasily between literary criticism and literary theory. Despite Jarvis's convincing case that 'Adorno is more aptly described as a philosophical literary critic than as a literary theorist', certain concepts or phrases from a relatively small range of his essays and radio talks have frequently been pressed into service of the analysis of literary texts.[43] Similarly, Robert Kaufman has warned of the danger of coopting Adorno on behalf of what he terms the 'critique of aesthetic ideology', which 'has at times seemed to make itself synonymous with Marxian or Marxian-inflected criticism in general', a critique which 'has assumed an identity between the *aesthetic* [. . .] and the process of *ideological deformation* of the material, the real, the sociopolitical'.[44] In contrast to this tendency, in this book I attend to the different ways in which Adorno uses form to analyze and theorize literary works, and to formulate their wider intellectual and socio-political implications.

The only monograph in English dedicated to Adorno's writings on literature is Ulrich Plass's 2006 study of the *Notes to Literature*, which seeks to examine some of the philosophical consequences of these writings, particularly in terms of the relationship between language and history. As I have observed elsewhere, Plass's study applies to Adorno's writings on literature conclusions drawn from his (earlier) writings on language without fully attending to the ways in which the investigation of literature might require that these conclusions be reconsidered, relying at times on a crude distinction between literary and colloquial language, and leaves unexplored the relationship between the *Notes to Literature* and a broader Adornian aesthetics of literature, such as in the conflation of the Kantian aesthetic judgment with Adorno's apparently broader categories of aesthetic or artistic experience.[45] There has been rather more attention paid to Adorno's literary aesthetics within individual essays. Chief among these are those collected in the 2006 collection *Adorno and Literature*, an attempt to take seriously Adorno's 'insistence on the possibility of making *value* judgements of literary works', judgments which are however themselves hostile both to what Cunningham and Mapp resonantly term the 'formalism' of traditional aesthetics and to the 'idea of an invariant or limitlessly applicable method through which literary works might be read'.[46]

This book seeks not only to pursue this tendency, but also to examine and reflect on the conceptual frameworks according to which such judgments can be made. In doing so I seek to take seriously Adorno's insistence that aesthetics 'is not applied philosophy, but philosophical in itself' (ÄT 140/ AT 91), and to make a case for the mutual implication of philosophical reflection and literary criticism, by means of the investigation of the terms and concepts with which we make such judgments about literature. My aim in doing so is not so much to develop an application of an Adornian aesthetics for the study of literature as to investigate this mutual implication by means of the interrogation of the deployment of the concepts of artistic, literary, and poetic form. I thus seek not only to site Adorno's writings on literature within the context of his aesthetics, but also to explore their consequences for his philosophy as a whole, and for our understanding of the relationship between literature and the wider world in which it is made and experienced. I am concerned, that is, both with the ways in which Adorno's writings on literature require a rethinking of other parts of his œuvre, and with the question of what the examination of the concepts with which we analyze literature might tell us about life more broadly.

Poetics

This chimes with the concerns of a growing body of work with the modes of knowledge production within the study of literature, with its broader intellectual and social consequences and implications. In some cases this work has involved methodological reflection on the methods or concepts involved in the study of literature; in some (not necessarily other) it has involved a focus on the relationship between literature and philosophy. In discussing Martin Heidegger's contribution to a potential reconfiguration of the ways in which we think about and with poetry, David Nowell Smith has made a persuasive case that what appears as Heidegger's dismissal of the traditions of aesthetics and poetics in fact turns out to be 'the catalyst for a far more developed thinking of precisely those phenomena with which "aesthetics" is concerned: form, but also the categories of beauty, artistic technique, the relation between artwork and equipment, the experience of an artwork, among others'.[47] This thinking toward which Nowell Smith points is 'a thinking of language and poetry beyond the limits of poetics', limits which 'belong to the very "essence" of poetics as a mode of questioning'; he finds within Heidegger's writings on poetry an impetus to 'rethink the basic questions of poetics' from the perspective that 'poetry's salient feature is its treatment of its language as medium, and as a medium that can open up a singular space for an encounter with beings, and thereby shape the ways in which we experience and comprehend the world'.[48]

For Nowell Smith, Heidegger's well-known dismissal of the concepts of aesthetics—among them form, beauty, metaphor—as 'metaphysical' is in fact a way of rethinking the phenomena in question, at and beyond the limits of the concepts that name them.[49] My point of departure in this study is not the dismissal of a concept, but rather the tensions that underlie the complexity of its deployment. I nonetheless share with Nowell Smith an orientation toward the potential for its reconfiguration that may lie within these tensions, and toward its implications for the ways in which we think about and with and through poetry. I thus attempt to examine the implications of the way in which Adorno reflects on, deploys, and alludes to one particular concept of aesthetics and poetics in his discussions of literature in particular, and of art and artworks in general—that of form. It is worth acknowledging that Adorno does not subject, either in *Aesthetic Theory* or his diverse writings on works of art, the concepts of aesthetics to anything like the same degree of explicit interrogation and critique as he does the concepts of metaphysics in *Negative Dialectics*. But as becomes increasingly clear through this study, this is at least in part because of the complexity in the content and structure of these concepts, a complexity which Adorno sees in Kant's *Critique of Judgment*, which, he argues, 'is revolutionary insofar as it, without going beyond the boundary of the older aesthetics of effect, at the same time restricts it by means of immanent critique' (ÄT 22/AT 10).

The critical potential of the *Critique of Judgment* is to an extent visible in Rodolphe Gasché's rethinking of the implications of the Kantian insistence that beauty 'should properly pertain merely to form'.[50] Gasché takes issue with what he terms the 'aestheticist and formalist interpretation of Kantian aesthetics', according to which beautiful form 'consists in the harmonious arrangement of parts into a whole, and has no other end than the pleasure it stirs in the beholder'.[51] He argues that Kant's separation of his conception of beautiful form from anything moral or sensible in fact breaks with the Aristotelian opposition of form to matter, that 'the concept of mere form encountered in the Third Critique [. . .] is anything but a free-floating form'.[52] This form, although it depends on (beautiful) objects, does not belong to the object, but is 'the form only of the organization of the faculties involved in a judgment of taste'.[53] It is not simply that form is no longer to be thought of as consisting in the explicitly harmonious arrangement of parts and whole, but that form, in this understanding, is shifted away from the object (whether the artwork or a natural occurrence), and into the subject who makes an aesthetic judgment. Similarly, Günter Figal has drawn attention to some of the ways in which the concepts of Kantian aesthetics frequently express more than they claim to, observing with Adorno that 'the Kantian analysis of the experiential side of aesthetic experience is always already geared toward understanding that which is experienced'.[54] I share with these accounts the conviction that the experience of works of art cannot but involve cognitive reflection and critique.

This, however, is not to argue for the subordination of the sensible to the supersensible. In this respect I share with Miguel de Beistegui a sense of the importance of the sensible in its own right and on its own terms, which he sets out in opposition to the tradition of what he terms the metaphysical aesthetics of mimesis that runs from Plato to Adorno, which remains confined within the space that stretches between the sensible and the supersensible. For de Beistegui, Adorno represents 'a particularly interesting, *limit* case' within this metaphysical tradition, 'insofar as his aesthetic theory throws mimesis into a state of permanent *crisis*, yet one that, in the end, he does not manage to extricate himself from, such is his unquestioned commitment to the very terms, concepts, and metaphysical framework that produced the theory in the first place'.[55] What de Beistegui reads as Adorno's unquestioned commitment to the terms and concepts of the aesthetic tradition I see as their immanent critique: in this respect I share with de Beistegui a concern with the limits of aesthetics—both the limits that Adorno investigates, and the limits of his thinking. I thus seek not only to make explicit the implications of the immanent critique that is at some points explicitly carried out and at other points implied by Adorno's aesthetics, but also to point or even clear the way for work that examines the implications of poetry for the ways in which we live in the world.

At the heart of de Beistegui's rethinking of aesthetics beyond the metaphysics of mimesis is his radically reconfigured understanding of metaphor as the 'image that opens up the time and space of art, the timespace of the hypersensible'.[56] Metaphor, according to this reconfiguration, is not 'reducible to a mere trope', not 'a trope amongst others, or perhaps the trope that encompasses all tropes', but understood rather as 'something altogether different—not a mere rhetorical figure, but a clue to "how things work"'.[57] Rather than being a trope, it is a way of thinking, an operation that consists 'in the ability to recognise something in something else, and see the beauty of an object in a different object'—'the operation that reveals or opens up that space and time, hidden or folded in the space and time of ordinary perception and cognition'.[58] This radically expanded and to an extent aporetic deployment of metaphor, which is 'drawn from the works of Proust and Hölderlin', is an indication of the extent to which literature—and the ways in which we understand and think with it—seem to us to hold a kind of hidden key to an as yet unlocked means of understanding the world.[59] As such it seems to reflect a sense that poetry represents a hitherto untapped and not exhaustively investigated resource for the rethinking not only of its own study, or even of aesthetic experience more generally, but also of the ways in which we know our worlds.

An exploration of one such poetic rethinking is Charles Bambach's reconfiguration of justice through an expanded sense of poetic measure: expanded beyond the metrical and understood 'as the "taking" of measure (*Maß-nahme*)', with the Heideggerian twist that it is strictly speaking 'less a "taking" than a *releasing* or a *letting-come* of that which cannot be thought in advance'.[60] This reconfigured justice, based on the affinities between 'the measured pacing of musical and poetic meter, in the medical practice of moderate intervention, in the archer's attunement to the tautness and amplitude of the bow, in the interpreter's reception to the mystery and paradox of the oracle', involves an attunement to that which is unknown and outside the subject, a 'middle-voiced rendering of justice' in which therefore '[b]eing as *dike* lets *adikia* into its order just as, in good middle-voiced reciprocity, *adikia* lets *dike* order it'.[61] The investigation of the resonances of the poetic (but, at the same time, never only or narrowly poetic) concept of measure reveals ways in which poetry not only reminds us of the limits to our conceptual and propositional ways of thinking, but also opens up ways of transcending these limits.

This brings into the foreground the question of how the study of poetry should relate to its object, of what poetics has to learn from poetry. One recent account of the specific contribution of poetry to its own theorization is Forest Pyle's investigation of what he terms a 'radical aestheticism', characterized as 'the experience of a *poiesis* that exerts such a pressure on the claims and workings of the aesthetic that it becomes (or reveals itself to be) a kind of black hole from which no illumination is possible'.[62] This experience is enabled by but not identical with what is variously termed a 'poetic reflection on the workings and effects of the aesthetic' and 'a powerful and sustained poetic reflection on and engagement with aesthetic experience'.[63] Similarly, Vittorio Hösle investigates the phenomenon of self-instantiation within accounts of literary aesthetics and poetics, departing from the observation that instructional handbooks concerned with the writing of poetry can themselves 'be formulated in verses and can thus exemplify that which they teach'.[64] For Hösle 'one of the secrets of the success of *Aesthetic Theory*' consists in the fact that it 'itself expresses that understanding of art' that is encapsulated in its writings on poetry, while he argues that although 'the rhetorical-poetical means of *Aesthetic Theory* in no way constitute proof of the consistency of Adorno's undertaking', they nonetheless 'show that Adorno had a sense for the poeticization of poetics'.[65] My investigation of Adorno's poetics is thus concerned both with his investigations of poetry and with the poetics of his own writings, in particular at the points where they themselves begin to resemble poetry.

I have recently drawn attention to the sheer variety of uses to which the term poetics is put, both within and beyond literary studies, and to the range of kinds of work that the term is asked to carry out.[66] This becomes particularly clear when comparing the conceptions of poetics, explicitly formulated or otherwise, with which these and other studies work, which range from the simple, even simplistic, to the diffuse and elusive. For Hösle poetics is unproblematically definable as the subset of aesthetics in general that is concerned with poetry in particular;[67] Nowell Smith charts how the conception of poetics rejected by Heidegger is where the disciplines of the history of literature and aesthetics converge.[68] John Arthos, in contrast, in his account of Gadamer's poetics, uses the term to signal a break from these very disciplinary conventions, clarifying that his 'use of the term poetics rather than aesthetics is meant to mark the distinction between Gadamer's theory of the work of art and the aspects of disciplinary aesthetics from which he wanted to distance himself':[69]

> The great contrast between Gadamer's poetics and disciplinary aesthetics is bound up in the idea of the work as an ontological category—the work's structure is so interwoven with the structures of the lives that engage it, that process, product, history, and identity become parasitic on and inextricable from one another. If we define the work by this capacity for metamorphosis, we have redefined it as its tradition, but tradition as much rupture as continuity, as much repression as enlightenment.[70]

My approach in this book is neither to seek to make or to assert a radical break from the disciplines of aesthetics or poetics, however construed, nor to assume their traditions and concepts as if unquestioned, but rather critically to examine the resources presented by one such concept. In doing so I seek to investigate the different ways in which the intertwining of process, product, history, and identity to which Arthos refers is revealed—and indeed obscured—by the concept of form and those against and in relation to which it is defined: in particular its relations to content, expression, genre, and material. In this respect my aim is to illuminate form from a variety of different angles in order critically to account for the range of its argumentative and analytical power.

I have referred elsewhere to what I term the pliability of the term 'poetics', the fact that it can be deployed without objection (and frequently without comment) for a wide range of (sometimes mutually contradictory) purposes, and that there seems to be something about it that enables people to resort to it in order to refer or point to matters that elude explanation.[71] This is in part because of the ability of the term to combine what I have tentatively identified as the objective and the subjective aspects of poetics, in which the former refers to the implicit principles that underlie the construction of a given body of work, the latter to reflection on the process of investigation of poetry (or to the making explicit of these implicit objective principles).[72] Indeed, Bruns's definition of (objective) poetics as poetry's frequently implicit 'concepts or theories of itself' already contains the beginnings of the link to the subjective experience, reflection on and formulation of these concepts: the experience of poetry frequently contains within itself something that seems to go beyond the bounds of what we think of as experience—the beginnings of a theorization of or reflection on the implications of that experience, or a spur to such a reflection.[73] A theme that recurs throughout this book is the adaptability of form such that it can refer at once to a manifestation of the activity of the artistic subject and to an objective force encountered by that subject as a constraint or limit. In analyzing and theorizing the relationship between subject and object, the relationship of poetics to poetry, I seek to proceed in the light of Werner Hamacher's claim that '[p]oetry is *prima philologia*', 'the most uncompromising philology'—that reading and reflecting on poetry is a stronger or perhaps clearer example of the truth of Hamacher's claim that 'philology must already be practiced by anyone who speaks, anyone who thinks or acts by speaking, and anyone who attempts to bring to light and indeed to interpret his and others' actions, gestures, and pauses'.[74]

Pyle's account of the literary reflection on aesthetic experience and Hösle's investigation of the phenomena of the 'poet who ascends to poetological reflection' and the theorist who is 'a literary example of that which he demands' are thus in a sense more explicit and deliberate investigations of something that is frequently implicit within poetry.[75] In some conceptions the link between subjective and objective is made primarily or exclusively through language: Bogel, for example, asserts that 'a properly formalist analysis must engage with that language no matter what it also takes the text to be—must show how it is the text's language that makes it any of those other things'.[76] Meanwhile, the genetically distinct New Formalism, the poetic movement of the 1980s according to which 'the revival of traditional forms' is seen as one possible response to the 'debasement of poetic language' that Dana Goia identifies in much US American poetry of the time, anticipates that its concerns would be taken up by literary studies more generally, where they would lead to an expanded sense of form, as he predicts that debates in literary form would soon begin to 'focus on form in the wider, more elusive sense of poetic structure'.[77]

In other reflections by poets on the implications of their practice, the concern is more explicitly social, as can be seen for example in some of the debates within and around Language writing as to the different ways in which 'choices of grammar, vocabulary, syntax, and narrative reflect ideology'.[78] Indeed the project outlined by Bernstein was in many cases at least as much a poetic as a literary-critical endeavor, insofar as many of the contributors to the discussions were trying not only 'to see the formal dynamics of a poem as communicative exchanges, as socially addressed, and as ideologically explicit', but also to address the question of how practitioners such as Bruce Andrews might go about 'making the form that's truly in question the form of society itself', or in Erica Hunt's work toward an 'oppositional poetics' which would 'form a field of related projects which have moved beyond the speculation of skepticism to a critically active stance against forms of domination'.[79] Common to these undertakings is the conviction that form constitutes a means of thinking poetry and society together, and to investigating and indeed altering the links between them. A significant concern of this book is to theorize this link, and to address the question of what it is about form that lends itself to such endeavors.

In setting out this poetics of form I thus seek to go beyond Rose's claim that 'Adorno sought to develop a sociology of artistic form', a claim which is perhaps an accurate characterization of his earlier writings on the sociology of music, but which does not begin to capture the rethinking, both explicit and implicit, of form within his later works.[80] In doing so I am deliberately working with the elusive and sometimes aporetic character of poetics, at once drawing on and theorizing its pliability and adaptability, and their intertwining with those of form, which of course can refer at the same time both to the unique features of an individual work and to that which it has in common with other works. Discussing form as it pertains to an individual work, for example, Derek Attridge argues that 'the notion of singularity is entirely bound up with the notion of form'.[81] Meanwhile, in approaching a villanelle by William Empson, Michael Wood confronts what he terms the 'need at some stage to ask what literary forms know or know of'.[82] Form's adaptability and pliability do not consist solely in the versatility with which form can be deployed to refer to apparently incompatible or mutually exclusive phenomena, although this versatility is an important aspect and indeed condition of the ways in which the term is deployed to make the link between poetry and its worlds.

Philology

Adorno ends the ninth of his 'Bibliographical Sketches' with what reads like a somewhat dismissive claim: 'Philology conspires with myth: it blocks the exit.' His critique is directed against the philosophical lexica—he gives as examples Rudolf Eisler's of Kant and Hermann Glockner's of Hegel—in which 'the most important formulations often slip through the cracks because they do not fit under any keyword' (NzL 352/Ntl 2: 26). Philological enquiry, however, reveals that this dismissal is not the end of the story. In the Odysseus chapter of *Dialectic of Enlightenment*, Adorno remarks that the philosophical critique that reveals the identification of epic and myth to be deceptive follows in the footsteps of recent classical philology, which had itself already dismantled the identification (DA 61/DE 35). In the opening paragraph of 'Skoteinos, or How to Read', the third of his studies on Hegel, he asserts that 'there is no Hegel-philology, no adequate textual criticism' (3SH 326/H3S 89). In *Negative Dialectics* he criticizes Heidegger's destruction, which 'falls silent before the philological education that he at the same time neglects and suspends' (ND 118/Ashton 112). In each case there remains the unarticulated possibility of a philological praxis adequate to the task of investigating the truth content of philosophical and literary works.

Such a praxis would of necessity distinguish itself from the two false sorts of philology that Adorno identifies. In *Aesthetic Theory* he writes of the danger of identifying the truth content of a work with the intention of its author: 'The philological procedure that imagines that it grasps the substantive content of the work as something secure by grasping its intention judges itself immanently by tautologically extracting from artworks what had previously been put into them; the secondary literature on Thomas Mann is the most repugnant example of this' (ÄT 226/AT 150). Meanwhile, while polemicizing against Heidegger in 'Why Still Philosophy?' he argues that Heidegger's unreflected philology 'cryptically becomes a philosophical authority' (E 463/CM 9). In his exposition of what he terms Nietzsche's philology of the future, James I. Porter distinguishes, in a conceptual schema that bears a striking resemblance to Horkheimer's account of theory, between traditional and critical philology.[83] Traditional philology is 'the agency that helps to sustain the mythical shape of the present, in part by alienating myth as an object of dispassionate study', and as such a form of forgetfulness. To distinguish itself from this—that is, to become critical—philology 'must become a self-reflexive, self-critical, and often paradoxical undertaking'.[84]

Such a critical philology would be characterized by a concern for the philosophical consequences of interpretation, without attempting to substitute for philosophy. It cannot afford to ignore what Peter Szondi terms 'the problematic of philological cognition', indifference to which is the explanation of his lament that philology so often tends toward an 'unreflected science'—that is to say that philology tends to lack hermeneutical reflection on its own procedures, focusing instead purely on its object.[85] The present study aspires to critical philology in three senses. The first consists in the fact that as a study of Adorno's writings on literary form, my investigative procedures are in some respects philological—my engagement with these writings draws on the resources including explication and elucidation, as well as literary analysis and textual criticism. I seek to illuminate some of Adorno's more enigmatic claims by means of attentive close reading and the examination of both their resonance and their frictions with other aspects of his work. In this sense I am concerned with what a certain kind of philological practice can reveal about the truth content of Adorno's work, and it at this point that both my concern and my methodology are closest to those of some of the works trading under the name of the new formalism. The second sense is that I investigate Adorno's writings on aesthetics and literature as an instance or prototype of critical philology—that is to say, not only as a means of analyzing texts but also as a reflection on the cognition embedded within and presupposed by such analysis. And where their shortcomings are revealed I seek to bring them closer to this aspiration. The third relates to the second, in that it seeks to outline the implications of Adorno's thought for a rethinking of some of the ways in which we study. In this respect it proceeds both with and beyond Adorno's work, on the one hand formulating and making explicit the implicit principles that inform his readings of literature, and on the other hand pointing to ways in which the tensions and aporiae within his work are representative of limits (whether to his writings or to the concepts and traditions with which he works) that might be transcended.

An investigation of this kind is in many respects the correlate of Hösle's account of *Aesthetic Theory* as an instance of self-instantiation: recognizing the poetic character of Adorno's writings on literature (and on art, and on aesthetics) implies that they require some kind of poetic or literary analysis. But where Hösle warns that concentration on what self-instantiations say can all too readily lead to the neglect of what they are, I deliberately leave this question of what they are open.[86] In doing so I am guided by the closing words of the 1961 essay 'Vers une musique informelle', later cited in *Aesthetic Theory*, that the utopian moment consists in the attempt 'to make things of which we do not know what they are' (QF 540/Livingstone 322, ÄT 174/AT 114). In this book I seek to explore the potential of this unknown quality not only of the creations that result from artistic processes, but also of those analyses that seek to know and come in some or other (frequently undefined) respect to resemble them. In doing so I take seriously Adorno's recognition that the essay's 'emphatic work on the form of its presentation' that is compelled by acknowledging the nonidentity of representation and matter leads it to resemble art (NzL 26/NtL 1: 18), not advancing what Jameson rejects as a literary reading 'in the restricted or trivialized sense', but nonetheless attending to the formal moment or style of his sentences.[87] This study thus shares a concern with Jameson's account of Adorno's sentences as 'individual "shots", edited into a larger formal movement (the constellation or model, as we shall see shortly), small- and large-scale dimensions through both of which the absent totality perpetually feeds', and also with studies such as Steven Helmling's account of the way this is played out in Adorno's own writerly practice, both in his focus on the how alongside the what of critique, and in his orientation toward the narrative of the coming to be of a 'now unimaginable future'.[88]

This sense of a philological practice oriented toward a future that cannot be grasped by the concepts with which we currently think is motivated by similar concerns to those of Hamacher's radical rethinking of philology, a term which signals (in a manner similar to Arthos's appeal to poetics to mark a departure from the conventions of disciplinary aesthetics) a break with the entrenched and established—disciplinary—ways of thinking. For philology, in Hamacher's conception, 'no matter how entrenched in the academy, is not a discipline'; it is 'a longing for language, for everything grasped by it and everything it could still touch, a longing that recoils from every totality, and which, speaking for another and yet another, critiques everything that has been achieved and can be achieved'.[89] This longing marks not only an affective relationship—'a *philia*, a friendship with or befriending of' language—but also a relationship of affinity toward and resemblance of language.[90] As such, in Kevin McLaughlin's terms, it aspires to raise 'the possibility of a communal human being arising from the feeling of a communicability—of a philological sociability and a *socius* emerging out of philology—that is threatened by the divisive finitude of incommunicability'.[91]

A consequence of writing on Adorno in a language other than German is that the requirement to interpret and explicate is doubly present. A sizeable proportion of this study consists in my own translations and commentary on the translation as a means of interpreting the original text. There are points at which my translations are substantially less elegant than the standard English-language translations. To take a single example, Rodney Livingstone renders the sentence from the fragment on music and language that I use as the epigraph to the fourth chapter—'*Form ist nur eine von Geformtem*' (QF 255)—as '[f]orm can only be the form of a content' (Livingstone 6). This is in almost every way superior to my own offering, 'the only form is that of what is formed'. I have opted for my rather more awkwardly phrased version because it is important for the purposes of this study that Adorno is opposing form not to either of the German words for content—*Inhalt*, the paraphrasable content of a work, or *Gehalt*, its broader significance of substance (I examine this distinction more closely in the first chapter, in the discussion of Adorno's conception of form as 'sedimented content')—but simply to that which is formed: he does not introduce a new term or concept in opposition to form, but refers solely to the object of this process, an object which is not defined except with reference to its being formed.

This is not a work of translation, what Walter Benjamin terms translation as form, but one in which translation is a process deployed in the service of philological commentary.[92] Indeed, in writing a study of Adorno I am at a considerable advantage in relation to those who have taken on the daunting task of translating his works into English. This advantage consists primarily in the fact that I have been able to choose which sections to translate, and that I have the opportunity at each point to offer the sort of commentary on the difficulties of translating a particular word or passage that is not often available when preparing a translation of a work. This is particularly helpful when confronted in the introduction to the second chapter with the bad choice of rendering *Vergeistigung* as spiritualization or intellectualization, both of which are in different ways unsatisfactory, or in discussing Adorno's use of *vertreten*, to represent, substitute or stand for, in his interpretation of the secularization of sacrifice in the Odysseus chapter of *Dialectic of Enlightenment* (to which I return in the discussion of abstraction and exchange in chapter 5 below).

In translating I have nonetheless sought to bring Adorno's German as far into English as I can. In translating the notoriously problematic *aufheben*, for example, I dissent from the idiolectical 'sublate' in favor of the more idiomatic 'suspend' (which contains within it many if not necessarily all of the ambiguities and contradictions implied by the German term). Similarly, I have generally taken the risk of translating problematic terms rather than leaving them in italicized German, as Jameson does, for example (and wholly justifiably), when discussing *Schein* (semblance, appearance) in *Late Marxism*, with the intention that this will illuminate or magnify more than it obscures. In this respect (and many others) I am in accord with Benjamin's remarks on the relationship between a translation and its original:

> The true translation is translucent, it does not obscure the original, stand in its light, but lets pure language, as if amplified by its own medium, fall on the original all the more fully. This can be achieved above all by literalness in the conveying of syntax, and it is precisely this that renders the word rather than the sentence as the primal element of the translator. For the sentence is the wall before the language of the original, literalness is the arcade.[93]

In a foreign-language philological commentary that is not a work of translation, but in which translation is an indispensable aspect of its work, the aim is one of amplification, illumination, and elucidation—by means not only of translation, but also of a range of other kinds of commentary. In translating I have aimed first and foremost at as literal as possible a rendering of the syntax, while seeking to preserve fluency in English. I have also drawn attention to points at which tensions between this aspiration toward fluency and that of conveying a particular resonance or nuance of Adorno's German reveal something about the ways in which Adorno's thinking relates to the language within which it is written. As such my aim differs from those great English-language translators of Adorno such as Rodney Livingstone and Edmund Jephcott, whose versions of Adorno speak in an elegant and lucid English: in my translations in particular I hope that there can be seen something akin to what Benjamin terms the 'transformation of the translator's mother tongue'.[94]

Constellation

Discussing the relationship that concepts have to one another in *Negative Dialectics*, Adorno insists that it is deceptive to speak of a sort of process of progressive gradation from concept to concept toward a universal subordinating concept, but that concepts rather 'enter into constellation', a web of interrelation between concepts (ND 164/Ashton 162). This motif is adopted from Benjamin's *Trauerspiel* study, as Buck-Morss notes, and from the *Arcades Project*.[95] However, Adorno's use differs from that of his friend and intellectual mentor in that whereas for Benjamin constellation is a means of thinking the relationship of past to present without recourse to historical thinking (it is the result of the sudden collision of 'that which has been with the now'), Adorno relies on a more spatial way of thinking concepts around their referent.[96] He advances a model of thought according to which concepts are not determined in advance of an investigation, but go through a process of defining, refinement, in relation to one another, around the object that they attempt to stand for. 'Only constellations represent, from the outside, what the concept has cut out of the inside—the "more" that the concept wants to be just as strongly as it cannot be it' (ND 164/Ashton 162). Constellations of concepts, that is, offer a means of illuminating that within the object which conceptual thought cannot itself grasp, of 'attaining by thinking that which thought necessarily excised from itself' (ND 165/Ashton 162). Jameson refers to this excised part as that which the concept cannot say but must nonetheless 'somehow, by its imperfection, be registered within it (just as the monadic work of art must somehow "include" its outside, its referent, under pain of lapsing into decorative frivolity)': the resemblance of this account of constellation and conceptuality to the artwork is one aspect of the affinity between the practices of poetry and those of studying it on which both the capaciousness of form and the frequently diffuse uses of poetics rely.[97]

This book is not, then, a first philosophy of literary form that proceeds according to the sort of foundational logic that starts with form in general and works toward particular manifestations of literary form by further determining and refining the concept. I attempt rather to consider form within the constellation of concepts that exist around it. Jameson has analyzed some of the ways in which particular contrasts, distinctions, and oppositions illuminate different aspects of Adorno's thought, remarking on the fact that 'the opposition between montage and meaning, for example, expresses a specific historical moment in the development of modern art;

but it also emerges at a specific "historical" or narrative moment in Adorno's text, so to speak, and is thereby as situational and as provisional in the text as it is in some "external" history of form.'[98] Similarly, Paddison and Bruns have in their different ways examined form with respect to the way in which it appears in opposition to material, the former focusing primarily on Adorno's musical writings, the latter on the ways in which examination of *Aesthetic Theory* rethinks this relationship.

I seek to build on and develop this work, and to illuminate form as it appears from a more extensive range of perspectives. In the first four chapters I thus offer four separate but interrelated examinations of form as the term is deployed within Adorno's œuvre, considering in each one form in opposition to content, expression, genre, and material. As can be seen from some of the ways in which the chapters interact, the distinctions between them are to an extent arbitrary. The material that is formed within a poem, for example, is by no means devoid of content, while it is difficult to think of the process of forming as completely distinct from subjective expression. Indeed, the points at which the different chapters overlap are themselves particularly fruitful areas of investigation, since they facilitate a sort of conceptual triangulation or simultaneous illumination of form from different directions.

In the first chapter I address the relationship between form and content, focusing primarily on the discussion of Hölderlin in 'Parataxis'. I explicate and discuss the consequences of Adorno's formulation that form is the 'sedimentation of content', and consider the role played by form in his distinction between propositional and substantive content. In the second chapter I examine form as it appears in opposition to expression, concentrating on Adorno's critique of literary expressionism and his writings on Kafka. The focus of the third is his conception of literary forms and genres: I discuss his theory of aesthetic nominalism and his understanding of the relationship between universal and particular, before examining the consequences for his theory of form of his discussions of the culture industry, the novel, and the essay. In the fourth I offer an account of the relationship between form and material as it is implied by his aesthetics of music and literature, paying particular attention to the significance for these aesthetics of his understanding of language, and discussing his interpretations of the work of Borchardt and Valéry.

What emerges from this illumination of form from four different angles is a complex web of dynamic conceptual interactions. Form has its origin in content, as the sedimentation of content. Form mediates expression, out of which emerges in turn a further expression of form. Form is a force that draws different works together: they come together or congeal into forms, which then themselves exert forces that are experienced as constraints or determinate influences. Form shapes and dominates material, which itself exerts a reciprocal constraint over the subject who seeks to form it. Form does all these things at once. As such it encapsulates a wide range of frequently divergent artistic and social processes: the poetics of form developed in this book seeks to reveal the diverse ways in which form brings these together without effacing their divergence. As such form offers a way of thinking beyond the metaphysics of the concept.

It is to the implications of this poetics that I turn in the book's final sections, in which I seek to draw together some of the consequences of the first four, examining the significance of Adorno's poetics of form for the relationship between art and society in the broadest sense. In a kind of constellation of constellation, Helmling has drawn attention to the antithetical implications of Adorno's varying references to constellation as 'unconscious ideological synthesis' and 'consciousness-raising estrangement', as object or subject of critique, and has suggested that these variations 'are themselves a kind of constellation implying or encoding, concealing or de-familiarizing a narrative'.[99] Accordingly, in the fifth chapter I examine the implications of the complex constellation of form as it comes to appear in the first four. By bringing this constellation of literary and artistic form into comparison with the commodity form I seek to open up and theorize possibilities for intervention into the narratives of political economy and its critique, focusing in particular on the implications of Adorno's enigmatic assertion that artworks are 'products of social labor'. In the concluding coda I set out some of the implications of the book's argument both for the study of literature and more broadly, considering the significance of Adorno's elusive writings on the lyric for what I term a poetics of the wrong state of things.

1

Form and Content

It is only through the hiatus, the form, that content becomes substance.

—NzL 470/NtL 2: 129

At the beginning of the second half of his essay on Hölderlin's late hymns, Adorno sets out the basis for his own elucidations of Hölderlin's poetry, to contrast with those of Heidegger, the object of the critique that constitutes the essay's first half. Adorno outlines the two schemata in opposition to which he develops his account of poetic form in Hölderlin's work:

> In contrast with the crude textbook separation of content and form, recent poetology has insisted on their unity. But there is hardly an aesthetic object that shows more urgently than Hölderlin that the affirmation of unarticulated unity of form and content is no longer sufficient. (NzL 469/NtL 2: 128)

While the first of these models is something of a caricature, the second, as Gerhard van den Bergh has pointed out, is a pointed critique of Friedrich Beißner's introduction to Hölderlin's poetry in the *Kleine Stuttgarter Ausgabe*, in which he insists that 'one cannot and must not divide what is at one within the artwork'.[1] This raises the question first of how it is that Adorno thinks the relationship between form and content should be configured, and second and more significantly, how he conceives of form and content in relation to one another, how they are to be identified within the artwork, and how their concepts interact.

These questions are the concern of this chapter, which addresses Adorno's conception of this relationship between poetic form and content, and its implications for the study of poetry. I begin by addressing the polemical aspect of many of Adorno's discussions of Heidegger, outlining some of the specific charges he raises against Heidegger's rejection of form. Focusing on the former's treatment of the latter's essay on the origin of the work of art, I seek to cut through the rhetorical force of Adorno's polemic in order to clarify the points of contention and agreement between the two thinkers, and to elucidate the theoretical presuppositions of Adorno's use of form as an optic to approach poetry. I then discuss some of the background to the work presented in 'Parataxis', turning my attention first to the textual history of the essay in order to develop, in dialogue with Adorno, an approach to the analysis of poems that eschews the procedures both of an uncritical philology and of the application to poems of philosophical or theoretical methods that are indifferent to them.

I then turn to discuss different aspects of the construction of form in relation to content. I begin by conceptualizing the relationship between linguistic and poetic form, explicating some of Adorno's close readings of Hölderlin in 'Parataxis' to reveal their intertwinement through the constellation of form, style, and means or technique. I then turn my attention to the implications of Adorno's resonant formulation that form is the 'sedimentation of content', and of his historized reinterpretation of the Kantian purposiveness in general without any particular purpose. By examining Adorno's discussions in both 'Parataxis' and *Aesthetic Theory* I reveal the nature and extent of the influence on his literary aesthetics of both Kant and Hegel, and formulate the ways in which his analytical and interpretative procedures differ from those of both his predecessors. Finally I expound on the implications of my analysis for our conception of poetry and in particular of poetic language, setting out the role of form in theorizing and accounting for the transformation of the literal, propositional content of poems' words into their poetic content in the fullest sense.

Adorno and Heidegger: The Form of the Thing

Adorno's chief objection to Heidegger's readings of Hölderlin is the way in which Heidegger reduces poetry to its paraphrasable content, on which he then expounds philosophically: 'Whereas Heidegger accentuates to a great extent the concept of that which is composed, and indeed accords the poet himself the highest metaphysical dignity, his individual elucidations reveal him to be supremely indifferent to what is specifically poetic' (NzL 452/NtL 2:114). Here the distinction between that which is composed—*das Gedichtete*, or more literally that which has been poetized or written into poetry—and the specifically poetic—*das spezifisch Dichterische*, or that pertaining to the poet—contains in condensed form the accusation that Heidegger neglects the implications of the process of composition, of forming into a poem. Heidegger's indifference, Adorno argues, is a consequence of his approach to poetry, an approach which involves the application of a particular method to the poems under discussion:

> Heidegger's method is false insofar as it, as method, tears itself away from the matter at hand: it infiltrates that which in Hölderlin's poetry is philosophically lacking with philosophy from the outside. The corrective should be sought at the point at which Heidegger breaks off for the sake of his *thema probandum*, in the relationship of the content, including the conceptual content, to the form. (NzL 468–69/NtL 2: 128)

Here form—the form that Heidegger is accused of ignoring—is the correlate of the specifically poetic, the technique of poetic composition. Adorno's objection is not that Heidegger applies the wrong method, but rather that he applies a method at all. In 'The Essay as Form', Adorno sets out his objection to what he terms 'the traditional concept of method', an invariant set of procedures which is applied unchanged to every object of investigation (NzL 18/NtL 1: 11). Such an approach ends up telling us more about its own presuppositions than about the object on which it is supposed to shed light. For Adorno, this is enough to account for Heidegger's indifference to the material aspects of a poetic text: the application of even the most dignified philosophical method will elide what is particular about such texts, and simply reveal compatibilities in terms of their paraphrasable content.

However, this critique is at best abbreviated, for it conflates Heidegger's rejection of form with his the blindness to the specifically poetic that comes about as a result of his application of a method. Indeed, nowhere in his œuvre does Adorno discuss in any detail Heidegger's explicit rejection of the category of form in 'The Origin of the Work of Art':

> The tendency to take the matter–form structure as *the* constitution of every single being receives particular impetus from the fact

that on the basis of a belief—namely the biblical belief—that the totality of beings is imagined in advance as something created, and here that means something made. [. . .] The metaphysics of modernity is based on the matter–form structure, coined in the middle ages, which itself only calls to mind in words the buried essence of *eidos* and *hyle*. Thus the explication of the thing in terms of matter and form, whether it remains medieval or becomes Kantian–transcendental, becomes prevalent and self-evident. But for this reason it is no less than the other explications of the thingness of the thing discussed above an assault on the thing-being of the thing.[2]

This complements Heidegger's rejection of what he considers the other two prevailing conceptions of the thingness of the thing—the first being the thing as bearer of characteristics, the second the thing as the unity of a sensory manifold—his argument being that it is wrong to attempt to answer the question of what an artwork is by asking what kind of a thing it is. In his rejection of the intractability of the 'prevalent and self-evident' attempt to comprehend an object according to a preexisting schema, Heidegger takes up a position that shows close affinities with Adorno's rejection of method.

Adorno never explicitly engaged with the foundation of Heidegger's rejection of form. While it is not possible to conclude from a lack of annotation that a passage has not been read or thought about, it is nonetheless worth noting that in his copy of *Holzwege*, Adorno only made scant annotations to 'The Origin of the Work of Art', consisting of two question marks toward the end of the first paragraph, and a rule down the left-hand margin on each of pages 7 and 29.[3] Indeed, Adorno's engagement with Heidegger's essay as a whole is limited to a few comments in *Aesthetic Theory* and the 1967 essay on 'Art and the Arts', first given as a talk at the *Akademie der Künste* in Berlin on June 23, 1966. The 'Theories on the Origin of Art' included in the 'Paralipomena' to *Aesthetic Theory* begin with the claim that '[a]ttempts to found aesthetics on the origin of art as its essence necessarily disappoint' (ÄT 480/AT 325), an implicit but pointed rejection of Heidegger's essay, followed only by a dismissal of its argument in the most general terms—so general, in fact, that it mischaracterizes and neglects the force of Heidegger's essay, which is less an attempt to found aesthetics on the origin of art than a critique of 'aesthetics' itself.

The 1967 essay engages more specifically with Heidegger's account of the artwork:

The origin of the artwork, he claims emphatically, is art. Origin here should be taken to mean, as always in Heidegger, not the temporal genesis, but the provenance of the essence of works of art. His doctrine of this origin adds nothing to that of something that has emerged, and cannot do so, because it would otherwise stain itself with the same being that the sublime concept of origin would not like to permit. The cost of Heidegger's salvation of the moment of unity of art, of what is artistic about art, is that theory falls silent, awestruck, in front of what it is supposed to be. (OL 446/COL 381)

Here Adorno is arguing against Heidegger's prioritizing of the essential origin of art at the expense of attention to the particularities of individual artworks. As such he identifies in Heidegger's account a systematic indifference to the particular in comparison with the general, insisting against Heidegger that art 'can no more be boiled down to its pure unity than to the pure variety of the arts' (OL 447/COL 382). Adorno insists that Heidegger's concept of origin is one that must remain pure, uncontaminated by the concrete being of any individual work. This effectively neutralizes theory, which such a schema renders blind to differences between artworks. Theory, that is, which takes its cue from the material object which it confronts, adapting itself accordingly, is reduced to a shadow of itself, an invariant method.

While this argument outlines in more detail Adorno's rejection of Heidegger's conception of the origin of the artwork in art, and indeed attempts to account for Heidegger's indifference to the material characteristics of specific works, it nonetheless leaves unaddressed the matter of Heidegger's rejection of the concept of form. The closest to an engagement with this rejection in Adorno's work is found in the following long quotation from *Aesthetic Theory*, in which he addresses Heidegger's approach to the thing-character of the artwork:

> As something essentially spiritual, art cannot be purely intuitable. It must always also be thought: it thinks itself. The prevalence of the theory of intuition, contradictory to all experience of artworks, is a reflex against social reification. This prevalence amounts to the construction of a special department of immediacy, blind to the thingly layers of artworks which are constitutive of that which is more than thingly about them. It is not only as bearers that they have characteristics, as Heidegger claimed against idealism

[. . .]. Their own objectification makes them second-degree things. That which they have become in and of themselves, their inner structure, obedient to ever more immanent logic, cannot be accessed by pure intuition, and their elements which can be intuited are mediated through this structure; compared with the structure, their intuitable aspect is inessential, and every experience of artworks must go beyond it. If they were nothing other than intuitable, they would be subaltern effect, in Richard Wagner's terms effect without cause. Reification is essential to works and contradicts their essence as something that appears; their thing-character is no less dialectical than their intuitable element. However, the objectification of the artworks is in no way [. . .] at one with its material, but what results from the dynamics of the work, related as synthesis to the thing-character. (ÄT 152–53/AT 99)

This is a relatively oblique passage insofar as it takes issue not only with Heidegger, but also with a heavily mediated Kant. Comprehension is not aided by the difficulties in translation that come about in part as a result of the standard rendering of *Anschauung* as 'intuition' in translations of Kant: both in Kant and in this passage, it refers to the immediate sensory (and thus nonconceptual) perception of an object, as opposed to understanding it intellectually and conceptually.[4] Heidegger recognizes that artworks are not reducible to their thing-character, but does so in such a way that he neglects this thing-character in the name of what makes artworks more than things. For Adorno, on the other hand, it is the fact that artworks are undeniably and demonstrably things that enables them also to be more than things. It is through the close attention that they demand to their tangible—one could say thingly, to put it in Heidegger's terms—character that artworks are able to become more than things: 'For to the extent that artworks are works, they are things in themselves, objectified by virtue of their law of form' (ÄT 153/AT 100). Sensory observation of works reveals the presence of something that cannot be fully grasped by the intuition, something that demands reflective judgment.

The translation of *geistig* as 'spiritual' also has the potential to be misleading. An equally valid translation would be 'intellectual', which is indeed here the primary sense of the word, insofar as Adorno is working with the contrast between the sensuous and the conceptual character of artworks. His claim is that these do not exist in opposition to one another, but reinforce and enable each other to come to prominence.[5] That is, whereas for Heidegger the form–matter distinction is a means by which the thing-character of the work is subordinated and reduced to the schema according to which it is observed—and it is important to bear in mind that for Heidegger this is true of all approaches to the thing-character qua thing-character, which is central to his rejection of the question of what kind of a thing art is—Adorno sees the form–matter distinction as one means among many of approaching the artwork's tangible thing-character, an approach which is itself necessary in order to access the aspects of the artwork that lie beyond its sensuous, intuitable character. Since the attempt to understand the thing-character of the artwork is for Adorno not a barrier to grasping these aspects but rather the very means of access to them, the Heideggerian critique of the form–matter structure no longer poses a barrier to the consideration of the relationship of form and content as a means of analyzing the relationship of a work's intuitable character to the intellectual content that emerges from close consideration of the thingly layer. It should be observed, however, that even this elides what is perhaps the sharpest point of Heidegger's treatment of the form–matter distinction, namely that it functions as a sort of mythical structure that prevents us from experiencing the world, that does not allow the thing 'to rest in its own essence'.[6] I return, if somewhat obliquely, to this point in the final chapter, addressing the manner in which Adorno conceives the distinction between artworks and other made objects. For now, I turn to discuss Adorno's discussion of form in his reading of Hölderlin.

'Parataxis'

The text that was, in an extended form, finally published as 'Parataxis: On Hölderlin's Late Lyric', was first given as a talk at the eighth annual meeting of the Hölderlin Society in Berlin on June 7, 1963, the 120th anniversary of Hölderlin's death. Although the conference report mentions that there was heated discussion after the paper in the foyer of the *Akademie der Künste*, where the conference was held, Adorno was unable to remain for the formal discussion of his own paper, which took place in his absence.[7] The talk was not, as is customary, printed in the *Hölderlin–Jahrbuch*, but had already appeared in the *Neue Rundschau* by the time issue 13 of the *Jahrbuch* was published in 1965.[8] Adorno accounts for this anomaly in a letter to Peter Szondi, to whom the essay is dedicated, in which he explains that the Hölderlin Society had made an offer of publication in the yearbook, 'with the suggestion that he soften the passages on Heidegger', an offer which he 'politely turned down'.[9] Van den Bergh reports on a personal conversation with Emil Staiger, who described some of the controversy provoked by Adorno's intervention: a member of the audience 'stood up and interrupted the speaker, insisting that it was unbelievable effrontery to attack someone who was not present and thus had no possibility to defend himself', in response to which Szondi commented that in the light of the extent to which Heidegger had been cited on the day, it was a 'legitimate and usual mode of debate'.[10]

In his study of what he terms the avoidance of philosophical communication, Hermann Mörchen raises the as yet unanswered question of the 'original motivations' of Adorno's study, describing how in relation to Hölderlin, 'Adorno and Heidegger's accentuations differ noticeably but not completely', and that while it would be possible to 'wrestle over the precise authority of the equivocal words', it was 'precisely this that Adorno avoided'.[11] My intention here is not to reconstruct such a dispute, but to consider some of the significances of the manner of this avoidance, discussing less the matter of whether the particular positions that Adorno rejects are accurate characterizations of those taken by Heidegger, and more the force of the rejection of these positions, and of those that Adorno sets out in opposition to them, as well as—perhaps more significantly—the consequences of these positions for the study of poetics, and in particular the understanding of literary form.

Central to Adorno's argument is the tension between philosophical and philological knowledge, neither of which is adequate to grasping Hölderlin's poetry on its own. Adorno recognizes the temptation to proceed by philosophically analyzing the surface content of the poem, but insists that this is not an acceptable approach:

> The attraction of Hölderlin's hymns to the philosophy of being has a lot to do with the position of abstractions within them. They invitingly prefigure the medium of philosophy, which admittedly, if it were bound by its conception of what is composed, would have to shrink back in fear of becoming contaminated with intellectual material in poetry. (NzL 463/NtL 2: 123)

Again, 'what is composed' is my rendering of *das Gedichtete*, and serves here as a condensed rejection of what Adorno identifies as Heidegger's privileging of the intellectual content of poems' material over the way in which this content (and this material) is formed into the poems themselves. While it is not in doubt that Hölderlin's poetry lends itself well to Heidegger's philosophical interpretation, it is also significant, as Adorno notes, that there is a systematic tendency in Heidegger to downplay Hölderlin's affinities with the tradition of German idealism in order to erase or avoid aspects in which it does not fit so well (NzL 468/NtL 2: 127–28). This raises the question of the extent to which such an approach is appropriate, commensurable to the poetry it seeks to analyze. The question is not simply of whether the philosophy with which Heidegger inflects Hölderlin's poetry is true, or even of whether it is compatible with the content of the poems under discussion, but of whether it is appropriate to read the poems in this way in the first place. What is at stake here is whether a multiplicity of readings from different perspectives constitutes a legitimate approach to the lyric. Adorno's admittedly polemical claim is that Heidegger's philosophical approach fails not primarily because the philosophy is not compatible with the intellectual content of the poems, but rather because the existence of such a compatibility by no means constitutes an acceptable criterion of the success of an account of the poems.

This claim has considerable significance for a philosophically informed and inflected approach to poetry:

> While [. . .] like all emphatic poetry, Hölderlin's requires philosophy as the medium that unearths its truth content, the appeal to a philosophy that in whatever way confiscates this truth content is in no way suited to this purpose. The division of labor, which fatally divided philosophy from the humanities after the decay of German idealism, both induced the humanities, conscious of their own inadequacy, to look for help where they want or have to stop, and conversely defrauded them of their critical capacity, the only thing that would have allowed them to cross over into philosophy. (NzL 452/NtL 2: 113–14)

For Adorno, philosophy is undeniably necessary for the interpretation of Hölderlin's poetry, but there remains the question as to whether there exists a philosophy adequate to the task, a philosophy that would not confiscate the truth content of the work. Such a philosophy must be developed by and through the reading of the poems in question: the idea that philosophy might be provided from outside as an aid to accessing and interpreting the truth content of poems is an aspect of the division of labor that must be overcome. This overcoming is not so much a prerequisite to the adequate mode of engagement with Hölderlin's poetry as a goal toward which such an interpretation should strive: the practice of reading is at the same time the attempt to overcome the view of philosophy as a court of arbitration between the other disciplines of the humanities.

In opposition to the Heideggerian mode of elucidation that he rejects, Adorno insists on the importance of differentiating Hölderlin's poetry from philosophy. Whereas philosophy 'takes a stand on the negation of that which is', Hölderlin's poetry, 'by virtue of the distance of its law of form from empirical reality, complains about the sacrifice that it demands' (NzL 463/ NtL 2: 123). Already the distinction is couched in terms of the 'law of form', which places demands on the poem that are not raised of philosophical argument, distancing the work which is subject to it from the empirical world. The fundamental difference between philosophy and poetry here is configured in terms of their relationship to this empirical world, utopian philosophy aiming toward the negation of that which is, while poetry moves away from it, neither affirming nor negating. As such, philosophy cannot expect to be able to provide an approach adequate to poetry.

However, the corrective is not to be sought in philology alone, at least, not in the sense of a philology that is restricted to textual scholarship and exegesis:

> What philological explication is held to clear away does not disappear from that which first Benjamin and then Heidegger called what is composed. This moment, which extricates itself from philology, demands interpretation of its own accord. It is what is obscure in poems, and not what is thought in them, that necessitates philosophy. (NzL 450/NtL 2: 111–12)

Adorno is rejecting the view that philosophical interpretation renders exegesis unnecessary, arguing instead that philosophy is required not because of instances of philosophical material in the propositional content of poems, but rather in response to their very aspects that are philologically most challenging. That is, exegesis is thought of as leaving behind a sort of residue, which is the point at which poems require and demand philosophy, which is applied not to some sort of reconstructed or conjectural authorial intention, but to the poem as it is experienced, after the work of philological explication. The philology that Adorno holds to 'block the exit' (NzL 352/NtL 2: 26) is the philology that is content with and refuses to go beyond such explication. That is, while philology cannot alone uncover a poem's truth content—in Adorno's words 'the philological method is restricted in relation to the truth content' (NzL 447/NtL 2: 109)—it is necessary in order to be able to attain the point at which poetry demands philosophical interpretation. What Adorno terms 'interpretative reason' (ÄT 193/AT 128), that is, is not interpretation from the outside, but takes place in accordance with the requirements of the artwork in question: this is a reciprocal, mutually attuned relationship in which artworks and their truth content depend on this interpretative reason that is sensitive to their requirements.[12]

Philosophy's task in relation to literature does not consist in reconstructing or speculating as to the poet's subjective intention:

> As long as it does not objectify itself, subjective intention is scarcely recoverable; this is in any event the case to the extent that drafts and adjacent texts illuminate it. But precisely there where it is valid—where the intention is obscured and requires philological conjecture—the debatable points will generally deviate, and with good reason, from those which can be accounted for by parallels, and conjectures promise little, provided that they do not already have a hold on something that is prior to them, something philosophical; reciprocity rules between the two. (NzL 448/NtL 2: 109–10)

Adorno's argument is not, quite, that subjective intention is irrelevant, or even that attempts to recover it are necessarily misconceived, but rather that they cannot represent the full story, even in cases where they are unambiguously available. The point is that the content of what can be known differs depending on whether the procedures that lead to the knowledge are philological or philosophical. Adorno insists that philosophy and poems 'both have the same aim: truth content' (NzL 451/NtL 2: 112). The constitution of poems as literary artworks out of conceptual-linguistic material is such that neither conceptual-philosophical nor literary-critical-philological thinking can attain this truth content in its entirety. It is not merely the case that philosophy is useful in those instances in which textual scholarship cannot contribute further to the interpretation or elucidation of a text, but, more strongly, that any textual scholarship that aspires to a critical philology cannot afford to lose sight of its philosophical presuppositions and consequences.

This is inextricably linked to the conception of truth within the poem. The problem Adorno identifies with the Heideggerian philosophical method is that it seeks to add philosophy, a mode of non-poetic truth, to the poem from outside. Adorno's response:

> The truth of a poem does not exist without its structure, the totality of its moments; it is, however, at the same time that which transcends this structure, at one with aesthetic semblance: not from the outside, through spoken philosophical content, but by virtue of the configuration of moments which, taken together, mean more than the structure intends. (NzL 451/NtL 2: 112–13)

The truth content of the work must be understood according to two schemata which are in conflict with one another. It exists firstly in the relationship of the aspects of the artwork to one another—what Adorno calls the structure—but also in what he terms aesthetic semblance or appearance, that which transcends this structure. A helpful model would be to think of this semblance as what emerges in the experience of the work, while the structure reveals itself under analysis. But it would be abbreviated to take this to mean that the analysis of an artwork's structure can be thought of as explaining why it is experienced in a particular way, that the truth of the analysis of the work's structure consists in explaining the truth that takes place in the experience of the work. Rather, the two truths must be thought of as one and the same, existing at the same time both within the work's structure and as its aesthetic semblance. This is the significance of the claim made at the end of Adorno's essay:

> [T]he dialectical structure of the hymns, irreconcilable with Heidegger's elucidations, is neither a merely poetic principle of form nor a means of adapting to philosophical doctrine. It is a structure of form as well as of content. (NzL 485/NtL 2: 143)

There is a significant conceptual distinction between structure and form. Structure is used here at a higher level to form, to refer to the relationship of the form to the content. That is, while form is opposed to content, the dialectical structure to which Adorno here refers incorporates both form and content in configuration with one another. It is Adorno's configuration of the relationship between form and content that I address in the remainder of this chapter, beginning with the relationship of the form Adorno describes to grammatical and syntactical forms.

Parataxis and Linguistic Form

In the first examples introduced by Adorno in support of his claim that the corrective to Heidegger's inflection of Hölderlin's poetry with a philosophy of being should consist in the investigation of the relationship of the content of Hölderlin's poems to their form, this form is an almost exclusively syntactical phenomenon, observable at the level of individual clauses and the relations between them. In the very first example of parataxis on which he draws, the beginning of 'Brod und Wein', he argues that the 'silently presupposed epic objectivity' is altered 'by the linguistic configuration'—by which Adorno presumably means that the poem's first stanza contains no subordinating conjunctions, as clause follows clause without implication of causal or temporal relation in a single extended present[13]—'tinted as if it were far away, a mere memory like the lonely man's strumming as he remembers old friends and his youth' (NzL 469/NtL 2:129). In the two examples he gives, from 'Heimkunft' and 'Andenken', his analysis consists in the examination of the effects of joining together of two clauses without explicit or implied syntactical subordination. In the first he describes how what is familiar becomes unfamiliar by virtue of the way in which it is presented, while in the second he gives an account of the effects of the 'linguistic form' within the excerpt he analyzes. The text under discussion is as follows:

> Wo aber sind die Freunde? Bellarmin
> Mit dem Gefährten? Mancher
> Trägt Scheue, an die Quelle zu gehn;
> Es beginnet nämlich der Reichtum
> Im Meere.[14]

[But where are the friends? Where Bellarmine
And his companion? Many a man
Is shy of going to the source;
For wealth begins in
The sea.][15]

Adorno's commentary on this passage is as follows:

> While the sense of these lines is borne by the historico-philosophical construction that spirit can only attain itself

> through distance, externalization, the foreignness is expressed as substantive content by the linguistic form by means of the impact of the as it were blind, lonely man's asking after the friends in lines that don't stand in any immediate relation of meaning to that question, but only in a relation of something left out. (NzL 469–70/NtL 2: 129)

Adorno differentiates between the sense or meaning of the text of the extract and its content. The word which I have translated as substantive content is *Gehalt*, which means the poem's weight or substance, as opposed to its *Inhalt* or propositional content, the literal word-meaning of the poem's text, which would be—and indeed is, in the next sentence of the essay—equated with the poem's sense or literal meaning. It is perhaps helpful to think of this substantive content as closely related to what Adorno terms a work's truth content, which he insists in *Aesthetic Theory* 'cannot immediately be identified' (ÄT 195/AT 129). The linguistic form consists in no more or less than the particular words used, including the fact, for example, that two clauses are joined simply by a comma rather than by a conjunction. This form does not so much transform the propositional content as transpose it, creating with and out of it the poem's substantive content. In Adorno's terms: 'It is only through the hiatus, the form, that propositional content become substantive content' (NzL 470/NtL 2: 129). The hiatus, the act of breaking off and leaving unanswered the questions with which the extract begins, does not alter the literal meaning of the content, but rather the status it takes on.

Adorno makes a similar claim in his earlier discussion of 'Andenken' in the first half of the essay. He describes how it is through its 'pure grammatical form' that Hölderlin's use of 'Was bleibet' in the poem's last line comes to refer to something that is rather than to a being (NzL 459/NtL 2: 120).[16] Adorno is referring to the last line of the poem—in its entirety 'Was bleibet aber, stiften die Dichter.'—in which the use of 'Was bleibet' as opposed to any other linguistic form which would express the same or similar content—the participial noun-phrase 'Das Bleibende', for example—foregrounds the indefiniteness of the object of the sentence. The form in this instance consists in the particular grammatical construction used. Similarly, in discussing the use of the word 'Oder' in 'Brod und Wein', he contrasts the 'merely conceptual content' with the 'fixed judgment-form' in which it is in this instance not expressed (NzL 472/NtL 2: 131-32). That is, the expression of the content as 'mere content' rather than in the form of a synthetic judgment reinforces its status as possibility rather than asserted fact. This is what Adorno later terms the 'paratactical revolt against synthesis' (NzL 476/NtL 2: 132) as a dominant feature of language—that is to say, against the false image of language as permeated by the principle of identity that manifests itself in the unity of language called into question in Hölderlin's poetry. Adorno offers an analysis of the importance of this unity to language, but also of its limitations:

> Without unity, language would be nothing other than diffuse nature; absolute unity was the reflex response to this. In contrast to this, in Hölderlin it becomes apparent for the first time what culture would be: received nature. That Hölderlin's paratactical language falls under the a priori of form—a stylistic means—is only another aspect of the same situation. (NzL 477/NtL 2: 136)

Adorno's claim is that Hölderlin's poetry shows the inadequacy of conceptions of language either that ignore the synthetic function of its conceptual moment, or that seek to reduce language to this moment, and in doing so eliminate from language all trace of the nature it seeks not only to classify but also to imitate (cf. DA 34/DE 13). Stylistic devices are classified under the category of form. However, this is no transhistorical truth but rather a consequence of the particular trajectory of the development of the use and understanding of language. That is to say, the treatment of Hölderlin's poetry in terms of form and content is not an endorsement of a metaphysical separation between the two, but a conceptual separation that is necessitated by the particular extent of the mediation of consciousness through the principle of identity.

Even then the distinction might perhaps seem arbitrary. If it is clear that what Adorno refers to as a poem's form is, as he insists, fundamental to its meaning, the question arises as to the extent to which it can be conceived as even conceptually distinct from the content. The answer is perhaps best illustrated in relation to grammatical form, narrowly defined, which as syntactical or prepositional relation expresses the relationship between the elements it links, regardless of the content of the clauses that a conjunction connects or of the prepositional phrase. This is, however, not to claim that form, understood in this sense, can even conceptually be cleanly separated from content: prepositions and conjunctions both have on their own account something that could be thought of as a sort of content, at least to the extent that relation of whatever sort can be understood as content. But the particular significance of, say, a concession only becomes evident with the knowledge of what is being conceded. However, it is hardly less true to say that the content only becomes understandable with and through the grammatical relation in which it is expressed. As such the grammatical form can be said not only to take on meaning only in relation to the content, but also itself to alter, indeed even determine, the meaning of the content.

Adorno's account of form in Hölderlin is not limited to the grammatical scale. Discussing 'Hälfte des Lebens' he asserts that 'Hölderlin knows forms that could as a whole be called paratactical in a broader sense' (NzL 473/NtL 2: 132). Adorno claims that Hölderlin's verse is purged of what he terms 'mediations of the vulgar kind', mediations that take place beyond or outside the two mediated moments, in favor of a mediation that is internal to what is mediated. In the long footnote that accompanies this passage, he discusses the central importance of language in the becoming-concrete of what is composed:

> The function of language in Hölderlin qualitatively outweighs the usual function of poetic language. If his poetry can no longer naïvely trust either the poetically chosen word or living experience, it hopes to attain bodily presence from the constellation of words, indeed precisely from a constellation that takes no satisfaction from the judgment-form. As a unity, the judgment-form levels out the variety that lies within the words; Hölderlin is eager for connection, which lets the words that have been condemned to abstraction sound as it were again. (NzL 473/NtL 2: 339–40)

Here Adorno insists once again that Hölderlin's use of language works to dismantle the dominance of the synthetic unity of the judgment-form, but this time the process takes place not through parataxis in the narrow sense of the linking of clauses without the syntactical relation of subordination, but 'even when, as far as the grammatical form or the poems' construction is concerned, the paratactical has not yet emerged undiminished' (NzL 473/NtL 2: 340). The form, that is, which Adorno insists is 'at one with the content', refers not only to the grammatical form, but also to the results of the application of what he terms Hölderlin's 'technique of arrangement' (NzL 475/NtL 2: 134): the form consists here in the weight of the division between the two strophes of 'Hälfte des Lebens', a division which coincides with the 'antithesis in the content between sensual love and affliction', an antithesis which indeed 'breaks the strophes apart' (NzL 473/NtL 2: 133).

What Adorno here conceives of as form goes for the first time in this essay beyond the particular 'linguistic form' of individual clauses and their relation to one another, comprising at this point the division between the two halves of the poem, if not explicitly the positioning of each individual line-break.

Adorno's claim here is not restricted to an assertion of the mere coincidence of form and content, as if the two harmonize or reinforce one another as it were coincidentally. He insists rather, in a phrase that asserts an element of distinction from Beißner's conception of unity, that 'form and content prove themselves determinably to be one' (NzL 473/NtL 2: 133). Form and content are not two distinct elements that must be combined within the appropriate proportion; rather, they are two moments that depend on one another, that subsist within the same material. It is almost impossible to imagine a content expressed in words without form: such a formless content would have to consist at the very minimum in the abolition of syntactical relation. Adorno goes so far as to insist that the 'paratactical principle of form' is in fact 'an anti-principle', since it consists in the refusal of hierarchical relationships of grammatical subordination, but it is nonetheless an aspect of the form of Hölderlin's poetry. This form, for Adorno, is 'commensurable with the comprehensible content', while the paratactical principle 'circumscribes the sphere of coincidence of content [*Inhalt*] and form, their determinate unity in the substance [*Gehalt*]' (NzL 481–82/NtL 2: 140). This coincidence raises the question not only of how form and content, if they are to be thought of as 'as such neither separate nor indifferently identical' (NzL 469/NtL 2: 128), are to be distinguished from one another, both conceptually and empirically, but also of the way in which they—and their relationship to one another—come into being and develop.

Form as Sedimented Content

Adorno's conception of the fundamental relationship between form and content is to an extent historical: in the essay on Hölderlin he describes form as 'sedimented content' (NzL 469/NtL 2: 128). This formulation requires substantial explication. It is in the first instance a Hegelian claim— or more accurately, one that is based on an interpretation of Hegel's claim that art consists in an objective form of spirit.[17] Over a decade earlier in *The Philosophy of New Music*, Adorno alludes to Hegel in his insistence in relation to Schönberg that musical material is 'sedimented spirit', which he in the following sentence describes as the 'objective spirit of the material', itself equated with 'former subjectivity' (PnM 39/PMM 33). Adorno offers a model for understanding Hegel's theory of objective spirit according to which the spirit that is objectified in (in this case) the material that is shaped into the artwork consists in a subjectivity that has 'forgotten itself'. It is in this process of forgetting that subjectivity—spirit—is sedimented within the material, leaving traces of itself as it were in the layers of the matter that is formed into the artwork. The sedimentation of content into form must be understood similarly: form—which here means not only the specific form of a particular content, but also the development of formal traditions and conventions at the level beyond that of the individual work—comes into being through what might be thought of as a process of depositing content in the work, a process which perhaps masks but does not hide the subjectivity in which the content has its origin. Form is thus the result or mark of the process by which the work of art is made, but never appears as merely subjective or arbitrary.

Adorno's most detailed account of his conception of form as sedimented content can be found in *Aesthetic Theory*. In the book's opening section, 'Art, Society, Aesthetics', he confronts the problem of the relationship of art to the empirical world. While art stands opposed to empirical reality, artworks are undeniably constructed out of elements of this reality. Adorno approaches this aporia as follows:

> Art at once both negates the categorically imprinted determinations of the empirical world and salvages in its own substance that which empirically is. If art opposes the empirical world through its moment of form—and the mediation of form and content cannot be grasped without distinguishing between them—their mediation can be sought somewhat generally in the fact that aesthetic form is sedimented content. (ÄT 15/AT 5)

Here is raised the question of the relationship between the artwork and the empirical world in and out of which it is created—that is to say, between form and material—which I discuss in more depth in the penultimate chapter. What is significant for understanding the relationship between form and content is that the separation is arbitrary. Adorno's parenthesis is almost apologetic in the claim that the distinction between form and content is conceptually necessary in order to understand the mediation between the two, as if to acknowledge that what is at stake is no metaphysical attempt to explain the nature of the artwork as such, but rather a contingent means of understanding particular aspects of the artwork in the context of the dialectic of enlightenment. The claim that form consists in the sedimentation of content is here explicitly presented as a means of understanding and formulating the nature and extent of the mediation between the two. He elucidates:

> The forms which are apparently the purest, traditionally musical forms, date back in all their idiomatic details to matters of content such as dance. Ornaments were in many cases once cultic symbols. Attempts to relate aesthetic forms back to contents [. . .] should be undertaken more widely. (ÄT 15/AT 5)

Sedimentation refers here to a process whereby the content of what come to be artworks—and 'content' must here be understood broadly, to include the resonances of purpose and social function—ceases to be relevant (or even to exist), while the objects continue to be made with the same or similar features. It is significant that the objects or practices in question—three pages previously Adorno gives the example of cultic images that have been 'transformed into art over the course of history' (ÄT 12/AT 3)—are not necessarily in the first instance artworks, either because they start out as something else or because they predate conceptions of the category of the work of art as such. To this extent Adorno is using a conceptual framework to analyze objects that do not necessarily conform to its logic—an observation which serves not as criticism of his argument but rather to support his insistence that the conceptual dualism of form and content is historically contingent.

This becomes clearer when approaching his somewhat problematic assertion that dance or cultic symbols were once solely 'content' before they became 'ornament'. He offers a more specifically artistic example in the posthumously published fragments on Beethoven, arguing in relation to the development of the first movement of the second symphony that the entry of the theme of the second thematic group after a general pause 'sounds "*false*" in the formal sense, anticlimactic, rhapsodic' (BPdM 114, emphasis original/BTPoM 73), insofar as the development contains not the suspension of what has already occurred but rather its repetition in the same order as in the exposition. What Adorno describes as the failure of the consequent phrase 'negates' the antecedent phrase, and offers the following interpretation of the passage:

> Such relationships are an *essential* aspect of musical form. But they are sedimented *contents*: in this instance mockery, aping. (BPdM 114, emphasis original/BTPoM 73)

This account of form in Beethoven not only provides an example of what for Adorno can be considered to be formal in music—that is to say, in this instance, the order in which two phrases occur—but also indicates the way in which this form comes into being as, an objectification of what he terms 'intentional content'. While his analysis of ornament centers on the fact that the objects and activities in question were purposive rather than decorative, his discussion of Beethoven's music locates the origin of form in intentional meaning. In both cases, the fact that this distinction is conveyed through the use of the concept of form is an indication of the extent to which these concepts have established themselves within western traditions of metaphysics.[18] And in both cases, form results from the shaping of this meaning.

What is arguably Adorno's most detailed and extensively formulated treatment of the category of form takes place almost 200 pages later, in the 'Coherence and Meaning' section of *Aesthetic Theory*. It is not insignificant that this discussion follows directly from his historicizing reinterpretation of the Kantian formula 'purposiveness without purpose':

> The relationship of aesthetic purposiveness to real purposiveness was historical: artworks' immanent purposiveness came to them from the outside. Collectively honed aesthetic forms are in many ways purposive forms that have become purposeless, such as ornaments, which not without reason drew on mathematics and astronomy. This path is prescribed by the magical origin of artworks: they were elements of a praxis which wanted to influence nature, separated themselves from it in the beginnings of rationality, and gave up the deception of real influence. (ÄT 210/AT 139)

The trace of the historical and prehistorical mystical praxis in which artworks have their origins is visible within their form. I discuss the consequences of what Adorno terms artworks' turn away from praxis more extensively in the final chapter on the relationship between artworks and society; what is significant at this stage is the way in which the sedimentation of content—a formulation which Adorno repeats in the sentence that follows this extract—consists in the process whereby artworks lose or renounce an intentional purpose. Adorno endorses Kant's formulation almost paradoxically, as a critique of what he terms the 'methodological context' in which his theorems appear—that is to say, to the extent that the claim that the beautiful is what is purposive without a purpose is true, it is at the same time the refutation of the formalist framework within which it originates, according to which 'what is essential to all fine art consists in the form'.[19]

Insofar as Adorno is raising an objection to the Kantian understanding of form it is an oblique or even misdirected one: Kant does not explicitly oppose form to content (*Inhalt* appears once in the *Critique of Judgment*, *Gehalt* not at all). Adorno's insistence is not merely that form and content cannot be separated from one another, but that form has its origin in content: 'What is specific to artworks, their form, can as sedimented and modified content never completely disavow its origin' (ÄT 210/AT 139). And he makes clear that his response is directed as much against the opponents of formalism as against any defenders of the Kantian insistence on what Adorno considers to be an empty form:

> The campaign against formalism ignores the fact that the form which befalls content is itself sedimented content; it is this, and not the regression to preartistic ideas of content, that makes the priority of the object in art what it is. Formal aesthetic categories such as particularity, unfolding and the resolution of contradiction, even the anticipation of reconciliation through homoeostasis are transparently matters of content, even and indeed all the more so when they have detached themselves from empirical objects. (ÄT 217–18/AT 144–45)

What we think of as matters of form are undeniably also matters of content. Adorno's claim is that the identification within an artwork of an instance of the formal category of the resolution of contradiction, for example, is impossible without the particular example of a contradiction in the work's content. Indeed, the development of the formal aesthetic category of the resolution of contradiction depends on particular instances in which contradictions are resolved within artworks.[20] Of the examples of formal categories with which Adorno argues, the most prominent are what might tentatively be termed forms of argumentation, means of presenting particular aspects of a work's content, such as in relation to each other. To the extent to which the two can be separated from one another, Adorno focuses here on the rhetorical arrangement of a content that can be thought conceptually rather than the prosodic arrangement of a content that already exists in words that have identifiable physical characteristics. It is thus at this point unclear whether the arrangement of physical characteristics—the rhythmical properties of Hölderlin's words, for example, or their lineation and arrangement on the page—are to be considered formal aspects of an artwork, and thus also whether their origin also consists in the sedimentation of content.

This mutual interdependence of form and content is central to Adorno's objection to Hegel's aesthetics of content, which he expresses in the following terms:

> In the dialectic of form and content, the scale tips [. . .], contra Hegel, to the side of form, because the content [*Inhalt*], the salvation of which is not the last concern of his aesthetics, has meanwhile degenerated to a positivist given, to a cast of the reification against which art is according to Hegel's theory supposed to protest. The more deeply the content, experienced to the point of its unrecognizability, transposes itself into categories of form, the less the unsublimated materials are commensurable to the substantive content [*Gehalt*] of artworks. Everything that appears in artworks is virtually content [*Inhalt*] as much as form, while form remains that through which what appears is determined, and content that which determines itself. (ÄT 218/AT 145)

Content is unthinkable without form. As a result, attempts to emphasize content in such a way that form is pushed aside do not succeed in elevating or dignifying content, but rather degrade it. The problem is not simply that emphasizing content over form involves, precisely because of their mutual implication, a necessary insensitivity to the content that is supposedly privileged—although this is undoubtedly to an extent true. Rather, downplaying form can only take place by ignoring what aesthetic content is, in the dual sense firstly that it is through the content of an artwork that its formal aspects come into being (that is to say, that attentiveness to content cannot avoid taking matters of form into consideration), and secondly that this propositional content does not constitute the sum-total of what might be thought of as the content of an artwork as a whole. An artwork's content alone, to the extent that it is possible to conceive of such a thing, would not simply be subject to the reification against with Hegel seeks to invoke subjectivity as spirit, but, more damningly, a pale imitation of this reification. Conversely, it is through form—which itself arises in content—that the distinction between propositional and substantive content opens up, that the artwork takes on meaning that differs sometimes radically from the literal meaning of the words, for example, out of which it is constructed.

Adorno's insistence is not only that form and content are better thought with and through one another, but also that they are unthinkable in isolation from each other—to express it in Kantian terms, content without form is blind while form without content is empty.[21] It is through their form that artworks come to mean something other than what they—or their words—say, but this form has its origin within the content against which it works. That is, the form that transforms the propositional content of a work into the work's substantive content is not foreign or external to the propositional content, but develops out of it. Through this development, the form, historically secondary to and dependent on the content, takes on a priority over the content. Indeed, if Adorno's interpretation of Kant's formulation that the beautiful consists in purposiveness without purpose is to be taken seriously, it is necessarily the case that the propositional content, implicated with the purpose of the pre-artistic object, not only comes to be dominated by the form but also itself fades from prominence—not disappearing, but remaining sedimented in the work, visible only through examining the historical layers that constitute its historical development.

Parataxis in Adorno's Reading of 'Der Einzige'

The implications and consequences of this schema for Adorno's understanding of poetic form—and particularly of the form of Hölderlin's poetry—are most clearly illustrated with reference to a particular example. In his discussion of the second draft of 'Der Einzige', he insists that 'parataxes are conspicuous as artful disturbances which elude the logical hierarchy of subordinating syntax' (NzL 471/NtL 2: 131). The primary significance of this phenomenon consists in the fact that it enables a use of language radically different from the predication that dominates within prose, Adorno writing of 'the music-like transformation of language into a sequence whose elements are connected in a different way to those of the judgment' (NzL 471/NtL 2: 131). The claim that Hölderlin's language becomes music-like is in a way an inversion of Adorno's insistence elsewhere on the similarity to language of art and in particular music (cf. i.a. ÄT 304/AT 204, NzL 200/NtL 1: 171 for art, and NzL 107/NtL 1: 92, VW 47/SW 49, QF 251/Livingstone 1 for music); it is worth observing that the resemblance to music consists not in the melodious sounds and rhythms of Hölderlin's lines, but to the procedures by means of which the different clauses are joined together—I return to this distinction in my discussion of language and poetry of the fifth chapter.

The text to which Adorno refers is as follows:

Es entbrennet aber sein Zorn; daß nämlich
Das Zeichen die Erde berührt, allmählich
Aus Augen gekommen, als an einer Leiter.
Diesmal. Eigenwillig sonst, unmäßig
Grenzlos, daß der Menschen Hand
Anficht das Lebende, mehr auch, als sich schicket
Für einen Halbgott, Heiliggesetztes übergeht
Der Entwurf. Seit nämlich böser Geist sich
Bemächtiget des glücklichen Altertums, unendlich,
Langher währt Eines, gesangsfeind, klanglos, das
In Maßen vergeht, des Sinnes Gewaltsames.[22]

[His fury flares up, however; that is, so that
The sign shall touch the earth, gradually
Released from eyes, as though by a ladder.
This time. Wilful at other times, immoderately
Boundless, so that the hands of men
Impugn whatever is living, more than is fitting for
A demigod, the design transgresses beyond
What's divinely ordained. For since evil spirit
Has taken possession of happy antiquity, unendingly
Long now one power has prevailed, hostile to song, without resonance,
That within measures transgresses the violence of the mind.][23]

Adorno offers the following commentary on the linguistic form of this passage, which he cites as exemplary for the phenomena described above:

> The indictment of an act of violence on the part of the spirit that has become infinite and is deifying itself seeks a linguistic form which could escape the diktat of spirit's own synthesizing principle. Hence the blasted-off 'Diesmal'; the rondo-like associative connection of clauses; the twice-used particle 'nämlich', favored in late Hölderlin. The particle introduces explication without conclusion in the place of a so-called intellectual progression. This provides the form with its priority over the content, including the intellectual content. The content is transported into what is

composed through the form's act of shaping itself to the content and of reducing the weight of the specific moment of thought, of synthetic unity. (NzL 472/NtL 2: 131–32)

What is described here as form has its origin in what Adorno terms the linguistic form, by which he seems to mean nothing more than the particular choice of words used at this point. There is a content which 'seeks a form': the implication seems to be that the same content could be expressed in a different form, one that could not escape the synthesizing principle but rather remained bound by it. However, this would be to adopt a form of crude voluntarism, to attribute to the content an apparently arbitrary capacity to choose its form. Rather, Adorno's insistence that this content 'seeks a linguistic form which could escape the diktat of its own synthesizing principle' should be interpreted as a claim that the content has particular requirements which are expressed through the demands which it exacts of the form. Hölderlin's criticism of 'evil spirit' is for Adorno inseparable from what he identifies as the attempt within this section of the poem to escape the confines of conceptual synthesis. The synthetic judgment represents for Adorno the affirmation of the principle of identity, the assertion of the identity of the nonidentical—that is to say, of that which is not. Synthesis has become a lie (MM 162/Jephcott 142). However, it is not the case that the claims made by such judgments are simply false. Synthesis rather contains within itself a moment of subjective truth, as Adorno insists in the *Metacritique of Epistemology*: 'Every logical synthesis is expected by its object, but its possibility remains abstract and is only actualized by the subject' (ME 87/AE 80). The lie comes into being in the process according to which what can be subjectively actualized is applied to the level of the object, in the extrapolation from that which can be thought by subjective reason to something objectively valid. The 'synthesizing principle' of spirit starts from what Adorno in the introduction to the *Metacritique of Epistemology* terms 'the identity of spirit with itself' (ME 18/AE 10), from which it attempts simultaneously to derive and to assert the identity of everything else with its concept—which is to say, with spirit itself.

He identifies in Hölderlin a resistance to this domination of synthesis within language, a resistance that is not configured through a propositional argument, but which is rather held up as a counter-example. The particular phenomena which conduct the opposition to the synthetic development of a logically founded argument—the extra-syntactical positioning of the adverb 'Diesmal' outside either of the sentences that surround it; the juxtaposition of clauses without conjunctions; the use and repetition of the particle 'nämlich'—can be thought of as in some way additional to what might be thought of as the poem's content, since the same propositional content—indeed, in the cases of punctuation, even the same words—could be expressed without these phenomena. At the same time, they constitute an inextricable aspect of this content. For if the form consists in the words and punctuation marks used in a particular poem—the same words that constitute its content—it is inconceivable that a change in the content of a work would not at the same time be a change in its form. Indeed, even the aspects of the text that at first glance appear to have the least effect on the poem's semantic content—the punctuation marks, including the full points which separate 'Diesmal' from the sentences on either side of it—can themselves hardly be separated from any understanding of the poem's meaning.

However, the way in which they mean is not in the first instance completely clear. In his 1956 essay on punctuation marks, Adorno considers the functions they are able to carry out within a piece of writing:

> They are all traffic signals; traffic signals were ultimately modelled on them. Exclamation marks are red, colons green, dashes order to halt. But the error of the George-school was to confuse them with marks of communication for this reason. They are rather marks of performance; they do not assiduously serve language's intercourse with the reader, but hieroglyphically serve an intercourse that runs its course inside language, on language's own tracks. It is thus superfluous to leave them out as unnecessary: then they simply hide. Every text, even the most poetically woven, cites them of its own accord, friendly spirits on whose bodiless presence the flesh of language feeds. (NzL 106/NtL 1: 91)

Adorno differentiates between what might be thought of as the performative and the significative functions of punctuation marks. In rejecting the claim that they are marks or signs of communication, he is in no way denying that they mean, but rather making a specific claim as to how they mean. Adorno's model is one according to which language, rather than being a tool with which a writer communicates with a reader—a conception responsible for what Clive Scott has criticized as the preoccupation of much recent criticism 'with poetry as either a formal or interpersonal pragmatics'[24]—itself enters into communication with the reader. Language becomes something like a subject, and comes to speak. However, Adorno's conception of the way in which language comes to speak differs fundamentally from the mystical status of language in Heidegger's claim that 'language speaks'.[25] In contrast with the deixis of the Heideggerian 'soundless voice' of language that speaks by showing, the speech identified by Adorno comes about as the result of subjective vocalization, and takes place within language itself.[26] That is, the punctuation marks direct and thus foreground the subjective act of voicing the text, and in doing so offer resistance to the significative pole of the linguistic sign, instead pointing toward the presence of the subject within language, whether in the speaking voice or through the pictorial representation of hieroglyphs. It is to this extent that the intercourse served by punctuation marks is described as being interior to language: at stake here is not a conception of language that transmits to a subject that is external to it, but rather of the embodiment of the subject within language. Adorno does not so much object to the claim that language speaks as insist on the as-if character of this speech, and to Heidegger's mythologization of what Adorno views as a necessary semblance.

The particular uses of punctuation that Adorno highlights in the extract from the second draft of 'Der Einzige' serve two functions. The speaking voice is instructed to slow down, particularly around 'Diesmal' at the beginning of the fourth line of the extract. The use of 'sonst' two words later removes any potential ambiguity from the grammatical fragment, making it clear, but only after the fact, that 'Diesmal' is to be construed as referring to the three lines that precede it, but the punctuation nonetheless enforces a distinct separation between the adverb and the sentence to the action of which it refers. While the full point after 'Diesmal' serves to mark the contrast implied by the following sentence, the one which coincides with the end of the previous line can be thought of as masking or interrupting the connection between the complete sentence and the one-word fragment that follows it. At this point I hesitate to use the term 'signifies' of the function of either punctuation mark, for there is nothing either conventional or intrinsic about what or how it is that they mean. It is certainly not the case that sentences that end mid-line necessarily imply contrast or that those that finish at the end of a line are always indicators of a thematic connection. However, it would also be wrong to see the punctuation marks as merely reinforcing or confirming an already-existing meaning. As marks or indications of performance, they direct the voice in which the poem's words are articulated, which in turn inflects the meaning which they carry.

This is in many ways similar to the discussion of grammatical form in the last-but-one section. The distinction between voice and meaning is not absolute but conceptual—perhaps even conceptually necessary or indispensable. It is not the case that there exists some sort of meaning prior to the act of speaking the words, that the particularities of the voice merely modulate: this modulation is rather the instantiation of meaning.[27] While it is possible, even necessary to think of the speaking voice as altering the content, it in fact enables the content to come into being in the first place. This does not, however, mean that the conceptual distinction between form and content is necessarily invalid: the inflection of meaning through pointers to the voice can be thought of as distinct from that which we tend to presume inheres in the linguistic sign. It is the ability to think this distinction that validates—necessitates, even—the distinction between what Adorno presents here as form and content. It is for this reason that Adorno can insist on form's priority over content: if modulations in the voice, shifts in duration, intonation and pitch are not so much secondary alterations of a preexisting meaning in the words as central to the meaning that the words take on, those aspects of a poem that instruct or direct the voice, that force or restrict the possibility of performance and therefore also of interpretation, are not of secondary significance, as it were merely formal, but rather fundamental to the poem's ability to mean at all, to say nothing of the particular meaning it takes on.

However, this is not the only way in which the punctuation marks are able to mean. What Adorno terms the 'rondo-like associative connection of clauses' consists at least in part in the way in which punctuation is used to link clauses together, referring in this case both to the absence of conjunctions and to the particular choice of punctuation mark used between each clause. This is not only a matter of how the words sit in the voice, the particular inflection of the words of the poem, but also pertains both to the very combinations of words that are used and to the way in which the clauses are linked to one another. To this extent, questions as to the weight of particular punctuation marks are hardly separable from those as to the significance of the poem's words. Indeed, this is perhaps an apposite illustration of the following claim made in *Aesthetic Theory*:

> The artwork becomes language-like in the becoming of the connections between its elements, a syntax without words still in linguistic structures. What they say is not what their words say. (ÄT 274/AT 184)

At stake here is the disjunction between a work's propositional content—the meaning of its words—and its truth content. The language-like aspect of artworks—especially of poems—in no way consists in their being constituted of words. Rather, in a certain sense poems must overcome the signifying character of their verbal aspects in order to become language-like in this sense. Adorno's description of the process by which artworks become language-like starts with what he terms the 'languageless expression' of 'mimetic impulses'. In the poem, that is, the predominance of the signifying character of language must be overcome in order that the conventionality of words can give way to these mimetic impulses—I discuss Adorno's concept of mimesis in more detail in chapter 2.

This is helpful for understanding Adorno's elucidation of the verse-paragraph selected from the second draft of 'Der Einzige'. The conventional meaning of the words—and with it, the construable propositional content of the text—takes on in Adorno's analysis a sort of secondary importance to what can be interpreted from the words, an interpretation to which the words are phenomenologically prior. From the phenomenon of 'explication without conclusion in the place of a so-called intellectual progression'— a phenomenon which he could just as well attribute to the paratactical juxtaposition of clauses without conjunctions as to the repeated use of the particle 'nämlich'—Adorno interprets a mode of speech which is not predicated on logical deduction and inference, in which words and clauses are not evaluated in terms of what they imply or the uses to which they can be put. This is what is at stake in what he terms the form's 'priority over the content'. The content consists in what one might try to think of as the literal verbal meaning of the words of a poem. The form and its priority over the content consist not simply in the way in which these words are arranged in relation to one another, but in the implications in every sense of this arrangement for the speaking voice and thus for the status taken on by the words articulated by this voice, through which the form 'reduces the weight of the specific moment of thought, of synthetic unity'. The precise arrangement of the poem's content—and this content can of course hardly be separated from the words in which it is expressed—serves to establish a language in which the synthetic judgment no longer disposes over the dominance which it has in logical argumentation. This is a language in which the content is able to fade into secondary prominence behind not so much the form as its effect: the development of a mode of expression in which the 'specific moment of thought' (which here is to be understood as conceptual thought, permeated by the principle of identification) gives way to the possibility of subjective expression that is not mediated through identity thinking.

Consequences for Form and Content

In discussing Hölderlin's own rejection of the 'logical positioning of periods', that is to say the form of argumentation in which basis is followed by, in turn, becoming, goal and purpose,[28] Adorno insists that 'linguistic synthesis contradicts that which [Hölderlin] wishes to let speak' (NzL 476/NtL 2: 135), that the aim of his poetry is to move beyond the 'logic of tightly bound periods' and with it the narrow conception of language as bound to the principle of identity on which this logic is based. This, Adorno argues, he attempts through language, an attempt which involves harnessing the potential of language against itself, or at least against the synthetic principle that dominates within it:

> The paratactical revolt against synthesis has its limit in the synthetic function of language itself. The aim is a synthesis of a different type, its self-reflection, critical of language, while language nonetheless retains synthesis. (NzL 476/NtL 2: 136)

The claim of this apparently paradoxical formulation is that language is to retain synthesis within itself, while at the same time harboring a new form of synthesis, critical of the language within which it develops. The self-reflection within the new synthesis consists in its ability to recognize its own limits, an ability not present within the as it were original synthesis, that takes itself to be the only form of knowledge. This recognition involves not merely acknowledging but coming to terms with the fact that it is itself limited and inconclusive. The problem, that is, is not the existence of synthesis itself, but the assumption—which also inheres within conventional synthesis—of the conclusiveness of synthesis, that is to say the domination within language of the assumed identity between concept and object. Adorno's aim is not to destroy synthesis, but rather to reconfigure the relationship between synthesis and language such that the principle of identity no longer dominates and restricts expression.

He finds the model for the attempt to reconfigure this relationship in Hölderlin, who, he argues, recognized the semblance of liberation from the domination of identity in the rhetorical technique of periodicity, in the context of which he develops his technique of parataxis, noting that periodicity tends to disguise much more than it alters the fact that expression is subjected to 'logical compulsion'. Adorno identifies in Hölderlin the response, the sacrifice of the period, which 'represents poetically the sacrifice of the legislating subject itself' (NzL 477/NtL 2: 136). The phrase 'legislating subject' is used twice at this point in the discussion of Hölderlin's parataxis, but does not otherwise appear within Adorno's œuvre. It refers to the bourgeois subject of the Enlightenment, the Kantian freedom of the will that corresponds to the necessity of nature: indeed, it is from the separation of subject from nature and the concomitant attempt by the subject to dominate and classify nature that the restricted view of language as synthesis has become prevalent (cf. DA 34–35/DE 13). And the toppling of the legislating subject is at the same time the dismantling of the primacy of synthesis within language:

> With this sacrifice the poetic movement in Hölderlin shatters the category of sense. For sense constitutes itself through the linguistic expression of synthetic unity. The subject's intention, the primacy of sense, is ceded to language, along with the legislating subject. (NzL 477/NtL 2: 136)

Sense as we understand it is mediated through the prevailing understanding of language as determined by enlightenment. That we tend to equate intention with sense is historically contingent, a consequence of the domination of the principle of identity within language and consequently within the humanities. Adorno differentiates between the two, sense understood as the verbal aspect of meaning, intention as its nonverbal aspect—which can only be translated into words in a compromized form.

He expresses his rejection of what would a few years later be called the linguistic turn, the tendency to (over-)emphasize the role of language in cognition to the extent that, at its extreme, problems of philosophy are presented as or reduced to problems of linguistics:[29]

> [Language's] dual character reveals itself in Hölderlin's poetry. As conceptual and predicative, language stands opposed to subjective expression; by virtue of its generality it levels down what is to be expressed to something already pre-given and known. The poets rebel against this. They always want to incorporate the subject and its expression into language, to the point of its downfall. (NzL 477/NtL 2:136)

While Rorty insists on the achievement of the linguistic turn in helping 'shift from talk about experience as a medium of representation to talk of language as such a medium—a shift which [. . .] made it easier to set aside the notion of representation itself'[30]—Adorno takes almost the opposite approach. Rather than seeking the convenience of a reason to ignore the problem of representation, he foregrounds it.[31] In doing so he insists that language—or perhaps more accurately, our understanding of language as mediated through the dialectic of enlightenment—is inadequate to expression. The translation of intention into (conceptual) sense serves to eradicate the differences in the former, flattening the contours of the qualitatively different, nonidentical experience that is to be expressed to something expressible in the terms of the classificatory knowledge mediated through language. Adorno sees in Hölderlin, who serves here as a metonymy for poets in general, the wish to break this dominance of sign (the aspect of language which seeks to know and classify nature) over image (the aspect which seeks to resemble it (DA 33-34/DE 12-13)), the desire not to destroy language but to reconfigure our understanding of it, to break the dominance of conceptual knowledge over thought, the desire for a mode of communication in which subjective experience is not cleared away but central, a 'communication of what is differentiated', to use Adorno's own expression of speculation as to a utopian state of reconciliation (S 743/CM 247). This is the force of Bernhard Lypp's claim that parataxis is a historico-philosophical and not only a stylistic concept, in that it 'makes the language of a free co-existence of difference thinkable'.[32] Parataxis, perhaps thinkable as metonymy for poetry or even art in general, does not realize subjectivity in its non-damaged form, but allows us to think the possibility of the communication that would take place in a state of reconciliation.

However, the substantive content and truth content of a work are not identical with the subjective expression that is flattened in the linguistic mediation that results in its propositional content. One possibility would be to establish a relatively crude schema, according to which the substantive content could be thought of as the cognition that propositional content does not simply constitute the expression of subjective intention. This would however be to commit the same error of which Adorno accuses Heidegger: it would infiltrate that which in Hölderlin's poetry is philosophically lacking with philosophy from the outside. The relationship is in fact more complex. Adorno argues that the 'linguistic procedure converges with the antisubjectivism of the substantive content' (NzL 478/NtL 2: 137). This antisubjectivism consists not in the attempt to present some sort of immediate subjective expression, but in cutting language free from the subject which holds the delusion of its own immediacy and 'which can no longer speak on its own account' (NzL 478/NtL 2: 137). Adorno attempts to formulate the consequences this has for the way in which we might attempt to identify and relate to the substantive content of poems:

> A critique of Hölderlin, as critique of the truth content of the hymns, would have to investigate their historico-philosophical possibility, and with it that of the theology toward which Hölderlin aims. Such a critique would not transcend the poetry. The aesthetic *coups de main*, from the quasi-quantitative strophic division of the great elegies to the triadic constructions, are witnesses to an impossibility deep within. Because Hölderlin's utopia is not substantial in the Hegelian sense, not a concrete potential of reality in the objective spirit of the epoch, Hölderlin must impose it by way of the stylistic principle. The contradiction between the stylistic principle and the poetic form itself becomes a shortcoming in the latter. (NzL 480/NtL 2: 139)

The word which I have translated as 'form' in the final sentence of this extract is not *Form* but *Gestalt*, derived from a substantivized form of the past participle of the verb *stellen*, to place. To the extent that there is a distinction between the two words, it is that *Gestalt* tends to refer more explicitly to the internal construction of an object, *Form* to the external shape, but this differentiation is perhaps arbitrary and artificial. More often, the two words are used as synonyms, and indeed on the previous page Adorno refers to the triadic structure of the late hymns as a *Formprinzip*, a 'principle of form' (NzL 479/NtL 2: 138). The contradiction Adorno identifies between the stylistic principle and the poetic form consists in the fragmentary character of the late hymns, which he says might themselves be something 'constitutively unfinishable' (NzL 480/NtL 2:138). This consists specifically in Hölderlin's response to what Adorno terms the 'extremely modern difficulty of achieving articulated construction without recourse to pre-given schemata' (NzL 479/NtL 2: 138). The phenomenon to which Adorno draws attention is the appearance of logical consistency and completeness, in the absence of both: in a footnote he gives the example of Hölderlin's use of the particle 'denn' to imply a logical conclusion in situations where the order and content of the clauses preclude or negate the possibility of such a conclusion (NzL 480/NtL 2: 340). In his opposition of the stylistic principle of Hölderlin's poetry to the poetic form, Adorno appears to complicate the relationship between what might be thought of as forming and form, the technique employed in composition and the structure of the resulting work. But what he terms the shortcomings in the *Gestalt* of a work are to be differentiated from what might be thought of as inadequacies of *Form*: the shortcomings in the structure constitute rather the fragmentary aspect of the work in question, which is not to be considered an inadequacy of the work's form. As Rainer Nägele points out, *Gestalt* tends to refer to 'organic wholeness and inner formation more than external form and shape'.[33] This is perhaps best illustrated with a quotation from Adorno's radio discussion with Peter von Haselberg on the nature of the fragment, in which he argues that 'fragments are artworks which have the character of something incomplete, of something unfinished, regardless of whether this is intended or whether it's a matter of a genuine form sui generis, that is to say regardless [. . .] of whether the fragment is form or accident'.[34] Form here consists in the shape a work takes on deliberately, which can include what Adorno here conceives as shortcomings in the work's structure or *Gestalt*, the fragmentary character of the work, which he describes in the discussion with von Haselberg as 'art's true border with reality'. As the mark of the madness of works of art, form is what sets them apart from that which they are not.

This is for Adorno closely related to the work's truth content. What he terms the historico-philosophical possibility of Hölderlin's hymns determines the relationship between their form and their truth content, the way in which the form inflects and conditions the truth content. The contradictoriness that Adorno identifies in Hölderlin's deployment of devices that imply the existence of logical periodicity despite the fact that he abandons this periodicity and the logic of implication and deduction on which it depends is a historically particular phenomenon. The voice that the form directs instantiates an uncertainty that reflects or perhaps enacts the philosophical problems bound up with the work. Adorno's phrase the 'impossibility deep within' refers to the (historically contingent) philosophical antinomy that is Hölderlin's attempt to abandon the subjective lyric in disappointment with the subject in pursuit of a lyric objectivity, which the poem is unable to grant. It is in this light that Adorno can in the final sentence of his essay identify 'metaphysical passivity' as the substantive content of Hölderlin's poetry, a passivity which does not consist in resignation, but which 'allies itself, against myth, with the hope of a reality in which humanity would be free from the spell of its own imprisonment in nature, a spell which was reflected in humanity's conception of absolute spirit' (NzL 491/NtL 2:

149).³⁵ This echoes Adorno's claim earlier in the essay that 'the sublimation of primary obedience into autonomy is that extreme passivity that found its formal correlative in the technique of arrangement' (NzL 475/NtL 2: 135). The word I have translated as 'arrangement' is *Reihen*, which means to arrange in rows or in sequence, and refers here primarily to the arrangement of clauses in relation to one another. The obedience at stake here is to language as liberated from subjective intention, a constellation which I now address in closer detail.

2

Form and Expression

> Art is surely unthinkable without the subjective power to form, but this power has nothing to do with the attitude of power within the work's expression.
>
> —ÄT 65/AT 39

In a manner reminiscent of the dismissal of the 'crude textbook separation of content and form' discussed in the introductory section to the previous chapter, the 'Semblance and Expression' section of *Aesthetic Theory* sees Adorno reject attempts to apply a similarly simplified and inflexible schema to the categories of form and expression:

> The mediation of artworks' expression through their spiritualization, as significant early exponents of expressionism were aware, implies the critique of that clumsy dualism of form and expression from which not only traditional aesthetics but also the consciousness of many genuine artists take their bearings. (ÄT 173/AT 114)

Spiritualization is in many ways an unsatisfactory translation of *Vergeistigung*, just as spiritual was of *geistig* in the previous chapter. The process to which Adorno refers is in the first instance one according to which artworks take on what might be thought of as an intellectual character in opposition to their intuitable or sensuous aspects. The English expression the 'intellectualization of artworks', however, carries a certain derogatory implication, and suggests a process much narrower than that which is at issue here. This spiritualization consists in the movement of consciousness in art, and harbors, as Surti Singh has shown, a tension between the traditional sense of spiritualization as intellectualization, which represents the tendency toward the domination of nature by the human intellect, and the radical sense of the 'process that turns art against its history of domination' by means of a renewed encounter with that which is dominated.[1]

In a footnote Adorno makes clear that the particular genuine artist to whom he is here alluding is Alban Berg, who according to Adorno criticized 'the lack of expressive content in Schönberg's early twelve-tone compositions'.[2] It is notable that this discussion of Berg to which Adorno refers in the footnote in *Aesthetic Theory* contains no mention of either *Form* or *Ausdruck*, the words used in the citation from *Aesthetic Theory* above. The terms used in the discussion of Berg for expression and expressive are *Expression* and *expressiv*, while the closest Adorno comes to discussing form are the points at which he mentions twelve-tone technique—I consider Adorno's deployment of the concept of technique more concretely in the next-but-one chapter on the relationship between form and material. The composer's consciousness—in this case, how Berg conceives of compositional technique—is to be understood as distinct from what Adorno identifies as the significance of the compositions. What artworks say is thus not only not what their words say (ÄT 274/AT 184), but also neither what their creators say, nor necessarily what their creators want or think them to say. Artworks' expression is not identical with the subjective intention of their creators. The relationship between artistic subject and expression, the nature and extent of their mediation, is a central aspect of the discussion in this chapter.

As in the case with form and content, Adorno's understanding of the relationship between form and expression involves what might be thought of as a sort of transformation, as the boundaries between the two concepts that appear fundamentally opposed to one another are revealed as somewhat more permeable than the opposition of their concepts to one another might suggest:

> That which subjugated expression, the formal character of beauty, transforms itself with all ambivalence of triumph into expression, in which what is menacing about the domination of nature is wed to the longing for the defeated which flares up at that domination. But what is defeated is the expression of suffering under subjugation and its vanishing point, death. Beauty's affinity with death is located in the idea of pure form which art imposes on the diversity of the living that expires

within it. In perfect beauty, that which strives against it would have come to rest, and such aesthetic reconciliation is deadly for the extra-aesthetic. That is the sorrow of art. (ÄT 84/AT 52)

Whereas the discussion in the previous chapter concerned itself with Adorno's insistence that form has its origin in content, here his concern is not so much the origin of form as what it might be thought of as doing within the work. Form is presented as a sort of imposition on expression, not so much in opposition to expression as oblivious to it, willing—required, even—to subordinate the requirements of expression in its attempt to establish itself. In this account two things in particular become clear. First, that the form under discussion here is not the same as that discussed in the previous chapter, that arises out of the content of the artwork, but a principle imposed from outside. And second, that what might be understood as the expression of an artwork is not identical with the subjugated expression, but rather arises out of the process in which this expression is subjugated by the formal character of beauty: this expression of the artwork is as it were the result of the mediation of form and expression. This points to a certain affinity between an artwork's expression as described here, and the developmental concept of form outlined in the previous chapter. That is to say, the examination of form through its relationship to expression not only illuminates form from a different angle, but also investigates what must to a certain extent be thought of as a different phenomenon.

At stake here is not form as such but more specifically the formal character of beauty, which is equated first with the idea of pure form, and then with beauty itself. That is, Adorno is working here with a variation of a Kantian understanding of form as that which in the visual arts for example can be understood as opposed to color.[3] However, whereas for Kant form involves shape and play, the latter encompassing play both of what is shaped and the resulting play of the sensations, Adorno works here with a concept of pure form that seems to exclude anything that could be understood as dynamism or liveliness. According to this understanding, perfect beauty—for Adorno an aim that is neither attainable nor necessarily to be striven for—would require the eradication of all such liveliness, its irrevocable crystallization into a static form. As such it is clear that the form here under discussion is not to be understood as a general property or attribute of all artworks but rather as a particular manifestation or instance of such an attribute. That is, there is a distinction to be made between a more general category of form, according to which the formal attributes of every artwork can at least theoretically be assessed, and the particular idea of form that consists in what Adorno describes here as perfect beauty. It is not the general shape or construction of an artwork but a particular idealized static construction. This idealized pure form, however, exists as a tendency that inheres within all artworks and within their artistic domination of the material of which they are constituted; I investigate the nature of this domination more thoroughly in the next-but-one chapter, under the rubric of Adorno's concept of technique.

There is a similar ambivalence at play in Adorno's use of the concept of expression, which encompasses both the expression of a formed artwork and what might be thought of as the expressive impulses that are themselves formed into the work. Grasping the distinction between the range of ways in which Adorno uses the two concepts of form and expression is fundamental for understanding the productive contradictions within his conception of the relationship between the two. A somewhat simplified model of Adorno's understanding of this relationship as demonstrated by the quotation discussed above is that the imposition of form on these expressive impulses not only overcomes them, but also allows the emergence of a form which is itself expressive. It is this model that I describe, investigate, and complicate during the rest of this chapter, by elucidating the variety of the processes at work in the relationship between form and expression. In doing so I seek both to account for the diverse and sometimes opposed or contradictory workings of form within the work, and to show some of the ways in which these workings coalesce within form as a way of thinking, but in such a way that the complexity of their relationships is not effaced.

I begin the chapter by discussing Adorno's account of the trajectory of the relationship between form and expression as a relationship of mediation that has its own historical development. In the second and third sections I examine the workings of this mediation in more detail, focusing on his critique of the failure he identifies in literary expressionism. In the second section I contrast his accounts of literary and musical expressionism to reveal a doubling that underlies Adorno's account, a result of the second-order expression of the artwork that emerges from the mediation of form and subjective expression. In the third I set out the implications of this doubling, and in doing so draw out some of the political implications of the comparison between expressionism and surrealism, formulating an alternative to Benjamin's conception of the political potential of the latter. I follow this with an account of Adorno's analysis of Kafka's prose, developing a theorization of the relationship between literary form and reality that dissents from the opposition between formalism and realism that prevails within traditional Marxist literary theory. In the fifth section I consider the implications for this relationship—and thus for the relationship between art and society—of Adorno's use of the concept of mimesis, the 'antithesis of form', and its complex relationship to expression. Finally I elaborate on some of the consequences of the complexity of these relationships between form, expression, semblance, and mimesis for the understanding of the concept of form, indicating ways in which form is able to serve as a deposit for the complexity of these moments and processes that act in opposition to one another.

The Mediation of Form and Expression

The quotation from the 'Semblance and Expression' section of *Aesthetic Theory* with which I began this chapter continues with an account of a historical trajectory of the relationship of conceptual opposition between form and expression, and its consequences for artworks today. While form and expression, like form and content, are not metaphysically distinct categories, their opposition is nonetheless grounded in the experience of artworks:

> Not that this dichotomy is completely devoid of foundation. The preponderance of expression here, of the formal aspect there can hardly be argued away, especially in older art, which provided a container for the emotions. In the meantime the two moments have been intimately mediated through each other. Where works are not fully constructed, formed, they forfeit the very expressivity for the sake of which they dispense with the labor and effort of form; and the ostensibly pure form, which repudiates expression, clatters. (ÄT 173–74/AT 114)

Adorno acknowledges that form and expression are phenomena that can—indeed, that must, by any attentive observer of an artwork—be observed. The mediation between form and expression on which he insists so strongly is presented as a historically specific development. He provides no example for his not entirely convincing claim that older art 'provided a container for the emotions'. Indeed, in the rest of his collected writings he only uses the term container (*Gehäuse*) to refer to the work of Schönberg and his (unnamed) successors, and of Wagner. In the case of Schönberg, Adorno uses the term positively, referring in his 1930 account of 'The History of Style in Schönberg's Work' to the 'freshness of improvisation in the container of the form' in his earliest twelve-tone compositions (GS 18: 392). In 'Arnold Schönberg', written in 1952 and first published in 1953, however, he employs the term much more derogatorily with respect to Schönberg's contemporaries, saying of countless young composers that they used twelve-tone technique 'not out of the need of their own experience but as a container in which one seeks refuge' (P 152/WWN 149; cf. GS 10.2: 839). Meanwhile, he describes 'the core [*Kerngehäuse*] of Wagner's formal construction' as empty (VW 39/SW 42), but had in his 1933 'Note on Wagner' argued that 'the emancipation of sounds from the system of their ranks which took place in *Tristan* as the excess of the individual, freed music from precisely that container of individual expression in which the alchemist prepared his sounds' (GS 18: 208). The period of older art of which Adorno writes thus comes to an end at the latest with the première of *Tristan* in 1865.

While his caricature of earlier art (and music in particular) is not entirely convincing, it is nonetheless notable that *Tristan* marked the crossing of a particular threshold. In *Composing for Film* Adorno argues that the break he identifies between the bourgeois public and genuine bourgeois art-music 'can be dated back to *Tristan*' (GS 15: 59–60/CF 57), while in the Mahler book he insists that what he terms 'chromatization as the dequalifying of material' has been 'driving music along one-dimensionally since *Tristan*' (M 167/MMP 19). By chromatization Adorno simply means the transition away from diatonicism toward chromatic atonality, a concept that is rather easier to grasp than that of dequalifying, even if the dividing-line between tonality and atonality is not entirely rigid. The dequalifying to which this chromatization is supposed to lead consists in the elimination of individual qualities of particularity from the material out of which music can be thought of as being composed. It refers to the breaking down of preexisting formations within the material, which becomes what Adorno in *Aesthetic Theory* terms 'a tabula rasa for subjective projections' (ÄT 33/AT 17).

Adorno's expression 'a container for the emotions' now begins to appear in a slightly different light, the emphasis shifting from 'for the emotions' toward the concept of a container. That is to say, Adorno identifies before *Tristan* a certain rigidity in the formal construction of artworks, a structure that exists as it were independently of the expressive content of a work rather than being determined by it. This slightly different claim is nonetheless not without its problems, since it presumes that the forms of pre-*Tristan* works are both static and self-evident, ignoring questions of how they come into

Form and Expression 69

being and develop, particularly in response to the particular ways in which they are used, that is to say through the development of what becomes a tradition. It is not clear, that is, whether the characteristic identified by Adorno as specific to modern artworks is not perhaps also identifiable in earlier works. Perhaps the most prominent example is provided by the discussion in the previous chapter of Adorno's account of the consequences of the form of Hölderlin's poetry not only for its content but also for the incorporation of the subject and its expression into language. Similarly, there is no sense in the unfinished monograph on Beethoven that Adorno considers that his music can adequately be conceived as a mere vessel for emotional content (NS 1.1, passim). However, in his discussion of the final scene of *Faust*, Adorno argues

> But when the Magna peccatrix pleads 'Bei den Locken, die so weichlich / Trockneten die heil'gen Glieder' ['by the locks that so softly dried the holy limbs'], the form is imbued with the literal power of the adverbial modifier, receives the softness of the hair, a sign of erotic love in the aura of heavenly love. (NzL 131/NtL 1: 113)

The use of *erfüllen*, which I have translated here as 'imbue', has the primary sense of 'fulfill', but retains its literal meaning to a rather greater extent than its English cognate. That is, this sentence is to an extent an illustration of Adorno's understanding of form as a container. However, the decision to interpret the use of *weichlich* as filling the form rather than constituting it or (to remain within a three-dimensional metaphor) building it up seems arbitrary. Meanwhile, going further back in history, he narrates in 'Bach Defended from his Admirers' how the composer 'created the form of the fugue' (P 141/WWN 138), which he describes on the following page as 'thoroughly formed' (P 142/WWN 139)—that is to say, what Adorno describes as the form is something not only made but also honed and refined.

This sheds further light on Adorno's ambivalence toward the shift that he identifies as beginning with the composition of *Tristan*. He does not deny that a significant shift can be identified—one could perhaps call it the beginning of the transition from classical to late modernity—but rather calls into question the status of what we think we know about it. While this is not a question that I will be able to settle within the scope of this book, it is a matter that will remain close to the discussion as it develops, and on which my investigations will on occasion touch, if obliquely.[4] The mediation of form and expression, that is, is not necessarily as recent a phenomenon as Adorno claims—but this is not central to his argument. Indeed, if anything his discussion of a previous time in which the two were more separate from one another takes on the role of a concession, allowing him to advance all the more strongly the claim that they are now thoroughly mediated through one another. He attributes this mediation not only to their dependence on one another—within the artwork and not only conceptually—but also to their opposition. The desire to abandon 'the labor and effort of form' has its origin in the attempt to liberate expression from form's constraints, while the search for a 'pure form' is at the same time the attempt to reject expression. It is a reflection of Adorno's understanding of the depth of their mediation that he insists that there is no possibility that either of these attempts could succeed: form without expression must reconcile itself to the clatter of a shoddily constructed form, while formless expression is no expression at all.

However, this account of the mediation of form and expression has hitherto remained relatively abstract, focusing primarily on the conceptual relationship between the two. The consequences of Adorno's understanding of this mediation—and, indeed, some of the problems within it—can best be seen through examination of his discussions not only of particular artworks, but also of artistic movements and currents. Of particular relevance to his understanding of the relationship between form and expression are his writings on literary expressionism, which, he argues in the short text on expressionism and artistic truthfulness in the appendix to *Notes to Literature*, 'places the self absolutely, and demands the pure scream' (NzL 609/NtL 2: 257). It is to Adorno's critique of this movement, 'more powerful as an idea than in its products' (ÄT 270/AT 181), that I now turn.

Literary and Musical Expressionism

Discussing Karl Kraus's attitude to the relationship between linguistic sign and expression, Adorno compares his view to that of the expressionists:

> In contrast to Kraus, the expressionists strived to jump over their own shadows. They uncompromisingly asserted the primacy of expression. Their intention was to use words purely as expressive values such as relations of color or tone in painting and music. Language's resistance to the expressionist idea was so tenacious

that it was hardly ever realized at all except by the Dadaists. (NzL 434/NtL 2: 98)

Literary expressionism constitutes in Adorno's eyes an attempt, to put it in the terms of *Dialectic of Enlightenment*, to privilege the image character of language at the expense of its sign character. That such an attempt can for Adorno only end in failure is clear from the account of the split of language into these two characters as a result of the division of intellectual labor into science and poetry (DA 34/DE 13). To attempt simply to reverse or to ignore this split would be to act as if this division of labor had not taken place. In the light of the predominance of sign over image within what Adorno terms the scientific conception of language, the resistance encountered by the expressionist attempt to reject precisely this aspect of language is hardly surprising. In his essay on Bloch's *Spuren*, Adorno suggests a more nuanced understanding of the relationship between expression and conceptuality, arguing that the expressionist scream is simply drowned out by the fact that 'the universal concept, which washes away the trace and is hardly able to suspend it within itself, must for the sake of its own intention nonetheless speak as if the trace were present within it' (NzL 247/NtL 1: 213).

Adorno insists in his discussion of Kraus in 'Presuppositions' that everything linguistic bears the trace of the conceptual, 'even in its most extreme reduction to expressive value' (NzL 434–35/NtL 2: 98). Literary expressionism was in his view condemned to obsolescence by its failure to acknowledge that the conceptual element of language cannot simply be shrugged off, that emancipation from conceptuality can only exist as a moment, a tendency, a struggle. Artworks recognize in the concept something hostile to art, but success in this struggle would be impossible for a literary artwork, since it would require the elimination of conceptuality from language, and thus the end of language. 'Even the stuttered sound, insofar as it is word and not sound, retains its conceptual range, and the context of linguistic structures, through which alone they arrange themselves into an artistic whole, can hardly dispense with the conceptual element' (NzL 435/NtL 2: 99). Here both expression and form are presented as being hostile to conceptuality: expression because it cannot escape conceptual mediation, form because the concept, as the 'unity of tokens of that which it subsumes' (NzL 435/NtL 2: 99), retains its connection to that aspect of the empirical world which is foreign to the law of form and cannot be incorporated into the work. What Adorno sees as the failure of expressionism is perhaps best illustrated by his comments on Borchardt's opposition to it, in which he notes that the expressionists never resolved the contradiction posed by the production of works, despite their attempt to follow expression's hostility to its mediation through form and 'suspend the concept of the thoroughly constructed work' (NzL 552/NtL 2: 207).

However, this critique of literary expressionism sits somewhat uneasily with Adorno's remarks on Georg Trakl, of whose lyric poetry Adorno writes in *Minima Moralia* that in it 'the waves of dream crash together over the helpless verses' (MM 253/Jephcott 222). In his elusive discussion of Trakl in *Aesthetic Theory*, Adorno claims that in his poems 'the word "sonata" takes on a significance that it is only accorded here, by means of its sound and the associations that are steered by the poem' (ÄT 186/AT 122). Adorno points to the possibility of a poetic language that refuses to eschew signification without being limited to it. Signification would here fall short of, to use Adorno's phrase, 'what the word wants in the poem'. The suggestion of diffuse sounds rejects the possibility of imagining a single sonata, the word is rather 'formed out of fragments, shards of sonatas', the word sonata itself 'reminiscent of the sound that is intended and awakened in the work' (ÄT 186/AT 123). Something similar is at stake in Adorno's claim that in Trakl's poetry the copula is 'alienated in the artwork from its conceptual sense' insofar as the verb 'is' rejects existential judgment in favor of 'its pale after-image, qualitatively transformed to the point of negation' (ÄT 187/AT 123). Poetry enables the fundamental transformation of even the most everyday and apparently simple units of sense. In the 'Paralipomena' to *Aesthetic Theory* Adorno refers to this phenomenon as 'the distinction between aesthetic and discursive logicity', in which there is no uncontrolled 'cascade of associations', but rather the image-elements play a part in the formal categories of an aesthetic form that 'has its rationality even while associating' (ÄT 431–32/AT 290).

This poetic transformation of language qualifies to a certain extent Adorno's claim that poetry is 'linguistic'. If it is correct or helpful to say that poetry is linguistic, it is not so in the sense that poetry is simply an instance of language. Adorno's discussion of Trakl makes the case at least as strongly as his essay on Hölderlin that study of the significative character of language—that is to say, linguistics, according to most conceptions—is inadequate to dealing with poetry, which reveals that much of what we might otherwise think to be the case about language is at best not the whole story. That is to say, if poetry is linguistic, it is so in such a way that it challenges understandings of language, and calls into question the primacy of the conceptual and predicative moments within language, as discussed at the end of the previous chapter. Indeed, it is perhaps more accurate to put it in the terms of Adorno's remark when discussing Trakl in the introduction to the positivism dispute that 'the medium of poetry is language' (GS 8: 337; I discuss the relationship between poetry and language in more detail in chapter 4 below).

A similar tension underlies Adorno's remarks on expressionist music in his 1942 encyclopedia article on 'Musical Expressionism'.[5] However, whereas in poetry the expressionist moment is unable to dispense with the conceptual elements of language, in music it is the prospect of realizing the expressionist ideal that ultimately reveals its impossibility. Adorno identifies as the ideal of expressionist music 'the *immediacy* of expression', in the sense both of the 'the elimination of all conventional elements of traditional music'—that is, of everything that abstracts or generalizes from or transcends the particularity of the unique, individual case—and of the transformation of the content of music, for which is sought 'the semblanceless, undisguised, untransfigured truth of subjective impulse' (GS 18: 60, emphasis original/NM 275). Expressionist music thus takes subjective expression as its content, which it seeks to convey in a manner that is free from the mediation of form: its aspiration is a transcript or documentation, the unstylized recording of psychic or emotional content (GS 18: 60/NM 275).

Adorno returns to this documentary character of expressionism in his discussion of Schönberg's expressionist phase in the *Philosophy of New Music*. In Adorno's account, musical expressionism turns the compositional repertoire of romantic music against its romantic aspirations:

> Expressionist music had taken the principle of expression from traditionally romantic music so literally that it took on the character of a transcription. With this, however, it is inverted. Music as a transcription of expression is no longer 'expressive'. That which is expressed no longer hovers over it at an indeterminate distance, lending it the reflected glory of the infinite. As soon as music fixes that which is expressed—its subjective content—sharply and unambiguously, this content congeals under this music's gaze into nothing other than the objective, the existence of which music's pure expressive character denies. (PnM 53/PMM 49-50)

Adorno's model here is his account of the development of new music out of and in opposition to its predecessor. Its technical repertoire emerges and proceeds from the 'immanent movement' of that of traditional music, 'from which it absconds by means of a qualitative leap' (PnM 20/PMM 11). New music develops the procedures and techniques of tonality in accordance with their own logic: their qualitative transformation consists in the fact that the music comes to focus on them in their own right. The means of musical composition cease to be means for the expression of some other content, and become themselves the content of new music. This analysis reveals the modernist counterpart to and inversion of the becoming-form of content discussed in the previous chapter: as modernism dedicates itself the artistic investigation of artistic techniques and procedures, form in turn becomes content.

Expressionism, that is, represents the culmination of a process whereby the expression of a something, of a given emotional content, is amplified and concentrated into a determined and sharply focused dedication to the potential of expression itself. From one perspective it appears as formless, because its intensification of the principle of expression is effected by means of the renunciation of elements of formal convention, as expression without the mediation of form—indeed, in the encyclopedia article Adorno draws the link between this aspect of expressionist music and literary expressionism, describing music from which all conventional elements have been eliminated as 'analogous to the poetic ideal of the "scream"' (GS 18: 60/NM 275). From the opposite perspective it appears as contentless, in that its expressed content is replaced by its dedication to expression *tout court*. But in the elimination of the objective content of expression, expression can no longer be subjective, and at once ceases to express and is itself transformed into objective content. In this respect expressionism represents the determinate negation of romanticist expression.

Expressionism and Surrealism

The implications of this theorization come into sharper focus when placed alongside Adorno's dissent from Benjamin's praise for surrealist poetry's rejection of the utopian, moralistic metaphors of the social-democratic promise of a more beautiful future, in favor of the development of the political potential of associative images.[6] In a footnote to his discussion of Schönberg's expressionism Adorno seeks to account for the distinction between expressionism and surrealism by means of the claim that the two movements diverge in the stances they take vis-à-vis the organic:

> The 'tornness' of expressionism hails from its organic irrationality. It measures itself according to the sudden gesture and the inertia of flesh. Its rhythm is modelled on that of waking and sleeping. Surrealist intentionality presupposes the physiological unity of flesh as disintegrated. It is anti-organic and refers to what is dead. It destroys the boundary between flesh and the world of things in order to convict society of the reification of flesh. Its form is that of montage. This is completely alien to Schönberg. But the more subjectivity in surrealism foregoes its right over the world of things and confesses the supremacy of that world with its accusation, the more it is at the same time willing to accept its preexisting form. (PnM 54/PMM 51)

The organicism which Adorno locates in musical expressionism consists in the fact that in its transformation into the objective content of music, subjective expression becomes itself the material that is shaped into the architecture of the work. This transformation of expression into material helps to account for the divergence between his assessments of musical and literary expressionism: while the inability, common to both musical and literary expressionism, to present pure subjectivity without the mediation of form means that neither is able fully to live up to their theoretical aspirations, the technical repertoire of expressionist musical composition—Adorno identifies as examples Schönberg's use of reprise, ostinato, reposing harmonies, and thematic chords within *Die glückliche Hand*—means that expressionist music also exceeds these aspirations in a manner of which its literary counterpart is not capable. More specifically (and in terms which I discuss more extensively in the fourth chapter), the transcribed expression becomes 'material for construction' (PnM 53/PMM 50), as music's dedication to emotional expression culminates in the musical architecture in which this expression finds its negation. The success of musical expressionism thus consists not in the triumph of expression over form, but rather in the suspended self-negation of expression through form itself, as the mark of artistic composition.

In contrast with the form that results from this suspension, a form in which the unity of the variations and rhythms of the human body is preserved, Adorno identifies in surrealism a tendency toward fragmentation that breaks down the distinction between life and the non-living. This fragmentation is oriented against reification, and toward reconciliation, insofar as surrealism presents itself as the future resolution of the states of dream and reality, brought together in a single, contradiction-ridden appearance.[7] However, in Adorno's assessment surrealism allows itself, however inadvertently, to acquiesce to the conditions against which its theory is oriented—in the terms of Richard Wolin's helpful gloss, '"inorganicity" and "lifelessness" were the chief traits of high capitalism under conditions of total reification, which fostered *social* relations between things—commodities—and *objective* relations between persons'.[8]

At the heart of the disagreement between Adorno and Benjamin is thus the question of the evaluation of surrealism against its own aspirations, of the success or otherwise of what Jameson describes as the surrealist image's 'convulsive effort to split open the commodity forms of the objective universe by striking them against each other with immense force'.[9] Benjamin largely accepts the surrealists' account of their practice: its emancipatory potential consists in the fact that the surrealists alone have understood the present demands of the communist manifesto, and are thus the sole standard-bearers of a radical concept of freedom otherwise lost in Europe since Bakunin.[10] Adorno's dissent from this position—and in his 1956 essay 'Looking Back on Surrealism' he acknowledges that his theorization relies to a certain extent on historical hindsight, writing that 'after the European catastrophe the surrealist shocks have become powerless' (NzL 102/NtL 1: 87)—is based on the diagnosis that surrealism's technical repertoire renders it unable to express its objection to reification without to the same extent accepting and endorsing it.

Adorno's comparison between expressionism and surrealism enables the further illumination of the critical consensus that Adorno's reservations with respect to Benjamin's endorsement of surrealism pertain to its susceptibility 'to a type of object fetishism'.[11] Adorno identifies as the feature common to the painterly and the poetic manifestation of surrealism alike the use of montage, a technique or practice which has both aesthetic and political implications. More specifically, montage 'would like, perhaps in vain, but unmistakably in accordance with its intention, to produce perceptions as they ought to have been at the time' (NzL 103/NtL 1: 88). In this respect surrealism takes as its material not the bodily rhythms of expressionism, but rather images of what is outdated or obsolete, images which for Adorno are 'fetishes—commodity fetishes—on which something subjective, libido, was once fixated' (NzL 104/NtL 1: 89). Surrealism is unable to escape the affirmation of reification because it does not carry out its immanent critique or determinate negation.

Adorno takes issue with surrealism's relatively static deployment of montage, creating images that are 'true still lives' (NzL 104/NtL 1: 89 that lack dynamism and tend toward death. His objection here is twofold. First, the material with which surrealist montage works is outdated, a theme to which I return in the fourth chapter. Second, the montage itself as technical procedure has not gone through a process of formal development or innovation akin to the transformation of expression that is central to Adorno's account of the successes of musical expressionism beyond its theoretical aspirations, even taking into consideration its failure when measured solely against those aspirations. The objection to montage is that whereas the dedication to expression at the expense of the content that is expressed means that it ceases to be expressive, montage never loses sight of its material in this way. Surrealism thus remains constrained within the horizon of the outdated material against which it orients itself—of the world of reification and the commodity, however much it seeks to object to that world.

Adorno's objection is that—in contrast with the mediation of expression through form—surrealist montage is deployed statically, without having gone through a process of self-negation and mediation. In the words of Wolin's commentary, '[a]s a result of its renunciation of the category of mediation, surrealism accepts the material elements of bourgeois society as such and uncritically'.[12] This gloss helps to illuminate the critical force of Adorno's claim that 'surrealism's dialectical images are the images of a dialectic of subjective freedom in the state of objective unfreedom' (NzL 104/NtL 1: 88). Without mediation, surrealism cannot but fail to see the extent to which subjectivity and its freedom are nothing other than the counterparts to the objective unfreedom against which they seek to revolt. In asserting subjective freedom against objective unfreedom without accounting for their mediation, surrealism inadvertently also affirms the objective unfreedom against which it orients itself, accepting the relations of bourgeois society.[13] This unwitting affirmation results neither from an as it were merely theoretical error nor from a mistake in the use of technique, but from the fact that the specific technical repertoire of surrealism does not involve the adequate development of its use of montage.

This diagnosis of the absence of mediation as the cause of surrealism's failure measured against its own political aspirations is closely related to Adorno's formulation of his objections to the expressionist understanding of the lyric subject. I discussed in the final section of the first chapter how Adorno understands the subject as flattened by conceptual and predicative language, in response to which subjective expression must be incorporated into language. He places this in stark contrast with the approach of the expressionists, accusing them of refusing to accept what he terms the 'dialectic of genre and individual work' (NzL 552/NtL 2: 207), of an 'incapacity to shape' (NzL 610/NtL 2: 258), that is to say an incapacity to make an artwork recognizable as such, as a type. This reduces the expressionist work to something contingent, an 'arbitrary experiential impression', which in turn 'simply withholds the soul from the totality which the artist has undertaken to shape' (NzL 610/NtL 2: 258). This is the force of Adorno's identification in his discussion of Berg's *Lulu* of 'the expressionist point of departure, the objectless subject' (B 483/AB 129): a subject removed from the artistic material—that is to say, a subject free of all mediation through the object—is no subject at all. Adorno insists in contrast on a critical subject that can reflect on the fact that it is itself object, albeit 'in a qualitatively different, more radical sense than object' is (S 746/CM 249).

That objective mediation is central not only to the formulation of a concept of the subject but also to its constitution is true not only of the individual subject but also of what Adorno identifies as the subject of art. Writing of art's paradoxical task of at once bearing witness to and reconciling the irreconcilable, a task which it can only achieve through nondiscursive language, he claims:

> Only in this process does awe become concrete. But what speaks out of art is truthfully its subject to the extent that it speaks out of it and is not presented by it. (ÄT 251/AT 168)

Adorno distinguishes the subject of art from both the artist and any speaker or character presented by the work, insisting that as a nonempirical subject it cannot be reproduced. This accounts for Adorno's apparently paradoxical formulation discussed in the opening section of this chapter, that the form that subjugates expression itself becomes expression: at stake here is the expression of two different subjects. Adorno's criticism of expressionism is that it attempts immediately to transpose the subjective expression of the artist into the artwork, rather than allowing the expression of the artwork to develop through the mediation of form. It is through the process of forming that the subjective presence of the artist exists within the work—indeed, Adorno insists that 'art is unthinkable without the subjective power to form'—but this power is radically separate from the expression of the artwork (ÄT 65/AT 39).

A more extensively formulated version of this claim can be found in Adorno's attempt to understand Beckett's *Endgame*:

> *Endgame* implies that the individual's claim to autonomy and to being has ceased to be credible. But while the prison of individuation is seen to be at once prison and illusion—the stage-design is the *imago* of such self-reflection—art cannot break the spell of cleaved-off subjectivity; it can only make solipsism sensual. Here Beckett comes up against the contemporary antinomy of art. The position of the absolute subject, once it has been cracked as the manifestation of a comprehensive whole that produces it, is no longer tenable: expressionism becomes obsolete. (NzL 291/NtL 249–50)

The 'cleaved-off subjectivity' is that of the Kantian transcendental subject, divorced from all content, whose spell was cast by the development of Enlightenment reason. This analysis of Beckett provides a sort of counterpart to the task Adorno identifies in the preface to *Negative Dialectics*, 'to break through the deception of constitutive subjectivity by force of the subject' (ND 10/Ashton xx). Adorno recognizes that the deception must be broken immanently, by means of the transcendental subject itself: this is the force of the claim that its spell cannot be broken by art. It is through philosophical insight into the subject that expressionism becomes untenable, but conversely, this insight is itself made in a sort of artistic cognition. This comes about through the inversion of what Adorno terms the enigmatic character of the physiognomy of objective expression, in which the most extreme determinedness is combined with its own radical opposite. In *Endgame*, '[w]hat usually barricades itself behind a communicative façade is condemned to appear' (NzL 296/NtL 1: 254). Adorno describes the result as 'the physiognomy of what is no longer human', self-controlled drama in which 'terrified health defends itself against schizophrenia', a schizophrenia which is subjected to rational reflection. The work comes to expression through the cracking of the transcendental subject and the decay of the empirical.

Adorno's critique of expressionism serves also to reject the realism that Adorno identifies as its counterpart:

> What is on offer as socialist realism does not, as is asserted, go beyond subjectivism, but remains behind it and is at the same time its preartistic complement; the expressionist *O Mensch* merges seamlessly with ideologically seasoned social reportage. Unreconciled reality tolerates no reconciliation with the object in

art; realism, which does not even get close to subjective experience, let alone going beyond it, merely mimics reconciliation. (NzL 291/NtL 1: 250)

This critique should perhaps be seen in the context of the debates in more or less Marxist aesthetics that were taking place in German in the mid-twentieth century. Adorno responds to the controversy between Bloch and Lukács—the former championing the expressionism that he saw as inextricably linked to the possibility of an emancipatory politics, in Adorno's words 'a protest against the reification of the world' (NzL 244/NtL 1: 210), the latter arguing from 1931 onward in favor of a realism that represented for him the defense of the bourgeois values of the Enlightenment against the encroachment of fascism in the guise of experimental art—by rejecting both positions as two sides of the same coin, both relying on the same limited understanding of subjectivity.[14] Expressionism presents the reconciliation—albeit of the false subject—as already attained in art, a reconciliation that neither challenges nor offers an alternative to the unreconciledness of damaged life. Meanwhile, realism's mimicry of reconciliation—what Adorno terms extorted reconciliation in his critique of Lukács—consists in its attempt poetically to anticipate the reconciliation of subjectivity and objectivity, of consciousness and the material world (cf. NzL 266/NtL 1: 229).

In opposition to this mimicry, Adorno locates the political potential theorized by the advocates of realism in what seems to be anti-realist literature, such as in this example from the 'Paralipomena' to *Aesthetic Theory*:

> Priority of the object and aesthetic realism are today almost contradictorily opposed to one another, even according to the realist measure: Beckett is more realistic than the socialist realists, who counterfeit reality through their very principle. If they took reality seriously enough, they would grow closer to that which Lukács condemned when he supposedly said during the days of his incarceration in Romania that he had finally realized that Kafka was a realist writer. (ÄT 477/AT 322)

The priority of the object does not restore 'slavish faith in the external world as it appears this side of critique' (S 746/CM 249). Fidelity to the empirical world as it appears to consciousness does not so much oppose subjectivism as reinforce it, presenting in the place of reflected objectivity the illusion of an immediate subjectivity that masquerades as object. In the next-but-one section I discuss this problematic in more detail, examining Adorno's configuration of the representation of reality and its role in art through his deployment of the concept of mimesis. Before this I make a detour through Adorno's discussions of Kafka, paying particular attention to his treatment of reality and expression.

Kafka

That he describes Kafka in *Minima Moralia* as a 'solipsist without ipse' (MM 255/Jephcott 223) is perhaps itself indicative of the fact that Adorno considers the status of the subject and its expression within Kafka's work worthy of investigation and discussion. In the 'Notes on Kafka' he addresses the status of the subject in greater detail:

> Absolute subjectivity is itself subjectless. The self lives only in externalization; as secure remains of the subject that isolates itself from what is foreign to it, it becomes the blind remains of the world. The more the I of expressionism is thrown back upon itself, the more it resembles the excluded world of things. By virtue of this similarity, Kafka forces expressionism, whose chimerical aspect he must have sensed like none of his friends and to which he nonetheless remained true, into a complicated epic; pure subjectivity, which is necessarily estranged even from itself and has become a thing, he forces into objectivity, whose own estrangement comes to expression. The boundary between what is human and the world of things is blurred. (P 275–76/ WWN 262)

Adorno is not, here, discussing any particular extract or even work of Kafka's, but the rather more general 'hermetic impression of his writings' (P 274/ WWN 261). The hermetic principle at stake here is that of what he terms 'completely estranged subjectivity', that is to say subjectivity cut off not only from the world which it experiences, but also from itself: absolute subjective space and absolute subjective time, in which 'there is no place for anything that could disturb their own principle, that of inalienable estrangement' (P 275/WWN 261). It is to this extent that Adorno can argue that 'Kafka the epic writer pursues the expressionist impulse further than all but the radical poets' (P 274/WWN 261). The lyric subject is not so much revealed to be object, as Adorno argues in the quotation from 'On Subject and Object' cited in the previous section above, as transformed into object, a process that, paradoxically, takes place through its isolation and intensification as subject, pure inwardness, which in the absence of any determination is denied anything that might enable it to place a limit—let alone anything that might place an external limit—on its timeless and therefore interminable cycle of repetition. Adorno provides as an example of this phenomenon the early nightfall which catches K. unawares at the opening of the second chapter of *The Castle*.[15] The interruption of the expected passing of time is an event that Adorno considers exemplary of the instances of 'damage to the space–time continuum of "empirical realism" through a small act of sabotage' (P 275/WWN 261), which shatter the illusion of confidence in either subjective experience or the external world.

Adorno insists that Kafka's language, like that of Brecht, is far removed from that of the expressionists' attempt to seek recourse in some sort of 'primal sounds' that would supposedly convey subjective expression free from any objective or formal mediation. Kafka goes beyond the contradiction of attempting verbally to convey objectless inwardness in words that cannot shake off their vast conceptual resonance by use of what Adorno terms the 'visual element':

> As the element of gestures it asserts its priority. Only the visible can be narrated, during which process it is completely estranged into image. Truly into image. Kafka saves the idea of expressionism by, rather than listening in vain for primal sounds, transferring the habitus of expressionist painting onto poetry. (P 277–78/WWN 264)

This consists in the rejection of both dream and the aping of reality in favor of an 'enigmatic image' composed of the scattered shards of reality. Adorno makes these comments in analysis primarily of examples from *The Trial*, in which patriarchal society is revealed, through suspension of the rules according to which it can function, to contain a secret of 'immediate, barbaric oppression' (P 277/WWN 263). The enigmatic image referred to here is the one that arises in the moments of happiness within this oppression, moments that arise 'out of the astonishment of the hermetically sealed subject at the paradox that it can indeed be loved' (P 277/WWN 263). Kafka's expression arises out of the rejection of the techniques of literary expressionism in favor of the attempt to open up fissures in the grey fabric of damaged life through which light can shine.

Despite Adorno's close attention to Kafka's prose—he insists in the first of the 'Notes' that 'every sentence stands literally, and every sentence means' (P 255/WWN 246)—the 'Notes' hardly touch on the category of form. His only substantive discussion of form in Kafka took place nearly twenty years later in *Aesthetic Theory*:

> Kafka, in whose work monopoly capitalism only appears at a distance, codifies in the refuse of the administered world what happens to people under the total social spell more faithfully and powerfully than novels about corrupt industrial trusts. The claim that form is the locus of social content can be shown clearly with reference to Kafka's language. (ÄT 342/AT 230)

The comment concerning 'novels about corrupt industrial trusts' is a rejection of Zola that has a history within Marxist thought going back at least to Engels's statement in a letter to Margaret Harkness in 1888 of his preference for the realism of Balzac the Legitimist over Zola's socialist commitment.[16] However, Adorno explodes the opposition, prevalent within the tradition of Marxist literary theory, between formalism and realism, arguing that it is in the form of Kafka's works that their realistic element crystallizes: to the extent that they are realist, it is a realism that Adorno locates within the features of their prose.[17] Somewhat frustratingly, these features are left to a great extent undetermined, the discussion taking place without reference to any particular text. However, even without exemplary illustration of what he means, the force of Adorno's comments becomes clearer later in the discussion:

> The critique of the realistic features of Kafka's form, a critique which to activist ears seems all too artistic, has at the same time its social aspect. Through some of these features Kafka becomes acceptable to an ideal of order, perhaps of simple life and modest activity in one's allotted position, an ideal that itself became a mask for social repression. The linguistic habitus of something's being the way it is and not otherwise is the medium through which the social spell becomes appearance. Kafka is wisely wary of naming it, as if the spell whose insurmountable omnipresence

defines the space of Kafka's work—and which as its a priori cannot become thematic—would otherwise be broken. (ÄT 342/AT 230)

Adorno refers to the 'objectivity' of Kafka's language, an objectivity that comes into productive contradiction with the events he describes through their sober presentation. The linguistic habitus invoked here consists not only in particularity, but also in the sense of the removal of contingency, that there is no trace of anything accidental about the particular descriptions. That is, the form which Adorno identifies here is entirely compatible with the expression identified and discussed in the earlier 'Notes on Kafka', the transformation of lyric subjectivity through the challenge to the legitimacy of the experience of the empirical subject—a challenge that is linguistic insofar as it is through the strategy of narration, the nonsensationalist presentation of what would otherwise be sensational, that attention is drawn to the radical interiority of Kafka's subjects, such as in the disruption of the expected passing of time. This challenge simultaneously reveals and refuses to name the social repression that hides behind the ideal of order that Adorno describes. This repression not only becomes to an extent the object of an implicit or potential critique through its identification and presentation within Kafka's prose, but is also a necessary condition of this prose. Adorno's assertion that it 'cannot become thematic' is an insistence that it must not become a matter to be treated by the work as if from the outside, but must remain immanent to its form. Form is in this way in no sense opposed to content but hardly separable from it: to return to the conceptual distinction used in the previous chapter, the substantive social content of Kafka's prose that Adorno identifies in *Aesthetic Theory* is inseparable from the expression that he discusses in the 'Notes on Kafka'.

In this earlier text Adorno identifies as a linguistic feature of Kafka's prose 'the inversion of the historical relation of concept and gesture' (P 259/WWN 249). Rather than emphasizing the conceptuality of signification that develops from and eventually comes to dominate gestural expression, Kafka exposes the 'traces of experiences which are covered by meaning'. Gesture—in Hamacher's terms 'what remains of language after meaning is withdrawn from it', and thus the 'rest of language—and so language itself, language irreducible to meaning'[18]—reveals that the configuration of language that we tend to think of as truth is not only historically contingent but also broken and untrue. With the example of a sentence spoken by the warden to Josef K. in the opening chapter of *The Trial*, Adorno argues that '[i]nterpretation will one day have to follow the experiences sedimented in the gestures, recognize in their mimesis a universal repressed by healthy human reason' (P 259/WWN 249).¹⁹ This argument resonates in this much later claim from *Aesthetic Theory*:

> In its archaism, Kafka's epic style is mimesis of reification. Whereas his work can only fail in the attempt to transcend myth, it makes the web of delusion knowable in myth through the how, language. (ÄT 342/AT 230-31)

In the argument of both works it is clear that Adorno conceives of realism, to the extent that it is to be admired, as an attempt not to describe the world but to imitate it—that is to say, to redress the balance within language away from the significative pole, toward the mimetic, a mimesis that consists in the mechanics of the use of language at the most minute level. It is Adorno's understanding and deployment of the concept of mimesis that I now turn to discuss.

Mimesis

Adorno's concept of mimesis has been the subject of a range of investigations. Indeed, concept is in some ways a misleading word, since, for Adorno mimesis 'resists being defined by reason', and 'works through images rather than concepts and approaches the other [. . .] as something different yet related, more "powerful" than the self'.²⁰ Mimesis is better seen as a comportment than a concept, a comportment that is characterized by what Wolin terms a 'nonobjectivating relationship to the external world'.²¹ In Jay's terms this is a 'sympathetic, compassionate, and noncoercive relationship of affinity between nonidentical particulars'.²² Josef Früchtl has shown that the dynamic and changing force of Adorno's understanding of mimesis is regulated by the changing constellations in which it appears, which govern whether it functions according to a logic of compulsion or of playfulness.²³ In Wellmer's dense but suggestive formulation, mimesis is 'the name for the modes of behavior of the living that are sensuously receptive, expressive and that nestle communicatively'.²⁴

In the 'Theories on the Origin of Art', Adorno notes the historical point observable in the development of cave paintings at which point stylized features began to appear, a point which is central to his account of the beginnings of the separation of art from magic:

> A mimetic comportment must have preceded the early paintings, that of making oneself the identical with another, which is not quite identical with the superstitious belief in a direct influence; if a moment of differentiation between mimesis and superstition had not developed over a long period of time, the striking features of autonomous design in cave paintings would be inexplicable. (ÄT 487/AT 329)

Mimesis has its origin in religious praxis, but its separation from such a praxis has a long history. The development of the aesthetic moment visible in the first features of autonomous design does not overcome or move beyond mimesis, which is itself central to Adorno's interpretation of this phenomenon. Hohendahl insists that the rationality that consists in and codetermines art since the earliest works is 'a form of the rational that excludes instrumental reason and retrieves mimesis'.[25] Art, that is, harbors a sort of rationality that is not reducible to conceptual thought, but remains compatible with the mimetic comportment. This mode of rationality persists as a moment within artworks and their expression—not as mere imitation, but as the 'nonconceptual affinity between what is produced subjectively and its unposited other' (ÄT 86–87/AT 54). This affinity underlies not only the determination of art as a mode of cognition, but also the critical force of its social intervention, which I discuss in more detail in the fifth chapter.

What is perhaps Adorno's most extensive treatment of mimesis consists in the continuation of the quotation from *Aesthetic Theory* discussed at the beginning of this chapter, initially in the introduction and then in the first section. Adorno continues by relating the expression previously under discussion to his understanding of mimesis:

> Expression is a phenomenon of interference, a function of procedure no less than it is mimetic. Mimesis is on its own part summoned by the concentration of the technical process, the immanent rationality of which indeed appears to counteract expression. The compulsion exerted by unified works is equivalent to their eloquence, to the part of them that speaks, not a merely suggestive effect; moreover, suggestion is itself related to mimetic procedures. This leads to a subjective paradox of art: to produce what is blind—expression—out of reflection—through form; not to rationalize the blind but rather first of all to make it aesthetically; 'to make things of which we do not know what they are'. (ÄT 174/AT 114)

The appearance that Adorno describes and rejects is that of a simplified schema according to which the technical aspects of composition stand opposed to expression, in which mimesis is a central moment. However, this schema is blown up by the fact that mimesis is inextricably linked to the technical procedures of composition: the technique that is thought of as opposed to expression is revealed to be central to it. Adorno insists that the force of a carefully and successfully constructed work—a work, that is, that displays unity within its construction—is not something that intensifies the work's expression but is rather central to this expression. That this unified construction is not limited to a suggestive effect does not mean that it is not a suggestive effect at all. Indeed, Adorno's claim that such suggestion is 'related to mimetic procedures' reinforces his insistence that mimesis consists in the how of artworks, the way that they mean, rather than merely in description. That is to say, the modality of a literary work, central to its expression, is not a purely grammatical phenomenon, but to an extent dependent on the work's construction, which itself exercises a significant effect on whether the work is for example assertive, interrogative or suggestive.

The quotation with which this extract ends is the final sentence of Adorno's essay 'Vers une musique informelle', a nonprogrammatic manifesto for a music 'which has cast off all its external or abstract forms, all those which confront it rigidly', which nonetheless 'constitutes itself in an objectively compelling manner' (QF 496/Livingstone 272). The formulation 'to make things of which we do not know what they are' is Adorno's determination of 'the shape of every artistic utopia'—*musique informelle* 'would be the image of freedom' (QF 540/Livingstone 322). What Adorno terms the subjective paradox of art thus has explicitly emancipatory consequences that go well beyond the understanding of the bourgeois subject. That expression is described as blind is another instance of what Bernstein identifies as Adorno's rewriting of Kant's concept and intuition as form and content.[26] In a further rewriting of the Kantian formula, form without expression is empty, expression without form is blind. The subjective paradox consists in transforming subjective reflection into expression, without subjecting expression to the constraints of instrumental rationality—that is to say, of preserving the moment of expressive mimesis in such a way that it is not dominated by conceptual thinking.

And yet there is a very real sense in which the mimetic moment must be worked—dominated, in a sense—into the structure of the artwork. Refusing to do so would be to succumb to the same error as the expressionists. Adorno examines this issue in the light of the apparent contradiction between form and expression:

> What to theorists is nothing other than a logical contradiction is familiar to artists and unfolds in their work: disposal over the mimetic moment—the former summons up, destroys, redeems the latter's involuntariness. Willfulness within the involuntary is the vital element of art, the ability to achieve it is a reliable criterion of artistic capability, without wanting to veil the fatality of such activity. Artists are familiar with this capability as their sense of form. (ÄT 174/AT 114)

The mimetic impulse, that is, is involuntary, to an extent beyond either the control or the influence of the artistic subject. And yet it is of prime importance that it is not completely beyond the grasp of the subjective will. That is to say, the task of the artistic subject is to shape this involuntary, objective material, but not in such a way that the mimetic moment is subordinated to the instrumentality of subjective reason, rather by as it were incorporating willfulness into the involuntary. However, it would be inaccurate to conclude that the sense of form which Adorno evokes here can be attributed purely or even principally to a subjective voluntarism, regardless of the extent to which it is the means by which the involuntary becomes willful; I return to the question of subjective will and its restriction in the discussion of material and technique in the fourth chapter. He not only insists that fatality is a significant force within the process under discussion, but also emphasizes the role of the sense of form as an objective category:

> The sense of form is the reflection, at once blind and binding, of the object in itself on which that reflection must depend; the objectivity closed off to itself, which devolves to the subjective mimetic capability that for its own part strengthens itself through its opposite, rational construction. The blindness of the sense of form corresponds to necessity in the object. (ÄT 175/AT 114–15)

Adorno is reworking the Kantian opposition between the necessity of nature and the freedom of the will. The freedom of the subjective mimetic capacity consists in the freedom to act in accordance with the law of the sense of form, but this law is given not by pure subjective reason, but rather by the constraints of the object. The priority of the object is as important for artistic production as it is for philosophy: the sense of form that at first sight appears to belong solely to the subjective capacity to form is revealed to be the site of mediation—and it is primarily in this respect that Adorno distinguishes his theory from the Kantianism that he reworks—between subject and object. The subjective power to form is not only constrained but also conditioned by the requirements of the object that is formed.

Even to the extent that it is reducible to mimetic comportment, mimesis cannot be thought of as free from either conceptual or objective mediation. Mimesis would be impossible without the capacity for conceptual discrimination that consists in the cognition of what is to be imitated. Even though he understands Adorno's concept of mimesis as a mode of cognition without domination, Bernstein insists that Adorno neither needed nor desired to present it as free from either conceptuality or mediation:

> In thinking the intuitive moment in terms of a mimetic potential he is, rather, calling into question the necessity of construing the appropriation of particulars as subsumption and domination. Mimesis is never pure, never an immediate relation of particular to particular. Mimetic activity is always shaped by spirit.[27]

Spirit is neither an abstraction nor the elevation or hypostatization of the subjective principle, but the configuration of the relationship between sensuality and materiality. It is emphatically neither derivable from nor attributable to the synthetic function of the subject, but closely bound up with both the sense of form that guides the artist and the law of form that develops within the work, both of which go beyond the confines of the idealist subject. To remain within Bernstein's terms, spirit refers to 'what gets articulated in the nonrepressive synthesis of particulars through form'.[28] In the concluding section of this chapter, I now turn to consider the consequences of these investigations into both mimesis and expression for their relationship to form.

Consequences for the Theory of Form

At the beginning of this chapter I discussed the process whereby the form that subjugates expression itself becomes expression. Adorno describes a similar process in the case of form and mimesis:

> Everything language-like in artworks subsumes itself in form, and in doing so they cross over into the antithesis of form, the mimetic impulse. Form tries to bring the individual to speak

through the whole. That, however, is form's melancholy, particularly in the case of artists in whose work form prevails. Form always limits what is formed; its concept would otherwise lose its specific difference from what is formed. (ÄT 217/AT 144)

Form and mimesis are opposed to one another, mimesis here reinscribing the Kantian intuition that complements the conceptual status of form. But just as mimesis cannot exist in its specificity without a trace of conceptuality, nor can form afford to erase the traces of particularity out of which it develops. This is the force of Adorno's claim that aesthetic form is at once 'the objective organization of everything that appears harmoniously eloquent within an artwork' and the 'nonviolent synthesis of the diffuse' (ÄT 215–16/ AT 143). This nonviolent synthesis is one in which the particularity of what is synthesized is preserved 'in its divergence and its contradictions', rather than being erased in its subsumption under a higher concept. To the extent that form can be associated with what is subjective in art—whether through the artist's subjective power to form or the subject that arises within each artwork—it has nothing to do with the idealist subject that destroys what it hopes to know through the imposition of the principle of synthesis.

To return to Adorno's insistence that 'art is unthinkable without the subjective power to form' (ÄT 65/AT 39), form is the objective manifestation of this subjective power, the index of art's madness—but the relationship between form and subjectivity is a complex one. The discussion of the 'sense of form' in the previous section demonstrates the importance of the concept of mediation for Adorno's aesthetics, and particularly for his reinterpretation of Kant. The sense of form is no radically interior feature of pure reason, neither internalized nor externalizable, but a principle that begins and is guided by the requirements of the object. Nor is this to claim that form is merely derivative of what is formed. Referring to the tendency of form to limit what is formed, Adorno writes

> That is confirmed by the artistic labor of forming, which is always selecting, cutting away, renouncing: no form without refuse. This prolongs the guilty domination in artworks, which they would like to be rid of, form is their amorality. (ÄT 217/AT 144)

This subjective labor is a prerequisite of the artwork. While the sense of form that guides this labor has its origin in the object that is formed, it does not arise out of or lead to any sort of self-preservation of the object in its original form. It is this that designates the object as such: it is there to be formed, but there is no principle according to which parts of it cannot be discarded. The requirements and constraints of the object that condition the sense of form in the process of composing any particular work are thus not contingently objective (by which I mean: would appear to be subjective if the situation were observed from the other side) but necessarily so, since they can on occasion lead to the large-scale destruction of the object. It is in this sense that form and subjectivity are closely related to one another.

This foregrounds the importance of considering not only the conceptual relationship between form, expression and mimesis, but also of examining the ways in which they—or perhaps their referents—interact within artworks. Adorno presents this configuration in the following terms:

> Expression and semblance are primarily antithetical to one another. If expression hardly allows itself to be imagined except as the expression of suffering—joy has shown itself to be prudish toward all expression, perhaps because it is yet to exist, and bliss would be without expression—art has in expression the immanent moment through which it turns against its immanence under the law of form as one of its constituents. Art's expression comports itself mimetically, just as the expression of the living is that of pain. The features of expression that are inscribed in artworks, if they are not to be mute, are lines of demarcation against semblance. But because, as artworks, they remain semblance, the conflict between semblance—form, in the broadest understanding—and expression is unresolved and fluctuates historically. Mimetic comportment, an attitude toward reality this side of the fixed opposition of subject and object, is seized in art—the organ of mimesis since the mimetic taboo—by semblance and becomes, as complement to the autonomy of form, the bearer of semblance. (ÄT 168–69/AT 110)

Artworks contain within themselves the opposed moments of expression and semblance. Broadly speaking, mimesis is identified with expression and form with semblance, but Adorno's description of the web of interactions taking place reveals the situation to be somewhat more complicated. Perhaps the most important distinction to be made here is that between mimesis and semblance: the two are contrasted with one another, but because they do not appear in corresponding positions in the conceptual schema, their relationship cannot be seen as one of simple opposition. Semblance is opposed not to mimesis but to expression—and it is expression of which mimesis is a 'comportment'. The distinction between mimesis—or more accurately, the mimetic comportment of expression—and semblance consists in the fact that this mimetic comportment survives, if not in unaltered form, from before the rigid separation of subject from object, a separation which is not only a prerequisite for the existence of semblance, but also one that is reinforced by it. In contrast, semblance is the embodiment of the cognitive subjective attempt to observe, recognize, and copy the object as something foreign to itself. Insofar as it predates the separation of subject from object, mimesis does not share the rigidity of semblance: mimesis does not attempt to imitate a reality that it conceives as external to itself but rather to make itself the same as this reality of which it is a part.

In an example of the difficulty that is at times posed by Adorno's description of relationships and interactions between almost personified concepts, he offers an account of the encounter between mimesis and semblance in the artwork. As the representative of subjective rationality in the work, semblance attempts to know mimesis, an attempt which necessarily involves domination. This is form's attempt to subjugate expression, as discussed at the beginning of this chapter. The domination of the mimetic moment consists in its being known—perhaps more accurately, in its becoming known—as an object by subjective rationality. Expression, that is, is only able to remain within the artwork to the extent that it can serve the purposes of semblance. Expression is instrumentalized by rationality, which presses it into service of its own requirements. However, the sense of form can be thought of as a means by which this instrumentalization is, to the extent that such a thing is possible, attuned to the object, not in such a way that it counteracts the tendency to dominate the object, but rather ensuring that the domination takes place in accordance with the requirements of the object. At its most sensitive, form is able to preserve expression within the artwork as something that is not only hostile to subjective rationality but that also holds it at bay. The sense of form, which is in one sense the most subjective aspect of composition, is at the same time a moment of objectivity—perhaps more accurately, a moment of attunedness to objectivity—preserved within the subjective act of forming. This is the force of the insistence on the autonomy of form. With the instrumentalization of mimetic expression—its heteronomy—form can only become autonomous through the suspension of dominated expression within it.

This begins to illuminate the significance of Adorno's reinscription of the Kantian concept and intuition as form and expression. It is not simply the case that Adorno introduces the category of mediation to the Kantian schema, that the opposed counterparts go through what is nothing more than an extra cycle of exchange while the relationship between them fundamentally remains the same. Rather the nature of their mediation reveals the way in which the relationship between them begins to shift. Form and expression work toward the autonomy of the artwork by means of form's subjugation of expression. While it is undeniably the case that *Aesthetic Theory* does not rework and call into question the concepts of aesthetics to the same extent that *Negative Dialectics* does those of metaphysics, this should not be seen as the mark of an accommodationist tendency within Adorno's aesthetics, but rather a consequence of his insight that there is more to the concepts of aesthetics than to those of metaphysics. They are not pure concepts in the strict Kantian sense, but harbor the trace of the remainder that is left over when the priority of the aesthetic object refuses to merge with its concept. This is why the categories of Kantian aesthetics remain usable—why, indeed, they cannot be dispensed with—after the opposition between thought and matter has been suspended. They contain within themselves, and to an extent greater than recognized by either Kant or his critics, a truth about the refusal of the objective world wholly to submit to the conceptual rationality that permeates our thought, a refusal of which artistic autonomy is a prominent example.[29]

This autonomy is at the heart of the contradiction that is preserved within Adorno's concept of form. Form strives to be the universal and the particular at once. As the unique form of an artwork, dependent on its particular object, it seeks to emphasize its particularity. As an identifiable shared trait between artworks it stakes a claim to the universal. This contradiction, which I discuss in more detail in the next chapter, is present in Adorno's work at least since the publication of *Dialectic of Enlightenment*, in which the essay on the culture industry contains the following discussion of style:

> In every artwork its style is a promise. By entering, through style, the dominant forms of universality—musical, painterly, verbal language—what is expressed is supposed to reconcile itself with the idea of true universality. This promise of the artwork, to found truth by impressing its shape on the socially transmitted forms, is as necessary as it is hypocritical. It posits the real

forms of the existing order as absolute by claiming to anticipate fulfilment in their aesthetic derivates. The claim of art is to this extent always also ideology. Yet in no other way than through this struggle with tradition—in which style is sedimented—can art find expression for suffering. (DA 152/DE 103)

The contradiction between universal and particular manifests itself in the tension between the socially dominant forms and the individual works out of which these forms originally develop, but which they subsequently come to dominate. The struggle of an individual artwork against the established canon of forms is both necessary and futile, as long as the forms that constitute this canon are elevated to the status of an absolute. And yet this tendency toward absolutism is inherent within the development of form: the move beyond the confines of the uniqueness of the individual work in order to point to commonalities and affinities between works contains within itself a moment of the claim to universality. This moment is unavoidable, but nonetheless something that artworks must attempt to resist. Style cannot but sediment itself into a form that has a tendency to hypostatize itself: it is through the struggle against this hypostatization that artworks become capable of expression. This tension between universal and particular depends to an extent on that between subject and object.

Discussing the enigmatic character of artworks, Adorno claims that they 'discharge themselves into their objectivity by force of their subjectively mimetic, expressive moment; they are neither pure emotion nor its form but the coagulated process between the two, which is also social' (ÄT 198/AT 131). In a manner akin to the way in which the expression of the artwork does not emerge unchanged from the interaction of its expression with form in the process of the artwork's making, artistic form is itself the result of the mediation of the formal and expressive moments. More specifically, it is the objective form in which these two moments coagulate. Form is thus a site at which the unique particularity of expression combines with the universality of its form. It is on this note that I now turn to explore in more detail some of the ways in which this coagulation is social, examining through consideration of its relationship to type and genre its aspirations toward intersubjectivity and universality.

3

Form and Genre

> The more distinctive the work, the more faithfully it conforms to its type: the dialectical proposition that particular is the universal takes art as its model.
>
> —ÄT 300/AT 202

Up until this point I have concentrated on aspects of Adorno's concept of form that refer to the structure or shape of an individual work, its origin in the demands of the work's content, and the tensions between form and artistic expression. In this third chapter, I turn to address some of the ways in which form can be thought of beyond the individual artwork, considering what are often thought of as art-forms, artistic forms, genres, or arts. As Jameson remarks, this is one point at which the tension between the interest of philosophical aesthetics in 'identifying what is common to all genuine works of art and their experience, and producing some generic concept of the "artistic"' comes into tension with the concerns of recent literary criticism, which has 'tended to conceive its mission as the identification of what is unique in specific works, of their incomparability and radical *difference*'.[1] Form, as I have repeatedly indicated, offers a way of thinking both the singularity of the individual work and the shared characteristics of different works. Adorno's understanding of form reveals the links between these two aspects, as can be seen from the discussion of form as the sedimentation of content in the first chapter, in which it became clear that the process of sedimentation leads not only to the structural development of individual works, but also to the formation of what he terms 'collectively honed' forms, a formulation to which I return below. Indeed, the relation of conceptions of genre to both content and expression is a recurring theme of this chapter, particularly in the confrontation of these collective forms with the form of the individual work, a confrontation expressed perhaps most succinctly in Adorno's designation of Beethoven's forms as 'the product of the pre-ordained schemata and the specific formal idea of each particular work' (BPdM 97/BTPoM 60).

It is what Adorno refers to here as the 'pre-ordained schemata' which constitute the focus of this chapter, with the caveat that the manner of the appearance of their pre-ordination must itself be investigated. In other words: the process by which these schemata might be thought to come into being is not presumed as a given, but rather a central element of this investigation. While I agree to a great extent with Alastair Fowler's claim that consideration of developments within genre 'offers frequent reminders that works of literature come to us from literary communities, with which we in our turn have to form a relation', my aim is not 'to break the hermeneutic circle and to reconstruct old or difficult works'.[2] Nor do I wish, in the first instance, to 'recover a sense of the variety of literary forms', or to advance either an account of the different literary genres or a universal theory of genre, but rather more specifically to understand how Adorno's understanding of genre interacts with other aspects of his theory of form.[3] More particularly, my aim is to consider what the conception of form as genre has in common with other ways of understanding form, and to investigate the significance of the agglomeration of all these senses of form within a single concept.

Indeed, the intellectual significance of an understanding of genre is not limited to the literary-historical attempt to reconstruct the social and political conditions under which particular works of art or literature originated, but is more fundamentally related to investigations into the nature of thinking. Rose has claimed that '[t]he exposition of poetry and prose as literary genres draws on the contrast of social and political cohesion already elaborated as social precondition'. According to this Hegelian schema, poetry 'has an affinity with speculative thinking' in its grasping of opposites 'in their living unity', whereas prose 'is a form of abstract reasoning based on a distinction between means and ends', a form of reasoning that is based on relation rather than unification.[4] This chapter seeks both to develop and to refine ways in which understanding and theorizing genre can account for poetry's affinity with speculative thought, and to explore the possibility of prose that escapes the instrumental logic of abstract reasoning.

I begin by reconstructing and refining the theory that underlies Adorno's writings on art and artistic forms. Focusing explicitly on the aesthetic manifestation of genre, I attend first to the critical and theoretical implications of his persuasive account of the breaking down of the boundaries between the genres in the decades following the Second World War. On the basis of this account I then formulate a theoretical account of the origins of genres and forms: what emerges is a conception of the historical development of art and artworks that rejects the crude dichotomy between necessity and contingency, and in which the relationships between works of art and the subordinating concepts under which they are grouped further complicate the relationship between objects and their concepts. In the third and fourth sections of the chapter I address this complication in more detail, examining first ways in which works of art complicate Adorno's understanding of the relationship between universal and particular, and then the implications of his account of aesthetic nominalism. I then examine the implications of his discussions of the culture industry for his theory of form, focusing in particular on the implications of the combination of and interaction between aesthetic and commercial influences on cultural objects. In the chapter's final two sections I consider some of the consequences—both for the theory of form and for its wider implications—of Adorno's writings first on the novel, the 'nominalist and therefore paradoxical form par excellence', and then on the 'critical form par excellence' that is the essay.

The Fraying of Borders

Adorno's 1966 talk on 'Art and the Arts' at the *Akademie der Künste* in Berlin begins with the claim that the 'borders between the different artistic genres are merging' (OL 432/COL 368). It is significant that in his analysis it is the borders between the genres and not the genres themselves that are merging: the genres, that is, are presented not as natural or given categories that constitute their own limits, but as a consequence of more or less contingent boundaries. He qualifies this claim with what he presents as a more precise formulation that 'their lines of demarcation are fraying'. The verb Adorno uses is *sich verfransen*, an expression not found in the quasi-authoritative *Duden*, or indeed in any other German or German-English dictionary I have consulted. The word seems to be a coinage of Adorno's, and is based on *Franse*, a fringe or frayed edge, while containing an echo of *sich verfranzen*, to lose one's way.[5] It thus contains the sense not only of deviating from a genre, but also of a process whereby the genres themselves begin to unravel, particularly at their edges.

The shifting of generic boundaries is not a new phenomenon. Michael McKeon offers an account of a much earlier instance of what he terms the 'destabilization of generic categories' in seventeenth-century England, charting 'the complex development of the genre' of romance and its subsequent 'resolution into "romance" and "historical" elements'[6]—I return to the particular status of the novel later in this chapter. But this and other instances of generic development have been examined primarily as processes of the arising or subdivision of genres, rather than the merging of already existing classes, as is the case here. In this respect Adorno's account further develops and theorizes Benjamin's incipient investigation of the social and political potential of what he termed the fusing or recasting of literary forms in a talk at the Institute for the Study of Fascism in Paris in April 1934.[7] As examples of this process Adorno cites the similarity of the graphical notation of some contemporary music to visual artwork, the influence of musical serialism on the composition of novels, the movement of painting beyond the confines of traditional surfaces (OL 432/COL 368). It is particularly significant that he describes the use in novelistic production of techniques derived from serialism as a mode of 'compensation for the retreat of the narrated content'—this conception of the relationship between the means of composition and the narrative content of the work is in many ways familiar from the discussion of form and propositional content in chapter 1. Here, however, it is not the form of the completed work that is foregrounded but the manner in which the narrative content is worked, or the compositional technique—the essay's second sentence contains an explicit reference to the 'so-called informal techniques' employed in contemporary painting. I consider the status of Adorno's conception of the relationship between technique and form in more detail in the following chapter discussing his deployment of the concept of artistic material. The extent to which the status of artistic genres is bound up with the relationship between form and content becomes clearer in Adorno's continuation:

> Musical passages lose something of the reliability of their temporal sequence through exchangeability or changing configuration: they dispense with similarity to causal relations. Sculptors no longer respect even the boundary between sculpture and architecture that seemed to follow as a matter of course from the distinction between purposeful and purposeless[.] (OL 432/COL 368-69)

If Adorno's claim here is that the blurring of a previously rigid distinction between purposeful and purposeless was specific to the time of writing, it is a claim that stands in tension with his argument in *Aesthetic Theory* discussed in the first chapter that many collectively honed artistic corms have their origin in the becoming-purposeless of elements that were original purposeful, for such a process presupposes the possibility of a transition between the two. Indeed, the collective honing of these aesthetic forms implies that they are not pre-given or naturally occurring but rather undergo a process of development, a process which must not necessarily be thought of as complete.[8]

In his discussion of the dialectic of lightheartedness in art, first published in July 1967 as a contribution to the *Süddeutsche Zeitung*, Adorno makes it clear that the reconfiguration of generic limits is historically contingent:

> Given the events of the most recent past, art can no more be completely serious than it can continue to be lighthearted. Doubts arise as to whether it was ever as serious as culture had convinced humanity it was. It is no longer allowed, as Hölderlin's poetry does, which felt itself at one with the world-spirit, to equate the expression of mourning with the utmost joy. The truth content of joy appears to have become unattainable. That the genres are merging, that the tragic gesture seems comic and the comic doleful, is related to this. (NzL 606/NtL 2: 253)

As explanation for the decay of the tragic Adorno offers the fact that it 'raises a claim to the positive meaning of negation', a claim on which it is no longer possible to make good. He insists that the 'only art now possible' consists in the rejection of both lightheartedness and seriousness, an art that would constitute a move into the hitherto unknown. To conclude from a discussion of what seems to be a modal opposition between seriousness and lightheartedness that the 'genres are merging' reveals a certain conflation of modal and generic distinctions within Adorno's thinking. His claim is that the borders between the genres, that is—and to this extent also the genres themselves—are established and maintained by known artworks. Artworks that do not challenge these borders are thus implicitly in some way already known, familiar. Or, to put it the other way around, each new artwork worthy of the name will necessarily challenge or redefine the limits between the genres as established at the time of its creation. This is the significance of Adorno's claim that 'artists always work on art as well as on artworks'—a statement that is as true for any understanding of a particular genre as for what we might think of as art in general.

The particular manner and direction in which the generic limits can be worked on should not be thought of as an arbitrary decision, but as inextricably linked to the state of the world. But it would be a mistake to think of this in the terms of the Marxist conception of the determination of the cultural superstructure by the developments of the political and economic material base.⁹ Adorno rejects the model according to which artistic production is simply an epiphenomenon of developments in industrial production. He insists rather that the means of artistic production are themselves mediated through the relations of production in a manner similar to the mediation of the means of industrial production. His claim is that the (industrial) forces of production develop in tension with the relations of production in a process whereby labor constitutes the principal means of relating to nature, at once enabling and restricting human life. He argues that the impulse to begin with analysis of the forces of production results from the fact that they are so thoroughly mediated by the relations of production that the extent of this mediation is hardly visible, that the relations of production appear as essential, they 'have wholly become second nature' (GS 8: 365). This mediation is not confined to the economic sphere of industrial production, but is just as important for cultural and artistic modes of production—I discuss the significance of this mediation for the relationship between technique and material in the following chapter, while the relationship between artistic and industrial production (and analogously, between artworks and commodities) is the concern of the final chapter.

In his attempt to interpret the process by which the edges of the artistic genres come to fray, Adorno insists that 'it is at its most forceful where it is genuinely immanent, where it arises from the genre itself' (OL 433/COL 369). That is to say, where it involves more than simply the application to one genre of aspects borrowed from another. 'When compositions borrow their titles from Klee, one tends to suspect that they are of decorative nature, the opposite of the very modernity to which they stake a claim by means of this designation' (OL 433/COL 369). Adorno's suspicion of the tendencies represented by the *Gesamtkunstwerk* is directed well beyond Wagner, as shown by his comments on artworks that ignore what he terms the 'moment of the irreducible, of the qualitatively different' (OL 440/COL 375), a moment that is opposed to every principle of unity—including the artistic genres. Such comments are directed as much at Berg and perhaps even Klee as at Wagner, Adorno arguing that these artists, 'whose talent was not unmistakably bound to material' (OL 440/COL 375), have every reason to attempt to submerge what is aesthetic in general within a specific material.

He insists on the importance of what he terms the 'ether' that survives of this generalized aesthetics, that distinguishes the work of these 'artists of high standing' from those works which decay, 'dry up into philistine handicraft' (OL 440/COL 376). The significance of his comments on Klee is brought more sharply into focus by his discussion in *Aesthetic Theory* of the enigmatic character of artworks:

> It is through organization that works become more than they are. In recent debates, primarily about the visual arts, the concept of *écriture* has become relevant, probably inspired by Klee's drawings, which approximate scribbled writing. This modern category illuminates the past like a spotlight; all artworks are writing, and not only those that appear as such—they are hieroglyphic writing to which the code has been lost, and to the content of which the fact that it is missing contributes. Artworks are language only as writing. (ÄT 189/AT 124)

Adorno is discussing artistic purposiveness, which he here identifies with artworks' character as enigmas, riddles that suggest only the figure of an answer, avoiding the specific purpose that would consist in a determinate solution. This resonates with my discussion of philosophical explication at the end of the discussion of 'Parataxis' in the first chapter: the work of philosophical interpretation that is attuned to the artwork involves explication in response to the enigmatic character whereby the work seems to require decoding, yet never fully yields to it. Writing that can no longer be decoded is akin to the disappearance of a particular purpose in its transformation into the purposiveness of what becomes a formal feature. What Adorno describes as significant about Klee's work is the fact that the manner in which it resembles writing reveals a truth about all works, of all periods. This further develops a remark in the discussion of technology in the earlier section of *Aesthetic Theory* on the categories of the ugly, the beautiful, and technique, that Klee's work is the most prominent recent example of a tendency toward a radicalized reification, defined as an act of 'groping for the language of things', of approaching 'that idea of that nature which extirpates the primacy of the humanly meaningful' (ÄT 96/AT 60). Again, Klee's work is presented not simply as exemplary of a particular tendency, but as revelatory of a truth of artworks of all genres: their philosophical investigation orients itself toward the enigmatic character that nonetheless resists resolution.

The challenge to the unity of the individual artistic genre, a challenge in tension with which the genres are established and develop, arises not through looking to other works outside the genre, but through the singularity of the singular work, not in the relatively banal sense that all developments within a genre are manifested in individual works, but rather through the adherence of an individual work to its own law of form, the law that inheres within the established genre. It is through such works—Adorno gives as examples Ligeti's *Atmosphères*, Varèse's *Ionisation* and a string quartet by Donatoni—that questions of the type 'Is that still music?' arise (OL 434–35/COL 370-71): at the boundaries between the genres, the specific formal demands of the individual work come up against those of the genre within which they seem to originate. This raises more urgently the question of the ways in which Adorno conceives not only of the challenges to particular genres and forms, but also of the way in which they might be thought to come into being in the first place.

The Genesis of the Forms

Discussing the downfall of the genres in the opening paragraph of the penultimate section of *Aesthetic Theory*, on the relationship between universal and particular, Adorno offers the following account of the emergence and development of artistic forms:

> The substantial moment of genres and forms has its locus in the historical requirements of their materials. Fugue is thus bound to tonal relations; and after the setting-aside of modality it is as it were demanded by a tonality that has attained absolute and unlimited power in imitative praxis, as the telos of this praxis. (ÄT 297/AT 200)

As explication of this argument he offers the claim that the real or tonal answer of a fugal subject is dependent on the situation in which polyphony as it has been handed down and developed 'sees itself confronted with the tasks of suspending the homophonic gravity of tonality' (ÄT 297–98/AT 200), that is to say that it attempts to integrate tonality into its own sphere, and to introduce it to the hierarchies of harmony and counterpoint. More strongly: 'All properties of the fugal form could be derived from this necessity of which the composer was in no way aware' (ÄT 298/AT 200). It would be wrong to claim that Adorno loses sight of the role of the creative subject within the process by which (in this case) the fugue came into being. His claim is not that the potential and necessary future development of fugue was in plain sight for all at the end of the seventeenth century. That development did not result from the application of an arbitrary and external subjective intervention to the state of the musical tradition as it existed at the time, but rather from its attunement to the historical requirements of that tradition.

The emphasis on the requirements of the material is a theme familiar from the discussion of what Adorno terms the artist's sense of form in the second chapter. As in that case, the formal development comes about not as a result of subjective voluntarism, but of, to use Adorno's formulation, 'the reflection, at once blind and binding, of the object in itself' (ÄT 175/ AT 114). This unverifiable claim is at best speculative, at worst tautological. That is to say: if the criterion of artistic success is defined in advance—and this holds just as true for subjective theories of genius as for claims of objective attunement or reflection—then every instance of such success, every successful artwork, can be presented in evidence of the truth of the theory. Indeed, it is hardly possible to distinguish between the two claims that a work is successful because of the subjective genius of its creator, and that its success consists in its creator's sensitivity to the objective requirements of the artistic material. Both claims have about them something of a retrospective conferring of necessity of the sort of which Adorno's social theory, when it is at its most compelling, tends to be profoundly critical, an aspect I discuss in more detail in the final chapter.

In this case Adorno's emphasis is less on the composition of the individual work than on the resonance of this act for the composition of future artworks. It is clear that for Adorno, the moment of the individual artwork cannot be separated from that of the genre. Since the material with which artists work must be understood as handed down through a historical tradition—an aspect to which I return in more detail in the following chapter—attunement to the requirements of the material necessarily resonates beyond the bounds of the individual work. This clarifies what Adorno means by the sentence, quoted in part in the previous section, that '[a]rt merges in no way with artworks, to the extent that artists always work on art as well as on artworks' (ÄT 272/AT 182). The composition of each work alters the state of the material as it is available to future artists, with consequences not only for the particular work, but also for the general category to which it is thought to belong.

Adorno's original formulation of the interrelationship between genre and material makes even clearer that the emergence of forms such as the fugue is closely related to the function of the law of form within the composition and structure of individual artworks: 'The substantial moment of genres and forms comes into being through the sedimentation in them of the desiderata of their materials.'[10] This makes clearer the extent to which Adorno's understanding of forms and genres is at least as closely linked to the Hegelian tradition as his understanding of the relationship between form and content. The claim that form consists in sedimented content clearly goes beyond what might be thought of as the adherence of an individual work to the form that develops out of its historical content, but resonates also in the more general artistic forms. That it is a formulation that Adorno in the end rejected should warn against taking its consequences too literally. That is to say, it would be an oversimplification dogmatically or formulaically to extrapolate from the combination of this and Adorno's claim in *The Philosophy of New Music* that musical material is 'sedimented spirit' the conclusion that genre is sedimented material, which in turn is sedimented spirit (PnM 39/PMM 33; cf. the discussion in chapter 1 above). However, it is nonetheless fruitful to consider the ways in which some of the aspects of the mutual implication of the relationships form–content and form–genre can be illuminated through Adorno's deployment of the concept of sedimentation.

The formulation suggests the working hypothesis that while the form of an individual artwork as discussed in chapter 1 is the sedimentation of content, artistic forms are the sedimentation of material. That is, the unique form of the individual artwork and the form that consists in what is shared between artworks come about as the result of two different sorts of sedimentation—or perhaps more accurately, of the sedimentation of two phenomena that can be conceived as being opposed to form in different ways. To establish an over-simplified hypothesis once again, the singular form of the individual artwork might be thought of as resulting from the sedimentation of the subjectively chosen content—or perhaps the content as it is viewed from the perspective of the cognitive subject—while artistic forms consist in the sedimentation of a material that is encountered by the subject as objective to the extent that it is mediated through an external tradition. In a manner analogous to the discussion of the sedimentation of content in the first chapter, this depositing of objective material might be thought of as a process that masks its objectivity, such as in the appearance of an unrestricted choice from a range of handed-down material. I discuss in more detail both the relationship between content and material and the more general significance of Adorno's deployment of the concept of material in the following chapter.

However, the relationship between form and content is certainly not inconsequential to the as it were collective forms under which artworks can be classified. Against what he characterizes as the romantic claim that the earliest artworks were the highest and purest, Adorno argues that the earliest art-like objects were indistinguishable from objects put to pragmatic uses such as magical praxis and historical documentation (ÄT 11/AT 2). The purposiveness of the 'collectively honed aesthetic forms' that have become purposeless discussed in the previous section and in the first chapter consists to a great extent in their use within cultic praxis (ÄT 210/AT 139). Indeed, he identifies in Kant's formulation 'purposiveness without purpose' an antinomical character, unacknowledged by Kant: 'through their technification, which binds them inalienably to purposive forms, artworks come into contradiction with their purposelessness' (ÄT 323/AT 217). I discuss the relationship between art and technology with reference to what Adorno terms the prose-character of modern art in the context of the culture industry later in this chapter; what is significant at this stage is the way in which Adorno's understanding of this antinomy admits a specificity of purposiveness or even function that would be excluded by a more stringent adherence to the tradition of Kantian aesthetics with which Adorno is working. This admits into Adorno's aesthetics the possibility of considerations such as those of Gérard Genette, who argues that literary forms—in his terms, the four 'classes of imitation' of tragedy, comedy, epic, and parody—each correspond to a different combination of mode (dramatic or narrative) and object or aim, which can be higher or lower.[11] A more strictly Kantian conception of form would deny its links to any such specific purpose or aim. To Adorno's historicized reading of Kant—his insistence, that is, on form as the sedimentation of content, however purposive—corresponds a relationship between form and function that recognizes the mediatedness of aesthetic purposelessness with not only purposiveness in general but also the specific purpose or function of artworks, whether viewed in terms of their origins in cultic ritual or their social function today.

This brings to the foreground the question of how artworks might be thought to interact with one another, a question which Adorno addresses most directly in his discussion of progress within art:

> One can only speak desultorily of a transition from one work to another. There would otherwise be no place for spontaneity,

> the impulse toward the unknown, without which art cannot be thought; its history would be mechanically determined. (ÄT 311/AT 209)

The tradition in which the material is handed down through different artworks is not determined by any individual work, nor does it erase the possibility of subjective intervention within the individual work. The impulse toward the unknown on which art depends consists not simply in the general unpredictability of such subjective interventions, but more specifically in the tension that exists between the requirements of content and material, a tension to which it is the task of the artistic subject to respond. Adorno insists that even the trajectory of the œuvre of an individual artist must be seen as fragmented—regardless of the extent to which the particular artist works within a variety of forms.

It should not, however, be inferred from this fragmented trajectory that individual artworks are isolated from one another:

> No individual work is that which is praised by traditional idealist aesthetics, a totality. Each one is as insufficient as it is incomplete, excised from its own potential, and this counteracts its direct continuation, if one perhaps neglects the planned series in which painters in particular experiment with a model according to its possibilities for development. (ÄT 311/AT 209)

Adorno insists on a conception of the historical development of artistic tradition in relation to which each individual artwork must be seen. And yet at the same time each work is more than simply a contribution to such a tradition, a tradition that depends on and consists in individual works. He argues that the discontinuity of the artistic tradition is 'no more causally necessary than it is accidental' (ÄT 311/AT 209). The discontinuous relations between artworks—the fact that they are discrete from one another without existing only in isolation—must be seen as both deliberate and noncontingent. This raises the question of how best to conceive of subordinating concepts—forms and genres—in relation to the ways in which artworks interact not only with one another but also with these subordinating concepts. It is a question that is perhaps best seen in relation to the much broader philosophical problem of the tense (and, as Jameson has observed, complex and mutually implicated) relationship between universal and particular, a problem which is present throughout Adorno's work, and to which I now turn.[12]

Universal and Particular

The relevance of the relationship between universal and particular to the status of forms, genres, and arts finds its most explicit expression in the penultimate section of *Aesthetic Theory*, in which Adorno addresses the tension between the creative artistic subject and the power of the established forms:

> The forms predominate over the subject until the images' coherence no longer coincides with the forms. The subject explodes them for the sake of coherence, a coherence derived from objectivity. The individual work did not do justice to the genres by subsuming itself under them, but rather through the conflict in which it spent a long time justifying them, then engendered them, and finally liquidated them. The more specific the work, the more truly it fulfils its type: the dialectical proposition that the particular is the universal has its model in art. (ÄT 300/ AT 202)

The relationship between universal and particular is presented as mediated through the artistic subject. The primary point of contact between genre and artwork consists in the power or hold over the subject exercised by genre. This power is derived not by the law of form as it results from the needs of the subjectively chosen content, but rather through the forms that have been established in response to the requirements of the material as it has been worked. However, the subject is able to break through the constraints imposed by this power—but this attempt is bound by the requirements of the object for coherence. That is, the singular form of the individual work comes into conflict with the artistic form that is established by previous works, a conflict that is played out at the level of the artistic subject. It is true that the artistic forms result from individual artworks, but the forms do not come about through a process by which these artworks group themselves together and classify or arrange themselves under a particular genre. Adorno offers a more dynamic account of the process in which the genres are established and ultimately broken or shifted by the tension of the singular individual work against the emergent and then dominant categories.

His reference to the 1966 Berlin talk in his elaboration in *Aesthetic Theory* of the prerequisites for a potential future theory of the artwork foregrounds the tension between artworks and genres, emphatically insisting that the relationship between universal and particular is not one of passive identity:

> The antinomy of the pure and impure in art can be classified under the more general antinomy that art is not the subordinating concept of its genres. They differ just as specifically as they merge with one another. (ÄT 271/AT 182)

The word I have translated as 'merge' is again *verfransen*. This time it is not the borders between the arts that are fraying but the artistic genres themselves, a fraying characterized by specificity—a specificity which, in turn, is fundamental to the ways in which they differ. The central aspect of Adorno's argument here is the tension established between general and specific, universal and particular. In his account in *Negative Dialectics* of what he terms the spell of constitutive subjectivity, he contends that the universal, 'by which the particular is compressed as by an instrument of torture until it fragments, works against itself, because it derives its substance from the life of the particular' (ND 339/Ashton 346). If the universal concept succeeds in crushing the particular, the concept becomes simply an empty shell.

He accuses Hegel of positing the immediate identity of universal and particular and in so doing of 'taking sides with the universal' (ND 320–22/ Ashton 326-29), an accusation that prompts Rose to raise a profound objection to the procedures of his thought:

> Adorno does not relate these oppositions to each other as they come to light in a dynamic historical development but argues that they are frozen—'regression under the spell'. [. . .] He thereby preserves them under the spell and brings mediation to a standstill.[13]

My concern here is less whether Rose's criticisms of the argument Adorno sets out in *Negative Dialectics* are directed at the correct target, and more with the reformulation of Adorno's position in *Aesthetic Theory*.[14] If it is the case that the Adorno of *Negative Dialectics* brings mediation to a halt, the same criticism cannot be made of his account of the relationship between specific and general within the artwork—a further indication of the potential contribution to be made by Adorno's aesthetics to the critique of metaphysics. Both the concept of art in general (in relation to the artistic genres) and these genres themselves (in relation to individual artworks) can be considered to be manifestations of the general. Meanwhile, the specific is represented not only by individual artworks but also by the individual genres. And in the latter case, this specificity is the site not only of the differences between them, but also of the ways in which their edges begin to fray. Adorno recognizes the mutual interaction and tension between the 'abstract subordinating concept' and the 'discretely detached moments' whose movements the subordinating concept seeks to restrict. In turn, 'the movement of art is most lively when it breaks down its subordinating concept' (ÄT 271/AT 182). This orientation against its own concept helps to account for the difference between Adorno and Hegel's response to the fraying of boundaries as analyzed by Hammer: 'whereas Hegel takes the waning of formal requirements in art to be an expression of the modern world's demand for free spiritual content (most directly conveyed in the form of philosophical thinking), Adorno considers responsible, advanced art to remain in a painful lyrical state of self-reflection and formally oriented self-dissolution, resisting the move beyond art'.[15] The tendency to strive against and break down the generality of the subordinating concept starts within the particularity of the work, a particularity which enables art to escape the constraints on philosophy as a discursive, conceptual medium.

Central to the determination of such subordinating concepts—whether artistic genres or the concept of art itself—is the question of the constitution of artworks. Adorno insists that the stability of these subordinating concepts is challenged by poems, for example, that 'on account of their relatively autonomous discursive element, are not only artworks, and not artworks through-and-through' (ÄT 272/AT 282). Similarly, he complicates Benjamin's distinction between artworks and documents, the former being internally determined by the law of form, arguing that some documents are in fact 'objectively so determined, even if they do not appear as artworks' (ÄT 272/AT 282). And he makes an even stronger version of this claim when discussing a work's belonging to individual genres rather than to the overarching category of art, insisting that '[t]here is probably no significant artwork that has completely corresponded to its genre' (ÄT 297/AT 199). Indeed, this is most emphatically true of those cases—Proust is an example to whom Adorno repeatedly returns—that seem to move the form with them rather than deviating from it. They shift or alter the form without breaking it or rupturing its spell, a process which Nicholas Brown characterizes with the thesis that subverting the genre 'means doing the genre better, just as every modernist painting had to assume the posture of sublating all the previous modernisms'.[16] This noncorrespondence of artworks either to the concept of art or to any individual genre or form is equally applicable to the relationship between genres, arts, and art: 'The genres and forms do not vanish without trace in any single art any more than the arts as such vanish in art' (ÄT 297/AT 199). Adorno does not deny that each artwork can be attributed to a genre or form, then to one of the arts, and finally to art itself, but insists that the elements of which this schema is composed cannot be fitted neatly inside one another according to a simple linear hierarchy.

Adorno recognizes in the universal concept a normative tendency to work against the particularity of the individual artwork. But his account of the relationship between universal and particular as it is played out in the tension between artwork and genre does not consist simply in the application to aesthetics of the dialectical principle that 'objects do not go into their concept without leaving a remainder' (ND 17/Ashton 5). Artistic genres explicitly make use of and preserve the specificities of the objects that are classified under or assigned to them:

> The genre stores up the authenticity of the individual works within itself. However, the tendency toward nominalism is not simply identical with the development of art into its concept that is hostile to concepts. But unlike the hazy concept of the symbol, the dialectic of universal and particular does not do away with its distance. (ÄT 299/AT 201)

At the heart of Adorno's argument is the claim that not only art but also its concept itself is hostile to concepts. The account in *Aesthetic Theory* of the relationship between universal and particular is to this extent a (largely unspoken) renegotiation of Adorno's account in *Negative Dialectics* of the nonidentity of concept and object—or perhaps more accurately, a preliminary delineation of the limits of the application of the negative dialectic. It is significant that the artistic genre is not presented as something that effaces the particularities of artworks, but as a site of their preservation. But while the genre has its origins in the individual work, the work retains an element that is hostile to the genre. This is closely related to—if not wholly accounted for by—the fact that artworks resist the logic of being-for-another, as seen most clearly in Adorno's famous account of the potential of the bourgeois aestheticist claim of *l'art pour l'art* to stand outside and therefore challenge the dominance of the context of commodity relations by virtue of the autonomy of the work that refuses accommodation to the market (cf. NzL 425/NtL 2: 89; I return to this conception of art's resistance to the dominance of exchange in the fifth chapter).

This resistance constitutes the foundation of Adorno's claim that the concept of art is itself hostile to concepts. This hostility has significant consequences for the status of Adorno's concept of form. Indeed, it is possible to recognize from an Adornian position that Heidegger's critique of the concept of form discussed in the first chapter is valid, that the concept of form does indeed do violence to the dignity of the object by inflecting it with the madeness presupposed by a thinking that is indebted to Thomistic theology.[17] The violence done by conceptual thought to its object is central to Adorno's thinking. The necessity of the concept of form is inextricably linked to the ontology of the wrong state of things. We cannot but think of forms of art because of the configuration of the relationship between universal and particular that is predominant within the ontology of what Adorno terms the 'false whole' (NzL 141/NtL 1: 123). His deployment of the concept of form might be thought to carry out an analysis of art within damaged life from a position that is avowedly within this life. It is speculative in the Rosean sense that it reveals something about damaged life—Rose's formulation that the object of Hegel's exposition is 'the *speculative experience of the lack of identity* between religion and the state' might tentatively be rewritten to refer to the lack of identity between concept and object—from a position within the experience of that damage.[18]

But the hostility of individual artworks to their subordinating concepts is not limited to the general (or generic) opposition of art to identity thinking. Adorno also identifies a nominalist moment in both art and artworks, a nominalism that is hostile to any conception of artistic genre. Recognition of this nominalist moment within art must not be seen as an endorsement of a nominalist denial of abstract subordinating concepts or categories. It is rather an insistence that artworks display and embody not only an affinity to generic categories but also a resistance to them. From the nominalist moment comes first an insistence that we recognize the abstractness—and therefore limitedness—of conceptions of genre, and second a challenge to their dominance. The tension between universal and particular within Adorno's account of the category of genre is neither an endorsement of the category's abstract character nor a wholesale rejection of it on account of this character. In order further to illuminate this tension between artwork and genre, I now turn to discuss in more detail Adorno's account of aesthetic nominalism.

Nominalism and its Discontents

Aesthetic nominalism is for Adorno not a theory or standpoint external to the work of art, according to which it is wrong to classify any singular artwork under the subordinating concept of an artistic genre. Such an understanding would involve the imposition onto artworks and their relationship with one another of a standpoint of identity thinking. Adorno understands aesthetic nominalism rather as a tendency or moment within the individual artwork that is hostile to the formation of genres, a hostility to the genesis of artistic genres that exists within individual artworks. It is not, therefore, a nominalism in either of the senses with which the term is commonly used within metaphysics—the denial of the reality of universals, or of abstract objects. It is not so much a nominalist theory of art as an account of a nominalist moment within art. Jameson's claim that Adorno's nominalism involves 'the repudiation of the universal' is thus misleading: it is much less a repudiation than a recognition of a moment that is opposed to the universalizing moment that establishes genre.[19] The relationship of these two moments is perhaps encapsulated most succinctly—and most enigmatically—in comments such as that found toward the end of the first half of 'Parataxis' that Hölderlin's anti-nominalism, like Hegel's, has both developed and arisen—in the term Adorno borrows from Hölderlin it is *entsprungen*—and is 'mediated toward nominalism' (NzL 466–67/NtL 2: 126). The truth content of the nominalist moment consists in the realization within the artwork of spirit's tendency to 'bring something that is not, something abstract, into being' (ÄT 165/A 108), a tendency that is central to the way in which spirit becomes semblance within the artwork.

This immanent nominalism is the result of the 'philosophical critique of unreflected nominalism' on which Adorno insists (ÄT 239/AT 159). Indeed, there is an important distinction to be made between nominalist theories that might be applied to artworks, and art's inherent nominalist moment:

> Art wants what has not yet been—but everything that art is, has already been. It cannot jump over the shadow of what has been. But what has not yet been is what is concrete. At its most profound, nominalism might adhere to ideology in that it treats concretion as given or at least at hand, and deceives itself and humanity that the course of the world hinders that peaceful determinedness of that which exists, a determinedness which is only usurped by the concept of what is given, and is itself beaten by abstractness. (ÄT 203/AT 134–35)

Nominalist theories of art are false to the extent that they presuppose a process by which spirit has become tangible in the artwork, without examining the procedures by means of which this process takes place. Art's nominalist moment is closely bound up with its emancipatory aspirations—a theme to which I return more extensively in the fifth chapter. What is significant at this stage is the manner in which the nominalist moment relates to the possibility of a life beyond things as they exist at the moment: in this respect art is oriented not toward that which exists, but toward that which is to come. But this orientation is found within art as it is. Art's emancipatory aim of radical change to life as it is lived—its remorseless critique of all that is—is situated within the concrete, actually existing being of the artwork.

This opposition is closely related to art's nominalist tendency, a nominalism that cannot be straightforwardly opposed to the universalism of artistic forms, for in their relationship of opposition they also mutually reinforce one another. Adorno argues in *Aesthetic Theory* that the nominalist attack on the idea of the unity of form was central to Beethoven's tightening of this very unity (ÄT 212/AT 141). This is what Adorno in the fragments on Beethoven terms his 'superiority over Wagner in the richness of structure, the concrete abundance of relationships as opposed to the abstract filling of time with dynamized identities', a formal superiority which cannot be understood in isolation from the superiority of Beethoven's content, its abundance and concreteness compared with what Adorno identifies as the '*emptiness* of Wagner's expression' (BPdM 115, emphasis original/BTPoM 74). What Adorno means by the tightening of a unity becomes somewhat more concrete in his discussion of Beethoven's Fantasia for piano op. 77, which he claims can be thought of as a 'transcription of actual fantasizing at the piano', whereas in fact 'a form is *essentially* immanent' to the Fantasia (BPdM 107–08, emphasis original/BTPoM 67-68). As in the discussion of musical expressionism in the previous chapter, the form carries out determining work even—especially—in moments where it seems to have been eliminated, as the particular is brought into relation with the universal.

Adorno begins the discussion in *Aesthetic Theory* of the relationship between universal and particular with an extended paragraph discussing nominalism and the demise of the genres, in which he sets out a preliminary definition of what he means by the nominalism of art and its consequences for our understanding of the relationship between universal and particular:

> The principium individuationis in art, its immanent nominalism, is an instruction and not an established fact. It does not simply promote the specification (and with it the radical design) of individual works. By lining up the generalities by which these works oriented themselves, it at once smudges the line of demarcation

against what has not been formed, the raw empirical, and does not threaten the design of works less than it releases it. The rise of the novel—nominalist and therefore paradoxical form par excellence—in the bourgeois age provides a prototype for this; all new art's loss of authenticity can be traced back to it. The relation between universal and particular is not as simple as the nominalist move suggests, but also not as trivial as the doctrine of traditional aesthetics according to which the universal must become particular. The simple disjunction between nominalism and universalism does not hold. (ÄT 299/AT 201)

The fact that the nominalism under discussion here is a moment or tendency rather than a fixed property is central to the tension between universal and particular in art. Adorno's rejection of the 'doctrine of traditional aesthetics'—and here he is primarily referring to Hegel's claim that artworks give sensuous form to universal spirit—is in the first instance an attack on universalist anti-nominalism.[20] But he opposes anti-nominalism not by reasserting a dogmatic nominalist position against it, but rather by means of the claim that the relationship between nominalism and universalism must be understood as more nuanced than one of simple opposition. Central to this relationship is the claim that art's nominalist tendency goes well beyond conceptions of the singularity of each individual artwork as nothing more than a tendency that is manifested merely in radical artistic innovation. It is significant that Adorno insists that the tendency works not toward artworks' rejecting or distancing themselves from the empirical world, but toward the blurring of the dividing line between what can and what cannot be thought of as falling under the concept of art. Although this is not surprising—a rigid conceptual distinction between art and non-art is profoundly anti-nominalist—it is nonetheless notable that the tendency toward the weakening of this conceptual distinction is presented as itself inherent to artworks. The nominalist moment of artworks is central to art's hostility both to conceptuality in general and to its own concept in particular.

Adorno's account of the mechanism by which the nominalist tendency enacts this opposition requires some unpacking, for this passage presents an undeniable difficulty. The third quoted sentence is particularly dense and complex, if anything more so in the German, in which the 'works' appear merely by means of a demonstrative pronoun whose referent is in the previous sentence. Adorno's claim is that art's nominalist tendency 'lines up the generalities' that artworks use to orient themselves, and in doing so blurs the boundary between art and not-art. The word I have translated as 'line up' is *aufreihen*, which means to string (pearls, for example), or to arrange in a row. What Adorno means by this is perhaps best revealed by his account of the result of this process: the loss of art's loss authenticity, the dissolution of the distinction between art and its other, a process to which Adorno claims the rise of the novel is central. The lining-up, then, is a process of bringing-together and of arrangement, the establishment of (in this case) literary forms. These forms arise and develop in relation not only to the works that can be classified under them, but also to the other forms against which they can be defined. What is at stake, then, is at the same time the establishment of a schema of subordinating concepts according to which individual works can orient themselves.

This does not, however, account for Adorno's insistence on the relationship between this establishment and the dissolution of the limits of the concept of art, which stand together in a causal relation that is sufficiently problematic that Hullot-Kentor elides it in his translation, replacing Adorno's insistence on causation with a claim to mere synchronicity: 'Bringing together the universals by which artworks are oriented, it at the same time obscures the boundary against unformed, raw empiria and thus threatens the structuration of works no less than it sets it in motion' (AT 201). But to ignore the causal relationship neglects the significance of Adorno's formulation of his claim that the novel is the 'nominalist and therefore paradoxical form par excellence'. The paradox does not consist simply in the fact that the nominalist tendency both arranges the subordinating concepts and works toward their dissolution, but in the fact that it is precisely by means of the establishment of the constellations of artistic genres and forms that the conceptual limits, not only of these genres but also of the concept of art, begin to be erased. To help clarify this paradoxical character I now turn to discuss the implications of Adorno and Horkheimer's critique of the culture industry.

Bourgeois Art and the Culture Industry

This notion that the novel is paradoxical is not new to *Aesthetic Theory*, but can be found in Adorno's work as early as 1942, in the essay on the schema of mass culture, a continuation of the culture industry chapter of the *Dialectic of Enlightenment*, published as an appendix to the third volume of the *Gesammelte Schriften* (cf. DA 336). The relevant quotation is as follows:

> Aesthetic truth was bound to the expression of the untruth of bourgeois society. In fact, art really only exists to the same extent that it is impossible by virtue of the order that it transcends. This is why the existence of all great forms is paradoxical, that of the novel more than all others, the bourgeois form par excellence, which film has usurped. With the extreme growth of tension, the possibility of artworks has today itself become entirely questionable. Monopoly is the executioner: it erases tension, but does away with art along with the conflicts. (DA 316/CI 67)

The impossibility of art to which Adorno refers is the dissolution of the line of demarcation between art and its other, and is closely related to what Adorno understands as the commercial character of culture, in which the distinction between culture and practical life disappears. The precise cause of this disappearance is the loss of aesthetic semblance, which in the culture industry is reduced to 'the sheen which advertising lends to the commodities that absorb it' (DA 299/CI 53)—and with this reduction, the moment of independence found within aesthetic semblance is lost. The claim here that the limits of the concept of art become unclear calls into question less the distinction between the artwork and the raw empirical than that between artworks and other (and radically different) formed products of social labor—commodities. I discuss the nature and consequences of the relationship between the artwork and the commodity at greater length in the fifth chapter; what is significant at this point is the difference between the accounts advanced in *Dialectic of Enlightenment* and *Aesthetic Theory*. The emphasis in the earlier text on the identity of art and commodity in the culture industry becomes almost three decades later a much more general claim as to the impossibility of distinguishing between art and not-art. That is, the claim in *Aesthetic Theory* is less a critique of art's cooption by or accommodation to the culture industry—a complaint, that is, about the role taken on by art within society—than an account of the social conditions of the possibility of such a cooption in the first place, the possibility that artworks might come to take on such a role.

And yet in both cases the novel is presented as archetypal, in the earlier text as the epitome of bourgeois form, in the late work as exemplary for the paradox of nominalist form. The continuation of the culture industry essay condemns the 'parasitic character' taken on by bourgeois art in the aftermath of the liquidation of its opposition to empirical reality (DA 302/CI 56). The loss of aesthetic semblance consists in art's assertion that it is not semblance but reality, but Adorno nonetheless distinguishes carefully between mass culture and the bourgeois artworks that are central to his account of the de-aestheticization of art:

> It is precisely because of the strictness of the immanence of their form that the bourgeois artworks which mass culture removes from circulation on account of their lack of fidelity to reality were not adequate to themselves: Kant's theory of the sublime expresses this most penetratively. True to reality, mass culture appropriates truth content and wears itself out in the material, but the only material it has left is itself. Hence all the musicals and biopics and biographies of artists. (DA 303/CI 56)

Products of the culture industry have been thoroughly absorbed into the instrumental logic of the reality of damaged life. Through their fidelity to this reality they abandon that which distinguishes them from it, renounce their claim to be different from the world. The tendency Adorno identifies within what he refers to as the bourgeois novel is that of the artwork that proclaims itself to be reality without entirely renouncing either aesthetic semblance or the adherence to the immanent law of form. His argument that the novel dissolves the conceptual limits of art is not based on a claim that it has become so inflected with or permeated by attributes of culture-industrial production that it is indistinguishable from these elements of instrumental rationality—instead it foregrounds its distance from this reality. The force of Adorno's claim in *Aesthetic Theory* that the novel represents a nominalist and therefore paradoxical form is that the individual work displays a radical specificity in its adherence to the law of form.

This, however, is not to deny the fact that the novel has superficial similarities to or affinities not only with some of the products of the culture industry, but also with other not cultural artifacts that stake little or no claim to be art—such as biography and reportage. Adorno pays little attention to the nature of these similarities, which he discusses as if they are accidental, or even as if the products of the culture industry are engaged in a mere aping of the novel. This seems ignorant of the novel's origin in other forms of narrative, an origin which McKeon discusses in terms of three transitions, from hagiography to spiritual biography, picaresque to criminal biography, and Christian pilgrimage to scientific travel.[21] Ian Watt discusses some of the particular similarities that can be identified in the work of Bunyan and Defoe, the 'simple language, realistic description of persons and places, and a serious presentation of the moral problems of ordinary individuals', arguing that the fundamental transformation that distinguishes the first novels from their predecessors in Puritan fiction consists in the loss of the 'transcendental scheme', according to which the details of the fictional reality display a significance that is primarily allegorical.[22] Indeed, McKeon's discussion of the novel's claim to historicity—a claim that is necessary in order for works 'to effect any moral and spiritual improvement'—traces the relationship of a formal characteristic of the genre to its social function and purpose.[23]

The affinities Adorno identifies consist to a great extent in what he terms the prose character of the novel, a character that goes well beyond the fact that most novels are not written in verse. Here it is necessary to draw a distinction between Adorno's use of 'prose' as an epithet and his concrete analyses of the prose of, for example, Kafka, Beckett or Proust.[24] Its scope is not confined to literature: Adorno argues of Schönberg in 1952 that his composition 'really becomes athematic, "prose", without degenerating into contingency' (P 174/WWN 167). He deploys the concept of prose character most frequently in reference to film and new music, repeatedly arguing that the former is in some way exemplary for the latter. In *Composing for Film* he contends that new music approaches film's prose character through its 'capacity for unfettered characterization' (GS 15: 45/CF 39), and insists that for music to take on such a prose character it does not suffice to abandon the formal elements of repetition that exist within (for example) the tripartite song-form, but must involve a fundamental reorganization of the way in which music is constructed (GS 15: 93/CF 96). Indeed, in *The Faithful Chorus-Master* the relationship between tonal music and the 'free, autonomous course' of Schönberg's early twelve-tone compositions—the example given is the second piano piece of Op. 23—is presented as a mode of musical secularization, analogous to the difference between verse and prose, which one reads 'by giving oneself up to the course, without lying in wait for evident symmetries' (GS 15: 199).

The prose character of works of the culture industry is conceived somewhat differently. What is at stake here is less a prose character in the sense of a perceivable asymmetry, but rather a tendency toward what Adorno describes as prosaic. His understanding of this tendency finds what is perhaps its most explicit formulation in the fifth sentence of the essay on the schema of mass culture:

> Since the industrial age an art has been in vogue that is adept at promoting its loyalties, that has made an alliance with reification by attributing to the demystification of the world, to what

is prosaic and even banausic, a poesy of its own that has been nourished on the work-ethic. (DA 299/CI 53)

What Adorno identifies as the prosaic character of the world consists in its demystification as represented by the increasing mediation of the experience of everyday life through the twin structures of automated production and the commodity form. He identifies within the works criticized a tendency to accommodation with this mediated world, a tendency which loses sight of the possibility of reconciliation. The prosaic stands for the increased social mechanization, which the art of the culture industry simply inflects with a poetics that is as it were superimposed. Adorno's objection is not to the inflection of art with elements of industrial production, but to the instrumentalization that takes place in the culture industry's uncritical absorption of and hence support for things as they are.

This nuances of this distinction become clearer by the time of *Aesthetic Theory*, in which Adorno addresses a similar constellation from the perspective of the prosaic moment in new music:

> The emphasis on technique in art alienates the philistine in his sobriety, for which art's origin in prosaic praxis, dreaded by art, is all too visible. Nowhere does art make itself so guilty of being illusionary as in the inalienable technical aspect of its magic, for it is only through technique, the medium of its crystallization, that art distances itself from the prosaic. (ÄT 321–22/AT 216)

What is at stake here is not the subjection of artworks, pressing them into service of a moment of accommodation with capitalist production, but rather a recognition of the contribution that developments in the means of production can make to art. I address this relationship more directly in the discussion of artistic technique in the following chapter; what is of consequence at this point is the status of the prosaic within Adorno's argument. Art is depicted as a movement made out of revulsion at its own origins in prosaic praxis. This praxis consists in the attempt to influence the world through ritual, the renunciation of which coincides with the development of aesthetic purposiveness without purpose. At the same time, Adorno draws on the concept of art's prose character in order to insist on art's increasing distance from myth:

> With regard to its content, the ambiguity of natural beauty has its genesis in that of mythology. This is why genius, once

it has become aware of itself, can no longer satisfy itself with
natural beauty. In its ascending prose character, art disentangles
itself completely from myth, and thus from the spell of nature,
which at the same time continues in the subjective domination
of nature. (ÄT 105/AT 66)

Artistic technique—which, as will be seen in the following chapter, for
Adorno is closely linked to the state of development of the forces of production at any given time—is the means not only by which art comes
to distinguish itself from the prosaic, but also, as the point at which art
comes into closest contact with social production, by which it develops the
prose character that distinguishes it from unformed, natural beauty. Art's
prose character is thus to be distinguished from the prosaic origins of art,
and more specifically as the means by which art rejects these origins. The
ascendency of this prose character is for Adorno a manifestation, and not
simply an epiphenomenon, of the continued progression of the dialectic of
enlightenment. Artworks do not simply reflect a cultural transition away
from myth, but take part in this process themselves.

It is in this respect that what Adorno identifies as the novel's specificity
can be viewed not in opposition to but rather as closely bound up with, if
not a direct result of, its affinities with elements of particular products of
the culture industry. In the first chapter I discussed in relation to Hölderlin
the way in which the content of an artwork to an extent determines its
form by means of the particular demands it exacts. The affinities of the
novel with the products of the culture industry are not coincidental, but
inextricably linked to the novel's own content, defined in terms not only
of the paraphrasable content of each sentence or paragraph, but also of the
ways in which this content is arranged—that is, to the way in which the
relationship between artwork and reality is configured within the novel.
Just as epistolary narrative or free indirect speech, for example, cannot be
thought of as entirely separable from the propositional content that they
might be thought of as conveying—and with it, the form of each individual
work—they are also closely related to the ways in which we think of the
forms that link artworks with one another.

This relation of mutual implication between the particularity of an
individual work and the more general form of the novel is central to Adorno's
claims about the specificity of the bourgeois novel, the novel's unrivaled
power, to put it in McKeon's terms, 'both to formulate, and to explain,
a set of problems that are central to early modern experience'.[25] Adorno

addresses this specificity only in the most general terms, arguing that the artwork's adherence to the demands of the immanent law of form is what sets it apart from empirical reality, and that at the same time the agency of the law of form within the novel is inseparable from the novel's attempt to imitate empirical reality. The specificity that Adorno identifies might be seen as another way of describing what Watt has termed 'the formlessness of the novel, as compared, say, with tragedy or the ode', that is to say, 'the poverty of the novel's formal conventions', which he suggests is 'the price it must pay for its realism'.[26] This 'formlessness' is nonetheless defined in terms of the formal 'premise, or primary convention, that the novel is a full and authentic report of human experience'.[27] Similarly, McKeon insists that 'Defoe's claim to historicity oversees the narrative's formal procedures'.[28]

This attempt to imitate reality differs from that of the culture industry's proclamation that it is at one with reality in that the novel, unlike the products of the culture industry, retains the sheen of aesthetic semblance that in the culture industry is reduced to the sheen of publicity. This tension within aesthetic semblance between the artwork's imitation of reality and its attempt to set itself apart from reality, a tension that has been eradicated from the culture industry, is perhaps what is at stake when Adorno refers to the 'liquidation of conflict within mass culture' or claims that it can 'tolerate no conflict' (DA 314/CI 65). Adorno's emphasis in *Aesthetic Theory* differs somewhat from the position advanced in *Dialectic of Enlightenment*, arguing that 'aesthetic nominalism terminated in the crisis of semblance insofar as the artwork wants to be emphatically essential' (ÄT 156/AT 101). This goes to the heart of the distinction between the culture industry and bourgeois art, in which the 'inalienably bourgeois' elements of conflict, intrigue, and implementation play an integral role (DA 314/CI 65). I now turn to discuss this conflict as part of the constellation between form and genre by examining in more detail their deployment in Adorno's discussions of the novel.

The Novel as Form

Adorno begins his essay on the position of the narrator in the contemporary novel, first given as a talk on the West Berlin public radio station RIAS (Rundfunk im amerikanischen Sektor or Radio in the American Sector) and published in 1954 under the title of 'Form and Content of the Contemporary Novel', by outlining his aim, to bring together some thoughts 'on the present state of the novel as form' (NzL 41/NtL 1: 30). He describes the position of the narrator as a 'moment' of this form. This is significant not only because it reveals that Adorno considers such aspects of novels to belong to the 'novel as form' as well as to the form of the particular novel under discussion, but also because of the manner in which the term locates Adorno's understanding of form within a Hegelian conceptual framework according to which the form, in both senses, is constituted by the interaction of separate but mutually interrelated dynamic moments or aspects (and, as was the case in the discussion of both content and expression, form is frequently the name given to one of these moments, as well as to what results from their interaction).[29] This demonstrates a certain similarity with the way in which Adorno's understanding of the adherence of an individual work to its internal law of form, in contrast with the static 'idea of pure form' (ÄT 84/AT 52) discussed in the introductory section to the second chapter, involves, as he insists more explicitly in 'Parataxis', an understanding of the unity of form and content as a tension between the individual moments that can be distinguished from one another (NzL 469/NtL 2: 128). It is clear that Adorno does not think of artistic forms as rigid containers within the constraints of which artworks must be produced any more than the form of a single artwork can be thought of as a mere container for its content or expression.

This is better explicated with reference to Adorno's more specific remarks about this moment of the novel as form, in which he claims that the position of the narrator can now be characterized as paradoxical, the paradox consisting in the fact that the form of the novel demands narration, but that narration has become impossible (NzL 41:NtL 1: 30). This impossibility consists in the demands and constraints placed on the novel by the development of the culture industry:

> Just as many of the traditional tasks of painting have been taken away from it by photography, those of the novel have been taken by reportage and the media of the culture industry, especially film. The novel would have to concentrate on that which cannot be achieved by reporting. However, in contrast to painting, language imposes limits on the novel's emancipation from its object and to a great extent compels it to take on the fiction of a report[.] (NzL 41–42/NtL 1: 31)

This claim provides a more specific example of the interaction between bourgeois art and the culture industry. Adorno's claim that the novel's genesis in the 'experience of the disenchanted world in *Don Quixote*' (NzL 41/NtL 1: 30), to the exclusion of its origins in the medieval traditions of the romance and the novella, is an explicit attempt to link the novel with the bourgeois age. The substantive content of Adorno's claim is that the attempt to 'sink into' a description of concrete objectivity—he cites the work of Adalbert Stifter as an example—is no longer possible without lapsing into a sort of imitation characteristic of the applied or decorative arts. 'He would make himself complicit in the lie of delivering himself up to the world with a love that presupposes that the world is meaningful, and would end up with intolerable kitsch in the mold of *Heimatkunst*' (NzL 41/NtL 1: 30). This accentuates the complexity of the relationship between art-forms and the substantive content of individual artworks: changes in historical and social conditions that bring about the transformation of the new into the well-known lead themselves to tensions within the forms.

This reinforces the link between artistic forms and literary modes of address. For example, Adorno insists on the impossibility that those returning from war could tell their stories 'in the way that people used to tell of their adventures':

> The narration that presents itself as if the narrator had such experiences in abundance encounters impatience and scepticism on the part of its audience. Notions such as that of 'sitting down with a good book' are archaic. This is not due simply to the reader's lack of concentration, but to the content of what is communicated and its form. (NzL 42/NtL 1: 31)

The phenomenon Adorno identifies here could be seen as the literary analogue to what he at different points in his earlier writings terms the loss, sickness, necrosis, or decay of experience.[30] He insists that the particularity that is a central element to the successful telling of a story is no longer possible because of what he terms the 'standardization and ever-sameness' that permeate the administered world. In this account the individuation on which the novel depends comes into conflict with the social conditions in which it finds itself, conditions under which the mature, responsible subject has been replaced by its pale shadow, yoked to immaturity by the mediated domination of the being-for-another that is encapsulated within the commodity. To this extent the products of the culture industry are not a cause of the changes forced upon the novel but, like them, epiphenomena of the same social processes. In Adorno's terms, 'the ubiquitous biographical tripe found today is a product of the disintegration of the novel-form itself' (NzL 42/NtL 1:31).

However, this disintegration must not be seen as equivalent to the downfall or destruction of the novel-form, but rather as a shift not only in the conditions of its possibility, but also in its potential social impact and function:

> The reification of all relationships between individuals, which transforms their human aspects into lubricating oil for the smooth functioning of the machinery, universal alienation and self-alienation, demands to be called by its name, and the novel is qualified to do this as few other artforms are. (NzL 43/NtL 1: 32)

It is perhaps worthy of note here that Adorno's understanding of reification differs from that called into question by Cornelius Castoriadis's insistence that reification 'can never be wholly realized', that the realization of a completely reified world would by necessity involve the complete destruction of personal relationships and result in the swift collapse of production.[31] For Adorno, the retention of the human aspects is not the counterpole to reification that allows production to be sustained, but rather an integral part of it, as these aspects are subordinated to the requirements of capitalist production and reproduction. It becomes clear that the relationship of artistic forms to social conditions in which they come to prominence is inextricably linked to the relationship they have to their function and mode of address. I discuss the matter and manner of art's potential for resistance to the domination of capitalist social relations at greater length in the next-but-one chapter; what is significant at this stage is the way in which this resistance—which consists initially in naming the alienation that has come to permeate late capitalist society (a naming that does not function according to the classificatory logic of identity thinking, but rather proceeds speculatively, that is to say with an eye on the possibility that things could be different)—takes on a form that is if not determined by then to a great extent responsive to the very social conditions under which it originates and against which it works.

Adorno identifies at the heart of the novel a conflict between the lives of individual human beings and the rigid, petrified relations in which they exist. This has been the 'true object' of the novel at least since *Tom Jones* (NzL 43/NtL 1: 32).[32] Increased social alienation alters the relationships between people: in Adorno's terms, individuals come to view each other as more enigmatic, the more they are estranged from one another in atomized living conditions. The novel's attempt to decipher the riddle of external life is reduced to a struggle for an existence that is determined by the estrangement of the conventions of life with which we become increasingly familiar, an existence which at once both confounds and appears alien. This, for Adorno, is at the heart of the twentieth-century developments away from novelistic realism: 'The antirealist moment of the contemporary novel, its metaphysical dimension, is itself produced by its true object, a society in which human beings are torn apart from each other and from themselves' (NzL 43/NtL 1:32). Indeed, this antirealism might itself be thought of as realistic: discussing Beckett's prose in *Aesthetic Theory*, Adorno insists that 'a second world of images leaps up, as sad as it is rich, the concentrate of historical experiences that at the bottom line in their immediacy did not approximate the hollowing-out of the subject and reality' (ÄT 53/AT 31). This can be understood as realistic to the extent that Beckett's image-worlds contain 'the negative impression of the administered world' (ÄT 53/AT 31). It is a realism, that is, that functions not simply by the attempt accurately to describe this administration, but by revealing it through its own procedures.

The way this relates to Adorno's understanding of the novel as form is perhaps best seen with reference to the example of his short discussion of Proust within the essay on the position of the narrator:

> The more strictly his work is bound to the realism of what is memorized, to the gesture that claims 'this is how it was', the more every work becomes a mere 'as if', and the greater becomes the contradiction between his claim and the fact that it was not so. It is to precisely this that the author must necessarily lay claim—that he knows exactly how things turned out—a claim that requires verification, and Proust's precision, driven to the point where it becomes chimerical, his micrological technique through which the unity of the living is ultimately divided into its atoms, is a single endeavor on the part of the aesthetic sensorium to provide this verification without transgressing the spell of the form. (NzL 44/NtL 1: 33)

Adorno sees in Proust a rejection of and aversion to the similarity of the novel with reportage—to the 'form of the report', in Adorno's terms—an aversion that expresses itself by taking recourse in the minutiae that radically distance and distinguish Proust's work from reportage. Adorno insists that phenomena such as these that might appear to be 'idiosyncratic sensitivities' on the part of authors are in fact often the result of historical changes in the requirements of the form. Proust, for example, remains within the constraints of the novel while at the same time succeeding in staking a claim to accuracy through precision, an accuracy that indeed consists in the very precision with which he describes experiences that are undeniably and professedly subjective. Indeed, it is perhaps not quite accurate to assert that he remains within the constraints of the form: he rather makes a contribution to the novel in a way that shifts what we think of as the form, without rupturing its spell. Decisive historical shifts such as these result from the response of individual artists to the changing social requirements that come into conflict with the forms as they are found: the extent to which these artists function as indicators of what is required and what is forbidden the 'essential determinant of their rank' (NzL 43–44/NtL 1: 32).

Artistic forms, then, are part of a tradition that comes into being and develops—more accurately, perhaps, is developed, or worked on—in response to the particular social conditions and the demands they exact in terms not only of the content of what is to be expressed but also of the mode of address required by the moment of the artwork that seeks to oppose social domination, a moment which itself has a determinant effect on the development of artistic forms. This finds what is perhaps its most explicit expression in the closing sentence of the essay on the position of the narrator:

> The confiscation of aesthetic distance in the novel today, and with it the novel's capitulation to an overpowering reality that cannot be transfigured in an image but must concretely be altered, is required by the direction in which the form wishes to go of its own accord (NzL 47–48/NtL 1: 36).

Artistic forms are not merely a generalization from individual artworks, but contain a tendency toward the general that takes on an appearance of independence from the individual works that constitute them, an independence that here manifests itself in Adorno's account of the form's wish. This wish leads in this case to a capitulation: it is no longer possible—if it ever was—to attribute to society, even temporarily, aspects of reconciliation by means of presenting its positive image. What Adorno terms the capitulation of the novel comes about because it is unable to carry out the concrete change in society that it desires, a theme to which I return in both the final chapter and the coda, discussing some of the different aspects and moments of this opposition.

Theory of the Essay

Adorno's insistence in *Aesthetic Theory* that the novel is 'the nominalist and therefore paradoxical form par excellence' resonates with and against the claim in 'The Essay as Form', first published in the first (and in the first impression unnumbered) volume of *Notes to Literature* in 1958, that the essay 'is what it was from the beginning, the critical form par excellence' (NzL 27/NtL 1: 18). He takes issue on the one hand with what he describes as the 'guild' that only suffers to be called philosophy 'that which clothes itself in the dignity of the universal, the enduring, and today perhaps the originary, and which only gets involved with the particular artifact of spirit to the extent that it can be used to exemplify the universal categories' (NzL 9–10/NtL 1: 3), and at the same time, on the other hand, in an explicit rejection of Lukács's characterization of the essay as an art-form, with the conflation of the essay with its (artistic) object (NzL 11/NtL 1: 5).

Adorno begins the essay by recognizing that the complaint has often been made that the essay has become notorious as a 'hybrid product' and that it 'lacks a convincing formal tradition' (NzL 9/NtL 1: 3). Indeed, it is significant that despite Adorno's title, of the (excluding the title) thirty-five instances in which the word 'form' and its cognates appear, only a small minority pertain to the essay *as* form (and a substantial proportion of these are quotations from others' work). Moreover, when he does explicitly refer to the essay as form he does so by referring to the way it functions or what it achieves, rather than with reference to any externally determinable shape: for example, by likening the way in which the essay appropriates of concepts to 'the behavior of someone who is compelled, in a foreign country, to speak its language, rather than cobbling its elements together according to rules learned at school' (NzL 21/NtL 1: 13). This is consistent with the etymology of the essay as an attempt or trial or examination. Indeed, Adorno explicitly emphasizes the essay's resultant relationship to being mistaken: 'Just as this sort of learning admittedly remains exposed to error, so too does the essay as form; it must pay for its affinity to open spiritual experience with the lack of security that the norm of established thought fears like death' (NzL 21/NtL 1: 13).

To this extent the form of the essay does not consist in a pre-given mold or formula as much as in the procedures or attitudes according to which it works. These, in turn, must be distinguished from method in the sense of an invariable set of procedures that can be applied to all objects, such as the Cartesian injunction to break down the object of investigation into 'as many parts as possible, and as might be necessary for its adequate solution', a maneuver which is violent to the requirements of the objects of the essay, which 'refuse to surrender to elementary analysis and can only be constructed out of their specific idea' (NzL 22/NtL 1: 14).[33] Adorno sets out his conception of the way in which the essay represents an alternative to the false choice between this Cartesian attempt to break down the object of investigation into the smallest possible components, and the Kantian insistence on treating a work of art as an organic whole:

> In contrast with both, the essay orients itself to the idea of that reciprocal effect which rigorously refuses to tolerate asking after elements any more than asking after the elementary. Neither can the moments be developed purely from the whole, nor vice versa. The whole is both a monad and not a monad; its moments, as moments of a conceptual nature, point beyond the specific object in which they are assembled. (NzL 22/NtL 1: 14)

The essay, that is, privileges and hypostatizes neither the whole nor the elements of which it is composed, but rather concerns itself with the reciprocal interaction that takes place between them, and in such a way that it calls into question the notion that their relationship can be conceived in static terms, or that the work can adequately be grasped with reference solely or even primarily to one or the other. They are composed not of elements but of moments, and as in the case of the novel, this emphasizes the dynamism not only of the composition but also of the components, which interact with one another in such a way that that they cannot be isolated from one another. The fact that the moments point beyond the object in which they consist and the insistence that they cannot be derived from this object are closely linked, for both claims allow the essay to re-admit into its investigation a contingency that more orthodox Cartesian or Kantian procedures would tend to rule out of order.

This accounts to an extent for the fact that Adorno's essay is focused less on the essay-form as abstraction than on the form which can be identified within an individual essay. And this consists not only in procedures consequent with the fact that 'luck and play are essential' to the essay (NzL 10/NtL 1: 4), but also with a certain striving to mimic the object under discussion. Adorno insists, for example, on the necessity of a distinction between investigation of a given object and the intention of its author:

> Once one has allowed oneself to be terrorized by the prohibition on saying more than was meant at a given time and place, one already complies with the false intention that people and things have of themselves. In that case understanding is nothing more than scraping away everything around that which the respective author supposedly wanted to say, or at best around the individual psychological impulses that the phenomenon indicates. (NzL 10–11/NtL 1: 4)

It follows from this that not only that the procedures of the essay must allow it to account for this divergence, or at least take it into consideration, but also that in attending to any particular essay it is necessary to consider the possibility that it might mean more than its author meant to mean—that the essay itself cannot be constrained by and restricted to the intention of its author. In refusing to be content with the discovery or revelation of what the author of its object supposedly intended to say, the essay exposes itself to the danger of saying more than its own author intends. That is, it comes to resemble its object. While Adorno criticizes Lukács for failing to recognize that the essay cannot simply be subsumed under the art-forms (NzL 11/NtL 1: 5), he nonetheless opens 'The Essay as Form' with an approving reference to Lukács's description of the essay as the sister of poetry (NzL 9/NtL 1: 3), while the claim that the essay 'starts not with Adam and Eve, but with what it wants to talk about' (NzL 10/NtL 1: 4) is reminiscent of Horace's claim that the great epic poet does not begin the tale of the Trojan War from Leda's twin egg.

Against Lukács, Adorno insists that the essay is distinguished from art with respect to the medium with which it works, that of concepts (NzL 11/NtL 1: 5). But the way in which it embraces and deploys these concepts distinguishes it from non-essayistic, scientific-academic writing:

> [The essay's] transitions disavow conclusive derivation in favor of interconnections between elements for which discursive logic has no space. It uses equivocations not out of sloppiness, not in ignorance of their scientific prohibition, but in order to bring home that which the critique of equivocation, the mere separation of meanings, rarely achieves: that wherever a word covers a

> range of different meanings, what is different is not completely different, rather that the unity of the word warns of another unity, however well hidden, in the thing—this unity, however, must not be mistaken for linguistic affinity, as is the practice of contemporary restorationist philosophies. (NzL 31/NtL 1: 22)

Here Adorno both describes and adopts a fundamental characteristic of the essayistic thinking that he is describing. His own argument unfolds not according to a logic of deduction, but following and indeed making a path from one aspect to the next. There are very few linguistic or rhetorical pointers as to the nature of the relationship between the different clauses of this extract—even the use of a dash rather than a colon in the long second sentence refuses the subordination of the second half as mere explication of the first. The restorationist philosophies (Adorno uses the term 'restorationist' as a near-synonym for 'reactionary') mentioned are presumably a reference to Heidegger—in this instance Adorno not only avoids explicit engagement with the rejected philosophy, but also refuses to name it.[34] The deployment of concepts that Adorno praises is reminiscent of the discussion of constellation in the final section of the introduction above. The difference consists in the fact that Adorno locates in the essay a way of proceeding that relies not on deliberate constellation, but on equivocation, an as it were more literary and less scientific mode that does not so much illuminate the distinction between concept and object, but uses their noncorrespondence to mimic the object.

The sorts of transitions and interconnections that Adorno identifies and praises in the procedures of the essay are reminiscent of the discussion of parataxis in Hölderlin from the first chapter, a link that becomes even more evident a few lines later:

> But the essay develops thoughts in a manner different from that of discursive logic. It neither derives from a principle nor deduces from coherent individual observations. It co-ordinates the elements instead of subordinating them; and only the epitome of its substantive content, not the manner of its presentation is commensurable with the criteria of logic. If the essay, in comparison with the forms in which an already finished content is communicated indifferently, is, as a result of the tension between presentation and presented, more dynamic than traditional thought, it is at the same time, as a constructed juxtaposition,

also more static. In this alone consists its affinity to the image, only that that stasis is itself one of as it were immobilized relationships of tension. (NzL 31–32/NtL 1: 22)

Adorno does not use the term 'parataxis' or its cognates within 'The Essay as Form' (indeed, its use within the *Gesammelte Schriften* is confined to 'Parataxis' and the posthumously published *Aesthetic Theory*), but the claim that the logic of the essay relies on coordination rather than subordination could not be a stronger argument for the association of the essayistic thinking with parataxis. Moreover, Adorno insists, by means of his emphasis of the role within the essay of the 'tension between presentation and presented', on the connection between the content of the essay and its form, not only in the sense of its external and static shape, but also in the sense of the internal logic according to which it is composed and constructed, the procedures which it follows, and the shape of the paths taken by its argument. That is, the literary essay is paratactical in that it learns from the associative, nonscientific thinking of its literary object. It is in this sense that the essay can be thought of as 'the critical form par excellence': it involves reflection not only on its object, but also on the way in which it relates to this object. That is, it learns from and even mimics some of the procedures and habits of its object, seeking a mode of knowledge that depends to a great extent on imitation and likeness. It becomes clear that it is not possible to talk about the form of the essay as a form without referring not only to its external shape, but also to its internal procedures and dynamics.

But there is another sense in which the essay can be thought of as a critical form. It differs from art insofar as it aspires to a truth that is devoid of aesthetic semblance (NzL 11/NtL 1: 5). But nor is its truth that of scientific cognition. 'In its relationship to the scientific procedure and its philosophical foundation of method, the essay, in accordance with its idea, draws the full conclusion from the critique of the system' (NzL 16/NtL 1: 9). The essay is not only an alternative model for thought to the method of scientific rationality, but also a critique of and response to its domination over our lives. Before addressing the relationship between art, criticism, and society in the final chapter, I now turn to consider some of the ways in which the interaction of art and social reality can be seen and understood at the level of the relationship between form and artistic material.

4

Form and Material

> The only form is that of what is formed.
>
> —QF 255/Livingstone 6

The conceptual relationship between artistic form and material has significance beyond the mere arrangement in relation to one another of the elements that might be thought to constitute the artwork. Indeed, it is not possible to construct such a schematic without making a necessarily arbitrary decision as to the scale at which the notional elementary particles of artistic matter are to be determined. And even this presupposes a satisfactory resolution of the question of the nature of artistic material, since the phonic, graphic, conceptual, and other properties of literary artworks—properties which cannot be thought of either as identical with or as completely distinct from one another—each lend themselves to different and often mutually incompatible modes of subdivision. The relationship between form and material, that is, must be conceived significantly more broadly, as including not only the arrangement of elements within the artwork but also what might be thought of as the process of formation, the process by which what exists independently of the artwork is incorporated into it—that is, as the artwork's composition or creation.

The relationship between poetry and its material has long been a concern of poetics. Writing in issue 6 of *Poetics Journal* in 1986, Bruce Andrews acknowledges the social and political implications of the different ways in which poetic material is intertwined with the 'apparatus of domination' that holds a social formation together:

> Because writing's 'material' is discursively articulated, it's also culturally and politically articulated in the light of these limits.

> The materials—or the building blocks of sense—are related internally in society as distinctions within a whole; and they're also organized to be mutually interdependent. They require each other as the ground of their *possibility*.[1]

This character of poetry's linguistic material as embedded within particular (if not necessarily specific) cultural and political and social (and historical) contexts—as being 'pre-formed', in Adorno's terms—constitutes an inexorable link between the poem and its (and our) worlds. In Bruns's terms, 'precisely in virtue of its materiality, poetry enjoys a special relation with ordinary things of the world'.[2] But whereas Andrews proceeds from the assumption that the materials of poetry are thus 'building blocks of sense', Bruns has a more nuanced account of the relationship between poetry and language: 'poetry is made of language but is not a use of it—that is, poetry is made of words but not of what we use words to produce: meanings, concepts, propositions, descriptions, narratives, expressions of feeling, and so on'.[3] He is thus able also to conceive of language in terms other than of meaning, such as with reference to the 'sheer sonic materiality of language'.[4] Meanwhile, Jameson has drawn attention to the way in which Adorno's conception of the relationship between artistic making and social production offers the potential for a more sophisticated conception of the relationship between art and society. Criticizing the neglect of the concept of the productive forces by even social thinking on aesthetics, he argues that 'it is precisely this conception of production that for Adorno will subsume both the historical and the social dimensions of the work of art, whose relationship to history is marked and dated, as it were, by the advanced character of the production process, while its essential sociality is given in advance by the collective social nature of production itself'.[5] Such an investigation offers not only a response to Benjamin's 'call for theses defining the tendencies of the development of art under the present conditions of production', but also a means of rethinking the relationship between art and industrial production.[6]

In the words quoted in the epigraph to this chapter, 'the only form is that of what is formed' (QF 255/Livingstone 6). Within such a framework it is not possible to imagine the form of an artwork in the absence of the material from which it is composed, or even to attempt to abstract an artwork's form away from its material. Similarly, it would be a mistake to think of the material of which artworks are made as being in some way formless. Since form and material are conceptually mutually dependent, it is impossible to conceive of either in isolation from the other: each is mediated through the other, there can be no access to either except through the other. Moreover, the material through which form is examined in this chapter is not and cannot be entirely distinct from the content, expression and genre that were the concern of the previous three.

I thus begin this chapter by outlining the conceptual relationship between form and material, paying particular attention to the distinction between material and content and analyzing the different ways in which form comes to appear when viewed in conjunction with each. I then turn to the concept of artistic or compositional technique, a mode of subjective working of artistic material which is revealed as central to the constellation of form and material. Elucidating the implications of the concept of technique that underlies both *Aesthetic Theory* and some of Adorno's writings on music, I show how the concept encapsulates in condensed form the potential for a reconfiguration of the relationship between subject and object. I follow this with an account of the consequences of Adorno's writings on literature for his understanding of language, attending in particular to the peculiar status within artistic making of linguistic material and its conceptuality, before addressing some of the points in *Notes to Literature* where he addresses the relationship between form, material, and technique, focusing on his discussions of the work of Rudolf Borchardt and Paul Valéry. Finally, I consider the consequences of Adorno's concept of material for his poetics of form, outlining both its contributions and the aporiae that it leaves, both for literary criticism and more widely.

Material and Content

In the section of *Aesthetic Theory* on 'Coherence and Meaning', Adorno criticizes Hegel's 'disastrous confounding' of the concepts of material and content, and elucidates the distinction by reference to music:

> Its content is at most what happens—partial events, motifs, themes, developments—changing situations. Content is not outside musical time, but essential to it, as musical time is to content: content is everything that takes place within time. Material, on the other hand, is that with which artists work: the words, colors, sounds and connections of every sort up to every procedure ever developed, that make themselves available to them for use in the whole: to this extent forms can also become

material; material, that is, is everything that confronts artists, about which they have to make a decision. (ÄT 222/AT 147–48)

Whereas content, broadly speaking, is to be conceived as an aspect of existing artworks, material is in some way pre-artistic, that out of which not-yet-existing artworks are to be made. Adorno is here unambiguous in insisting that the material out of which literary works are made consists of and in words. But not only in words. If colors are the material of painting and sounds that of music, the account of the dissolution of the limits between the arts discussed in the previous chapter suggests that phonic and graphic elements of literary works might be considered among their material, at least at the points at which literature begins to merge with music and the graphic arts (cf. chapter 3 above). In 'Art and the Arts', Adorno gives the example of Sylvano Bussotti, the graphic artist who became a musician, in whose work 'the graphic character takes on a certain independence from that which is composed' (OL 432/COL 368); one might equally think of the compositions of Cornelius Cardew, John Cage, and Christian Wolf, or the sound poetry of Christian Morgenstern and Kurt Schwitters. Meanwhile, the emphasis Adorno places on 'connections of every sort' admits nonverbal elements into his concept of material, whether as punctuation or as the order and manner in which words and phrases are placed together. This allows the account of parataxis in the first chapter to appear in a different light. I discussed in that chapter how the content of a poem 'seeks a form' which itself contributes to the work's substantive content: the details of the form that is chosen are here construed as part of the material of the work.

Content and material, that is, cannot be thought of as completely separate from one another. The distinction between them exists at the conceptual level, not at that of the referents of the concepts. Material can no more be thought of as contentless than content as free from the material in which it is expressed; the meaning of a poem cannot be divorced from the words and sounds and traces of which it is made. Adorno's identification of content with that which happens in a work makes it clear that the concept of content refers primarily to the paraphrasable or describable elements that are found within it, its propositional rather than substantive content. Content tends toward subjective intention, whether conceived as meaning or purpose, while material tends more toward the objective aspects of the work. The distinction is perhaps most helpfully conceived in terms of the dual character of language as sign and image discussed in the final section of the first chapter. The content of a poem can be seen as referring primarily to the aspects associated with the sign character of its language, while the material pertains to the image character, the attempt to resemble the world.

I suggested in the previous chapter that artistic forms might be thought of as the sedimentation of a material that can be thought of as objective in such a way that its objectivity is masked. Adorno offers the following analysis of the act of making the choice of material:

> The idea, widespread among uncritical artists, of the arbitrariness of material, is problematic in that it ignores the compulsion of material and toward specific material, a compulsion which rules in compositional procedures and in the progress of material. Choice of material, its application and the limits in its use, is an essential moment of production. Even expansion into the unknown, development beyond the given state of the material, is to a great extent a function of the material and of its critique, which the material itself determines. (ÄT 222/AT 148)

The insistence is not so much that there are things that the artist simply is not allowed to do, that the artist does not have a free choice, as that not all decisions lead to a successful artwork. The compulsion of which Adorno writes can thus be seen neither as a moral nor a purely technical constraint. Indeed, given that if the artist were presented with an unrestricted, arbitrary choice, this would not in any substantive sense constitute a free choice, it is perhaps misleading to think of it as a constraint at all. It might rather be thought of as a criterion of aesthetic success, or, perhaps more accurately, as an inference that can be made from the judgment as to the aesthetic success of a work. Adorno's claim is not only that the physical properties of particular materials lend themselves to particular artworks—that certain musical themes are suited to the ternary form of the sonata, or that the rhythmic properties of particular words and phrases require and enable particular metrical schemata—but also that the material to an extent determines artistic development, seen on the level both of the creation of the individual work and of the evolution of artistic traditions and conventions.

It follows from this claim that the range of material available to an artist is historically mediated. In the first instance, this means that Adorno's concept of material is not one of 'raw' material:

> Of the abstractly available material only the very least is usable concretely, that is to say without colliding with the condition of

> spirit. Material is thus not natural material, even if it presents itself as such to artists, but historical through and through. (ÄT 223/AT 148)

The range of material available for use is historically contingent, but does not appear as such. This further illuminates the discussion (in the opening section of chapter 3 above) of the submersion of a general aesthetic within a specific material. The particularity of the material is determinate not only in the sense that the material chosen determines the process of artistic creation, but also that the very choice of material is itself a reflection of the 'condition of spirit', which includes the current state not only of intellectual but also of artistic developments. Artistic material does not exist outside the development of artistic production. As Adorno continues, a more concrete example makes clearer what he means by historical mediation:

> It is obvious how the composer, for example, who works with tonal material, receives it from tradition. If, however, he uses autonomous material—completely purged of such concepts as consonance and dissonance, triad, the diatonic scale—critically against tonal material, the negated is preserved within the negation. (ÄT 223/AT 148)

The material handed down by tradition is an as it were direct reflection of previous developments—in Paddison's terms, it is 'the precipitate or sediment of previous interactions between composers and the historical "figurations" they encounter as material, and thus represents social collectivity'.[7] This, however, is only half the story, for it fails to allow for the attempt to negate the received tradition. This negation appears as the attempt to remove all traces of the received material, in this case by the elimination of tonality from the material used in twelve-tone composition. Even the successful exclusion from the work of all tonal material leaves behind what might be thought of as the outline of what is excluded, and thus constitutes a form of obedience to the historical tendency that is to be negated.

That Adorno writes of material that is 'purged of such concepts as consonance and dissonance, triad, the diatonic scale' makes it clear that what he refers to as material cannot be assessed purely in terms of its measurable physical properties, in the sense not only that what is important here is as much tonal relations as the individual tones themselves, but also that both tones and tonal relations must be seen within the particular historical context in which they are used. Indeed, Adorno explicitly differentiates between material and the physical properties of sounds, asserting as early as 1930 in 'Reaction and Progress' that 'material, unlike the twelve tones and the mapped physical relationships of their overtones, is not a given that appears naturally invariable and at all times identical' (GS 17: 133/NM 219). That it now seems that the division of the octave into twelve tones is arbitrary and historically contingent is at this point irrelevant—indeed, Adorno's use of *naturhaft* leaves open the possibility that the twelve tones only appear to be naturally given—what matters is that for Adorno material is subject to a further degree of historical and social mediation, within the themselves already historically and socially mediated limits of chromaticism.

Adorno's point is not only that what artists encounter as the range of available material is historically, socially, and culturally determined rather than a natural given, but also that the matter and manner of this determination changes. This is perhaps best illustrated by a musical example. Adorno argues that 'roughly the same overtonal relation within the diminished seventh that, seen in relation to the state of material as a whole, could in Beethoven's time be deployed as a moment of extreme tension, has with material in a later state of development become harmless consonance' (GS 17: 133/NM 219); a similar sense of decay and obsolescence underlies the objection to surrealism's montages of outdated material as discussed in the second chapter. The material discussed at this point does not consist simply in the sounds that constitute the chord itself, taken in isolation, but rather takes into consideration the trajectory of the use of the chord up until the point at which it is employed. While it is correct to claim, as Michael de la Fontaine does, that in Adorno's pre-exile writings, 'material' refers to the state of the currently available musical material as handed down by the tradition of composers, it is important not to forget that the act of composing has itself a reciprocal effect on the available material, a claim that Adorno makes more explicit when returning to the changing potential of the diminished seventh in *The Philosophy of New Music* in 1949:[8]

> It is in no way the case that all combinations of tones that have ever been used are available to the composer today. Even the bluntest ear notices the worn-out shabbiness of the diminished seventh or certain chromatic passing notes in nineteenth-century salon music. For the technically competent ear, such vague discomfort is transposed into a canon of what is disallowed. (PnM 40/PMM 34)

The composition of new works both adds to the repertoire from which material can be selected and limits the ways in which it can be used in the future. This applies even on a scale as small as that of individual chords. Perhaps the most obvious example of such a phenomenon is that a previously unheard combination of sounds, deployed subsequently, will no longer sound new. Adorno expresses a similar idea in rather different terms two decades later, claiming that there is no such thing as a new chord, writing with reference to the image of a child sitting at a piano, looking for an unheard combination of notes: 'The chord already existed, the possible combinations are limited, everything is actually already present in the keyboard' (ÄT 55/AT 32).

However, this impossibility is not historically invariant, as Adorno makes clear in the 1954 talk on the ageing of new music:

> When late Wagner placed the minor ninth over the diminished seventh and Schönberg in 'Verklärte Nacht' used the dominant ninth in the forbidden second inversion, the potential in such chords of that which Webern called a sea of never-heard tones rose, toward which the 'Erwartung' then ventured. No tone today could so easily stake a claim never to have been heard. If an insatiable composer were to go looking for such a thing, he would succumb to the impotence that arises as soon as the material no longer expands out of necessity, but is instead used as a store to search through for the sake of new stimuli. (D 154–55/EoM 190)

The impossibility of writing a new chord is different today from how it was at the beginning of the twentieth century. During the exploration of dissonance and atonality, it was possible to deploy harmonies which were unheard, a possibility which for Adorno no longer exists, at least not within the limits imposed by the diatonic scale—this may at least partially account for the fact that the most significant subsequent developments in musical material, from Ligeti to Morphogenesis, have taken place by exploring timbre more than pitch, *pace* some of the recent explorations of microtonal tunings. In any case, what is at stake is the way in which particular chords can successfully be used, and this tendency does not apply only in one direction: each new composition not only opens up new possibilities but also, and just as importantly, sets new restrictions for future musical development. Indeed, there is no objective scale according to which the newness of chords can be judged: discussing the use of what is no more than a 'diminished seventh over a pedal-point of the secondary dominant' in *Der Freischütz*, Adorno writes that 'it sounds as if had not been heard before, such a swollen expression that there is hardly a polytonic chord since that comes close to it' (GS 17: 99/NM 58).

That is, there is no static canon of available material, which rather exists in a constant state of development, as do artistic forms and genres. In another statement that illuminates the discussion of the blurring of generic boundaries from the standpoint of material, Adorno insists that 'the extension of available materials, which mocks the old boundaries between the artistic genres, is simply the result of the historical emancipation of the concept of artistic form' (ÄT 223/AT 148). As form takes on independence it becomes part of the range of available materials. As Adorno writes in a letter to Peter Rühmkorf, 'because no matter, no idea, no form is any longer prescribed to it, art must, in order to be capable of that through which it would be more than itself, "concern itself with itself", reflect on itself and its procedures'.[9] As Peter Bürger has argued, this transformation brings about a certain tension within the concept of material:

> On the one hand, the concept of material signifies within Adorno's theory the place in which artwork and society meet; on the other hand, it serves as a means of understanding the development of art as autonomous, and at the same time as following the development of society as a whole. Put differently, the concept is supposed to perform both the mediation of individual work and society, and the mediation of the development of art and actually existing history.[10]

For Bürger, material is the objectification within the artwork of that which constitutes it. As such, material includes not only the individual elements of which the work is composed, but also the procedures through which this composition takes place. That is, what we might crudely think of as the form into which raw material is arranged must itself be considered part of the repertoire of material not only from which the work is produced, but also which remains visibly preserved within the work. Material cannot be thought of as simply opposed to the creative processes that work it: rather, these processes not only leave their mark on the material, but even incorporate themselves into it. This is what Adorno means when he claims that forms can also become material: what we might for now think of as the formal canon that develops through social artistic production becomes in turn itself something for future artists to work with. And as material, it can be experienced as a constraint, such as in Adorno's account of how in Schönberg's operatic fragment *Moses und Aron* 'it is no longer the composer who expresses himself, but the protagonists and antagonists, igniting the musical objectivity of the whole', in which the operatic form becomes a medium, a third factor or middle that mediates between composer and composition (QF 459/Livingstone 231). The question remains, however, of how Adorno conceives this process of working, the act of making decisions over the material, a question that is best addressed through his writings on the status of technique.

Technique and the Mastery of Material

In the section of *Aesthetic Theory* entitled 'Universal and Particular', two consecutive paragraphs—'Progress and the mastery of material' and '"Technique"'—begin by making the same equation:

> Without question, historical materials and their mastery—technique—progress; inventions such as perspective in painting, polyphony in music are the most obvious examples. (ÄT 313/AT 210)

> The aesthetic name for the mastery of material—technique, borrowed from the ancient usage that counted the arts among the artisanal activities—is in its current meaning relatively new. (ÄT 316/AT 212-13)

Adorno's conception of technique is clearly more specifically limited to the artistic sphere than the Greek τέχνη from which it is derived, which can refer equally to skill at a particular craft and to artistic capability. The term now 'bears the traces of a phase in which, analogously to science, method appeared to be independent of its object' (ÄT 316/AT 213). For Adorno, this independence is necessarily illusory, since art, as a means of resistance to the integration of all spheres of life into the capitalist economy, retains a connection to the medieval production of goods. As such, 'under the technological aspect converge all artistic procedures that form material and let themselves be directed by it' (ÄT 316/AT 213). Technique is thus not simply a means of processing artistic material according to a particular predetermined method, and Adorno's 'mastery of the material' not a subjugation or even simply a domination of that which is to be incorporated into the artwork, but a more reciprocal capacity that consists at least in part in attentiveness to the limits and demands of the material.

This resounds with a claim made almost a decade earlier in the *Introduction to the Sociology of Music*:

> Technique adjusts itself according to the state of the material and of the procedures. This state could be thought broadly comparable to the relations of production into which the composer is drawn, technique to the embodiment of developed productive forces, against which the composer verifies his own. Both are obedient to their mutual interdependence; the material is itself always a result of procedures, permeated with subjective moments; the procedures necessarily find themselves in a particular relation to their material, if they want to do justice to it. (EM 421/ISM 218)

Technique, that is, does not exist apart from the material which it works: the two must be seen as mutually interdependent. This pertains not only to the choice of the particular material of a specific work, but also, in the light of the discussion in the previous chapter of the tendencies represented by the *Gesamtkunstwerk*, to the particular medium, a concern which, as Bernstein has noted, 'is hounded out of aesthetics and eventually art by the reigning concept of the concept, a concept cut loose from its moorings in materiality and sensible experience, the abstract concept whose appearances include the increasing dominance of technological reason and rationality'.[11] It follows not only that technique and material are part of a conceptual constellation in which neither can be conceived without reference to the other, but also that they cannot wholly be separated from one another. From the fact that material is the result of the procedures applied to it follows the recognition that these procedures in turn leave their trace on material: there is no material that is not itself worked by technique. Similarly, there is no technique other than that which can be applied to particular material. Technique, that is, is not only the domination of material, but also something that itself becomes material. Technique and material cannot be seen simply in opposition to one another: each rather plays a part in the constitution of the other.

Equally important is Adorno's insistence on the relationship between technique and the current state of the forces of production. The comparison he draws is not merely an analogy: the claim is not simply that technique is to the productive forces what material is to the relations of production—whatever that might be. Adorno's claim is both more specific and more vague: the state to which artistic material has developed is 'broadly comparable' to the relations of production; technique, to the productive forces. More light is shed on the nature of this relationship by the discussion in the 'Technology' paragraph of *Aesthetic Theory*:

> Artistic technique is no cushy adaptation to an age that is foolishly eager to label itself as technical, as if its structure were determined immediately by the productive forces and not also just as much by the relations of production that hold the productive forces in their spell. (ÄT 94/AT 59)

Productive forces do not develop of their own accord, but are constrained by the relations of production. It would thus be an oversimplification to claim a general equivalence either between artistic technique and the productive forces or between artistic material and the relations of production. The relationship between technique and the productive forces is perhaps the most simple to grasp: procedures that develop within industrial production extend the ranges of procedures that can be used in artistic production. However, within artistic production, technique is not subject to quite the same restraint as the social productive forces: the artist, Adorno claims, 'embodies the social productive forces, without necessarily being bound to the judgments dictated by the relations of production, judgments which he always criticizes through the consistency of his *métier*' (ÄT 71/AT 43–44). However, the constraints imposed on technique by the material differ starkly from those imposed on the productive forces by the relations of production. The relationship of similarity between the relations of production and artistic material, however, is not quite so easily characterized. Whereas the relations of production impose limits on the potential for development of the productive forces and the rate at which this development can take place, the material's influence on technique is better construed as needs or demands than as restraints. To the extent that material is social, it must be thought of as mediated through the particular social relations of production, but it is also and just as importantly influenced by the development of technical procedures that allow the expansion of the material and indeed can themselves become part of the material available to the artist.

In concentrating on the role of technique in working the artistic material, it must not be forgotten that its effects are visible in the completed artwork. Indeed, technique is constrained not only by the demands of the material, but also by the content of the work that is to be created:

> How intimately technique and content, against the *convenu*, are constrained by one another, was expressed by Beethoven in his claim that many of the effects that are commonly ascribed to the natural genius of the composer are in truth simply due to adroit use of the diminished seventh; the dignity of such sobriety condemns all chatter about creativity; Beethoven's objectivity was the first to allow justice to be done both to aesthetic semblance and to what is without semblance. (ÄT 320/AT 215)

This is at once a demystification of the category of genius and, if not an obscuring of that of technique, at least a claim that emphasizes how elaborate the category must be. For if 'genius' can no longer be used to avoid having to account for the artistic success and influence of significant works, technique must be conceived as more than the simple processing of material. Matters of technique such as the selection of when and how to use, in this example, the diminished seventh, are not reducible to what might be thought of as mere technical proficiency, on top of which the adequate artistic expression must nonetheless be present, but rather bound up with this expression. Technique is itself a criterion of aesthetic success: it consists in the mastery of material in the sense not that the material must be subordinated to the artwork, but that it must be mastered in a manner consonant both with the material and with the artwork's expression.

That is, anything that might be thought of as a law of form that in some way directs the process of artistic creation must have its basis in artistic material. However, it cannot be reduced to the material:

> The criterion according to which artworks are judged is twofold: whether they succeed in integrating their material layers with the details of the law of form immanent to them, and in preserving within this integration that which fights against it, even with ruptures. Integration does not as such assure quality; in the history of art, the two moments have often parted company. (ÄT 18/AT 7)

Successful mastery of the material involves neither the subjugation of material to an abstract and externally imposed law of form (against what Bruns terms 'the anarchic resistance of material to any effort to bring it under control')[12] nor the application of a process dictated entirely from within the material. That is, while the criteria against which technique is judged have their origins within the material, aspects of the material fight against the attempt to master them. It is in this light that this claim made in 'Reaction and Progress' must be evaluated: 'The more closely an artist stands in contact with his material, the freer he is' (GS 17: 135/NM 222). Artistic freedom consists not in the ability to exercise arbitrary power over an arbitrary selection of material, but in the successful execution of technique, which must have its origins within the material but not be merely derivative of it. In this respect technique is never merely technical, a matter which is perhaps best illustrated by Benjamin's somewhat awkward attempt to engage with the political and social relevance of form when confronted by the growing power of fascism in the mid-1930s: discussing Brecht and Eisler's collaboration on *Die Maßnahme*, he suggests that a transformation in the political resonance of theatre represents 'a high point in musical and literary technique'; more specifically, Brecht's 'detection and shaping of the gestural means nothing less than the retransformation of the method of montage, decisive in radio and film, frequently merely a modish technique, into a human happening'.[13]

The force of Adorno's claim in 'Reaction and Progress' becomes somewhat clearer in the insistence in *Minima Moralia* that 'it is part of the technique of an author to dispose of even fruitful thoughts when it is demanded by the construction' (MM 95/Jephcott 85). This begins to reveal the extent of the mutual implication of form, content, and material. The act of forming must both be attuned to the requirements of the material—that is to say, the way it can be constructed—and willing to exclude aspects of it. A more concrete example of an analogous process in music is found in the argument in *Aesthetic Theory* that technique consists not in the abundance of accumulated means of working material, but rather in the 'amassed capacity to adapt oneself to the objective demands of the matter' (ÄT 320/AT 216). As an example of what he means by this he draws a comparison between Schönberg and Richard Strauss:

> With the magnificent ungainliness of their fresh approach, Schönberg's sparse piano pieces op. 11 technically surpass the orchestra of *Heldenleben*, of which one can actually hear only a fragment of the score, such that the means no longer serve their immediate purpose, the acoustic manifestation of what is imagined. (ÄT 321/AT 216)

This time what is renounced is not the obviously conceptual material that could be included in a novel but what Adorno describes as means, that is to say in this case orchestration. His distinction between means and technique is significant. Aspects of compositional practice that would colloquially be considered tools or techniques—here orchestration, but also brushwork in painting, metrical facility or the deployment of figures in poetry—are here considered means. The concept of technique is much broader than this, and includes the decision of which means to employ.

The relationship of means to form is developed in the discussion of the concept of articulation in the 'Coherence and Meaning' section of *Aesthetic Theory*:

> The means, without which form would simply not exist at all, undermine form. Works which renounce partial unities in order not to compromise their unity only evade this aporia: the most cogent objection to Webern's intensity without extension. Mediocre products, in contrast, leave their partial unities unchallenged under the thin shell of their form, disguising them rather than amalgamating them. (ÄT 220/AT 146-47)

The means constitute both a precondition of form and its opposition. Form develops as a result of the domination of material, as the (itself already preformed) material takes on a particular form within the artwork. The task of technique, however, is to employ these means to fight against the form's tendency to become settled and stagnate: in doing so, it will inevitably take part in the creation of new forms, which it will in turn necessarily attempt to oppose. Technique, that is, is complicit in the creation of the very form against which it strives. And the successful artwork is characterized by a particular sort of unity between form and material: one in which what Adorno terms 'partial unities'—that is, elements of the material that could in some way be considered complete in themselves, such as musical phrases—are neither renounced nor simply masked by the form of the work as a whole. The material elements of a work must be amalgamated: combined in such a way that they are themselves recognizable as elements, but within the unity of the form of the artwork as a whole, neither subsumed by it nor passively identical with it.

Equally striking is Adorno's description of artworks as 'products', which emphasizes not only their madness, but also the fact that the process of making is one that at least resembles the production of goods—and under capitalist relations of production, therefore, commodity production, a resemblance that I discuss in greater depth in the following chapter. At this point, however, the most relevant comparison is with what is strictly speaking a pre-capitalist mode of craft production:

> The threshold between craft and technique in art is not, as it is in material production, the strict quantifying of process, incompatible with the qualitative telos; nor is it the introduction of machines; it is rather the preponderance of free disposal over the means through consciousness, in contrast with traditionalism, under the shell of which this disposal matured. (ÄT 316/AT 213)

The comparison between artistic technique and craft production reveals that artistic technique is by no means identical with the development and use of technology in industrial production. Artistic technique is not a matter of producing higher volumes of artwork at a lower cost or in a shorter time, but rather of the use to artistic ends of procedures that are often derived from those of the production of goods. The development of artistic technique enables not increased efficiency, as in industrial production, but rather the appropriate means of working the material. That is, technique enables not quantitative increases in production but qualitative differences in what is produced. This is perhaps best seen in relation to the concrete example of Adorno's 1929 discussion of twelve-tone technique:

> [Schönberg's twelve-tone technique] is the rational execution of a historical compulsion undertaken by consciousness at its most advanced, to cleanse its material from the decay of its decomposed organic elements; twelve-tone technique cannot be considered ahistorical, but can be accounted for by the state of the material that Schönberg found and which he produced; it does not attempt unexpectedly to transform this decomposed material into order, which would necessarily be empty, but rather wipes out material's last pretence of order, in order to create space for the freedom of constructive fantasy; it is in no way a positive compositional process, but the historically current preforming of material, which must be implemented; it does not account for itself mathematically, but historically, and does not aim at a mathematical-formal region of music, but wants to make the composer's freedom possible. (GS 18: 364)

The historicity of technique is closely linked to that of the material: changes in the latter necessitate developments in the former. Adorno's claim is that the particular material change that necessitated the development of twelve-tone technique is the decay and decomposition of organic order within the work. That is, he identifies a particular organicism in early twentieth-century music, which can neither be prevented from decaying nor recreated anew. Twelve-tone technique is thus not a means of reestablishing order by reassembling the parts of a whole that no longer exists, but an attempt to destroy all semblance of order within the work. But it is significant that Adorno does not describe this process as the destruction of form: rather, it is a means of preforming—more accurately, the particular means of preforming that was current at the time of writing. And even if the currency of the technique might have changed during Adorno's lifetime, his understanding of it had not—he wrote nearly forty years later in *Aesthetic Theory* that 'twelve-tone technique effectively preforms the material through numerical relations—sequences, in which no tone can appear before another, and which are permuted' (ÄT 214/AT 142). The relationship between this preformation and the process of working the material that leads to the development of form within the artwork is somewhat complex. It is clear there are two different processes taking place, which seem at the same time both independent from and dependent on one another. Independent because Adorno's designation of the application of twelve-tone technique to the musical material as a preforming distinguishes it from the act of composing: twelve-tone technique predetermines the artwork and cuts short the process of composition. Dependent, on the other hand, because the way in which it preforms the material imposes particular limits on what can be expressed in the resulting artwork. The question remains, however, of the extent to which this conception of formation is helpful for the consideration of specifically literary form: how it might be possible to draw analogies between linguistic and musical material, and in what ways and to what extent the former might be considered to be preformed.

Language and Poetry

Literary technique involves the forming of (itself socially preformed) linguistic material—words—into literary works. In the 'Theories on the Origin of Art' published posthumously in *Aesthetic Theory*, Adorno addresses some of the problems raised by the constellation of language and art:

> The word *Sprachkunstwerk* [linguistic artwork], currently popular among Germanists, that through the mediation of language unceremoniously subsumes poetry into art, has something labored about it that arouses suspicion against this process, although it is without question that art unified itself during the course of the process of enlightenment. The oldest artistic pronouncements are so diffuse that it is as difficult as it is pointless to decide what should count as art and what should not. (ÄT 481–82/AT 326)

In a discussion of the term in the main text of *Aesthetic Theory*, Adorno notes that *Sprachkunstwerk* is a term for poems [*Dichtungen*] 'coined, not incongruously, by a literary historian', a term that, as discussed in the previous chapter, 'harms poems, which are artworks and at the same time, because of their relatively independent discursive elements, not only artworks or not artworks through and through' (ÄT 272/AT 182).[14] The ontology of the linguistic artwork, that is, cannot be thought of as a subset of that of the notional artwork-in-general, but is bound up with all the other things that a poem might at the same time be. Poetry cannot reasonably be treated as an unproblematic subset of art (nor poems of artworks) that happens to be made of words. This further complicates the claim also discussed in the previous chapter that '[a]rt merges in no way with artworks' (ÄT 272/AT 182). Indeed, it is only at the conceptual level that poetry and literature are able to be subsumed into art, 'through the mediation of language'.

Language is a central point at which to consider the relationship between the poem and empirical reality. As I discussed in the second chapter, Adorno locates the premature failure of expression in its attempt to escape its affinity with the empirical world. This affinity consists in the 'conceptual element' of language, that prevents poetry from becoming pure expression:

> The concept itself, the unity of attributes of everything subsumed under it, which belongs to the empirical world and does not fall under the spell of the work, has before any narration of the world something hostile to art about it. (NzL 435/NtL 2: 99)

Poetry is written within the empirical world, in and out of the language of the empirical world. Its affinity with this world, which it cannot but strive to escape, consists in the fact that the concepts of language are preserved within the linguistic artwork. Meanwhile, the impulse to absolute subjective expression strives to work against all forms of conceptual mediation. This tension cannot be resolved, since poetry cannot dispense with either expression or conceptuality. '[C]oncepts are indispensable to language' (NzL 435/ NtL 2: 99). Not even *poésie pure* is able to relinquish the material elements of which it is composed (NzL 60/NtL 1: 46). Poetry, that is, consists in the tension between conceptual language and the drive to eliminate conceptuality from language—the source of the clumsiness that Adorno recognizes in the juxtaposition of language and artwork in the term *Sprachkunstwerk*. The act of forming linguistic material into poetic works is the point at which this tension first arises, the site of conflict between expression and conceptuality.

This can helpfully be illuminated with reference to Bernstein's Adorno-influenced account of painterly modernism. Discussing Jackson Pollock's *Full Fathom Five*, Bernstein offers this interpretation of the materiality of paint after representation has been removed from painting:

> Paint-on-canvas is the exchange value that renders buttons and thumbtacks two-dimensional. But unlike money, it is also *like* the key or the pennies, material stuff—which is why, finally, painting can get rid of representation and remain painting: the paint-stuff can stand in for objects by being one of them; the forming of the paint-stuff into intensive patterns does for it what representation did for the objects represented.[15]

In analyzing the combination of paint with objects that include nails, matches and cigarette butts as well as the buttons, drawing pins, pennies and key that are mentioned, Bernstein distinguishes between representation of an otherwise absent object and likeness to a present object with which the paint is combined. Both of these modes of relation to an object depend on resemblance of one form or another—even the likeness that enables paint to 'stand in for objects' in a manner that does not require depiction is predicated on visible or even tangible similarity. This differs from Adorno's account of the conceptual, classificatory pole of language, in which concepts aspire and claim to stand in for their objects at the exclusion of resemblance. Moreover, Bernstein's recognition discussed in the previous section that the importance of aesthetic and artistic medium is driven out by the abstract concept must be further complicated in the case of poetry, in which conceptuality inheres and from which it cannot be expelled.

According to this account there are many more affinities between Adorno's project and that of Heidegger, particularly in Nowell Smith's formulation, than either figure was willing to acknowledge:

> The artwork's engagement with its medium is always an engagement with the limits of this medium; shifting the limits of what is intelligible within the medium, it shifts the limits of intelligibility as such. This limit is not simply semantic (and in this respect, it is striking that, for Heidegger, the sounding of Hölderlin's poem concerns the meaning of an individual word, *Denn*) but prosodic, the incursion of dissonance into euphonic singsong. The limit of language as medium is experienced as *noise*. If poetry is to exceed, and antecede, the conception of language as tool, and thereby attain the *aletheic* vocation through which it does not simply announce what is 'in' the open, but can shape the open itself, then this will require an engagement with the limit and opacity of that language out of which arises [*sic*].[16]

Both thinkers provide the resources for theorizing the way in which poetry calls into question any understanding of language as solely communicative and functional. For poetry reveals (not least by virtue of the fact that it does not only communicate, if indeed it communicates at all) the inadequacy of any conceptions of language that focus solely on the semantic element—in Adorno's terms, that reduce language to its sign character, and in doing so neglect that it can also—that it cannot but also—function as image. In Nowell Smith's account this reminder emerges through the incursion of dissonance into euphony, which contrasts with Adorno's contention (discussed in the account of Adorno's critique of expressionism in chapter 2) that in Trakl's poems the phonic properties of words and their associative connections alter their significance. In this account Adorno is working with a conception of a sort of second-degree significance, in which the interaction of the sense with the sound results in an effect which is nonetheless still construed according to an (albeit radically altered sense of) meaning—both of poem and of word within it. The becoming more than mere signification by means of the exploration of its limits is in this example at least still conceived in terms of signification. If this is a primarily terminological distinction, the differences in the two accounts of how the sonorous aspects of language come to the fore are more prominent. For Adorno it takes place by means not of the interruption of the (apparently otherwise unremarkable) harmonious rhythm, but of a more sustained heightening of the attention drawn to the material aspects of words and sounds over the course of the poem—a claim which is much more convincing than Adorno's renowned tendentiously polemical objection (hastily asserted as if in passing) to the '"musical" language of a

Swinburne or Rilke that imitates musical effects but is alien to the musical approach' in the fragment on music and language (QF 253/Livingstone 3). Meanwhile, his interpretation in *Aesthetic Theory* of the apparent taunt in Eduard Mörike's 'Mousetrap Rhyme' as a 'nonjudgmental reflex of language on a wretched, socially conditioned ritual' (ÄT 188/AT 124) is explained with reference not to melodic or prosodic interruption, but rather to the 'form, which joins the lines into the echo of a mythical saying' and thereby 'suspends their disposition' (ÄT 188/AT 124). Form here is not a single formal feature, but a condensed reference to the composition and construction of the poem as a whole.

The poetic act of forming has the ability to transform language, but does not always work in opposition to language's significative pole, which points to the potential for an element of discrepancy between that to which poetry aspires and that which it can achieve. In his discussion of Beckett's *Endgame*, Adorno shows how poetry does not necessarily fight against the division of language into sign and image, but sometimes contributes to it: discussing the figure of Hamm, he writes of how the image of a napping middle-aged man, whose eyes are covered with a cloth 'first becomes sign to the gaze that becomes aware of the loss of identity of the face, the possibility that its veiledness is that of a corpse, the repellence of the physical concern that by reducing him to his body, already indexes the living under the dead' (NzL 297/NtL 1: 255). The process described here differs from the tendency of Enlightenment thought to divide language in that it avoids hypostatization. Beckett does not reduce image to sign, but rather provides an example of how image can become sign, how signification can arise out of depiction. Indeed, in this example, there is no hint that sign displaces image, but rather an awareness as to how image can be preserved in the sign that emerges out of it. This is one possible interpretation of Adorno's characterization of artworks as 'language-like', a character that they take on through the process of forming (ÄT 182/AT 120).

In the final section of chapter 1 I discussed Adorno's account of Hölderlin's incorporation of subjective expression into language from the perspective of a poem's content. Adorno's discussion of Eichendorff's poetry offers a way of understanding the transformation of linguistic material within the artwork:

> The line 'Wolken ziehn wie schwere Träume' ['Clouds drift like heavy dreams'] gains for the poem the specific kind of meaning in the German word *Wolken*, in contrast with for example

> *nuage*: in this line it is the word *Wolken* and what accompanies it, and not at all the images that it signifies, that drift by like heavy dreams. (NzL 80/NtL 1: 65)

Adorno's claim is that the subject of the verb is not the imagined signified but the signifier. Ulrich Plass's assertion that in this passage the 'unique material signifier in itself actualizes the signified' is to this extent not quite right: it would perhaps be more accurate to say that Adorno's claim is that the materiality of the signifier enacts the unity, if not the identity, of signifier and signified.[17] This is a relationship that cannot be described in the terms of Saussurian linguistics, depending as it does on the rejection of the theory of the arbitrariness of the linguistic sign. Something similar pertains to Plass's commentary on Adorno's discussion of Eichendorff's use of the term *Rauschen*—the motion and sound of a rushing or rustling, a term which, as Shierry Weber Nicholsen observes, 'appears repeatedly in Adorno's writings on literature, where it stands for a similarly enigmatic and indeterminate phenomenon, namely, the appearance of an authentic poetic dimension of language'.[18] Plass claims that the 'notion of *Rauschen* signifies language as "pure" metonymy, as a meaning that is always in the process of transition from one segment of the chain to another, but in an unpredictable way' (p. 70). He concentrates on the experience of Eichendorff's poetry, considering what Adorno at different points terms *Sprachgefälle* and *Wortgefälle*, the falling or decline of language and of the word (NzL 84, 88/NtL 1: 70, 73). For Plass, this *Rauschen* 'becomes audible momentarily where the concept disappears' (p. 70).

However, it is not the case either in Eichendorff's poems or in Adorno's discussion of them that the material sound of words takes on prominence at the expense of conceptuality, and certainly not to the extent that conceptuality disappears. This can be seen perhaps most clearly in Plass's comments on Adorno's account of the incorporation of the expression of nature into language:

> The subject makes itself into *Rauschen*: into language, living on only in the instance of dying away, like language. The act of making the human being into language, a becoming-word of the flesh, incorporates the expression of nature into language and transfigures once again the movement of language into life. (NzL 83/NtL 1: 39)

Plass reads language here as a purely acoustic phenomenon, language as it is heard (p. 57). It is tempting to read Adorno's account, as Plass does, as a claim that conceptuality is erased from poetic language, but Adorno's argument is subtly different. What Adorno is opposing is not conceptuality per se, which is inescapable even in the *Rauschen* of Eichendorff's poetry, but rather the reduction of language to mere conceptuality. Eichendorff's poetry does not, as Plass claims, simply assert the priority of image over sign, but offers a glimpse of what language could be as the suspended unity of sign and image, in which language is no longer reduced to its signifying moment. This suspension involves the transformation of language from a means that serves the end of subjective communication, a transformation which requires what Nicholsen terms 'a certain voluntary renunciation or sacrifice [. . .] on the part of the human subject'.[19] The subject, that is, ceases to be wholly subject, as the material by means of which it seeks to communicate is transformed into something that is itself able to speak through the subject. It is in this way that the material of linguistic artworks must be thought, which I now address in more detail, in relation to Adorno's discussions of first Borchardt and then Valéry.

The Literary Manifestation of Form and Material

Literary technique consists for Adorno unambiguously in—if not only in—the use and manipulation of language to poetic ends, which should be construed as pertaining as much to the choice of words used as to their arrangement. In the second of his discussions of the use of foreign words in the appendix to *Notes to Literature*, Adorno insists that the author 'consistently uses the authentic, nonorganic foreign word as quotation' (NzL 645/NtL 2: 290), while he claims in the essay on the same subject in the second volume of the *Notes* that the author can 'take advantage of the tension between foreign word and language by including it in his own reflection and in his own technique' (NzL 220/NtL 1: 189). The tension of which Adorno writes is present, at least as potential, in the (socially preformed) linguistic material: the role of developed artistic technique is to make appropriate use of it. Adorno continues as follows:

> Through the foreign word he can productively interrupt the conformist moment of language, the turbid current in which

> the specific intention of expression drowns. The hardness and contouredness of the foreign word—just that, which it lifts beyond the continuum of language—is suited precisely to advancing that which is impending and that which is covered by the bad universality of the usage of language. Yet more. The discrepancy between foreign word and language can step into the service of the expression of truth. (NzL 220–21/NtL 1: 189)

Technique is as it were the interface between material and expression. It is on the author's act of forming the material in a particular way that expression depends, working against the hardening division of language into sign and image, through which language is divorced from the world it describes. In this particular example, this is achieved not by working toward a conception of language that involves both sign and image, but through the foreign word's assertion of its character as sign, thus working against the tendency of sign to stand for language in its entirety. In Adorno's terms, the foreign word 'starkly warns that all actual language has something of a token about it, by professing itself to be a token' (NzL 221/NtL 1: 189). It works against the tendency of sign to disguise itself, on which its claim to stand for language as a whole depends.

But Adorno's conception of technique goes well beyond the choice of words: he writes in 'Parataxis' of 'Hölderlin's ordering technique'—conformity—which can only with difficulty be attributed to the influence of Pindar (NzL 475/NtL 2: 134). Meanwhile, in his discussion of Borchardt's poetry 'Charmed Language', Adorno discusses technique as a means of potential continuity between poetic œuvres, focusing in this case on the influence of Hölderlin on Borchardt:

> The long poems transmit the musical idea of form as immanent to structure, not borrowed from anybody, to language. Language is literally composed. Several of these poems, like the *Bacchic Epiphany*, contained reprises in the musical understanding of the word. In this poem, the opening, 'Zwischen Greif und Sphinge schreitend' ['stepping between griffin and sphinx'], returns, altered, for the first time with the verse 'Zwischen Tod und Leben reisend' ['travelling between death and life'], and a second time, this time with concluding force, in the 'Zwischen Tod und Leben brausend' ['roaring between death and life']. It is uncertain whether in doing so Borchardt is also referring to

late Hölderlin, perhaps the technique of 'Patmos'; it is beyond question that he never distinguished himself from the George-circle, foreign and hostile to music, as deeply as in this layer, in which he wanted to meet the Viennese Hofmannsthal. But it is an original phenomenon of Borchardt's modernity, which transforms every thought of the Alexandrine reanimation and the excavation of its nonsense. The musically forming procedure revolts against the traditional primacy of sense in the lyric, and moves toward absolute poetry, which in his poetry was still restrained by the traditional moments. (NzL 539–40/NtL 2: 196–97; the Viennese Hofmannsthal is the Austrian author, poet, dramatist, and librettist Hugo von Hofmannsthal (1874–1929))

Adorno's understanding of Borchardt's technique consists in the latter's ability to deploy allusion and recurrence to develop effects which Adorno can only describe in the terms of music. This is even more explicit in 'Parataxis', in which he describes how the ninth strophe of 'Patmos' 'knows something like a reprise' (NzL 470–71/NtL 2: 130), in which the sound of the line 'Und fernhin über die Berge zu gehn' ['to go far away over the mountains'] provides an unmistakable means of acoustic connection to the lingering memory of 'gehn', 'Bergen', and 'Hinüberzugehn', all used in the poem's opening strophe. It is in this way that technique itself cannot be considered merely as the means with which an artist works the material, but also part of the repertoire of material at an artist's disposal: just like more tangible conceptions of material, technique is something that can be passed down or alluded to, a means of artistic continuity and influence.

This quotation also shows more concretely the relationship between technique, material, and form. While Adorno insists that technique is something that can be handed down, he describes here how Borchardt's poetry takes on 'the musical idea of form as immanent to structure, not borrowed from anybody'. That is, the application of a technique conceived as in a certain way shareable is understood to enable the resulting form to become independent and unique. While Adorno is open to the possibility that the technique of incorporating something like a musical reprise into poetry is something that Borchardt has learned from Hölderlin, he insists that it results in an 'original phenomenon of Borchardt's modernity'. This uniqueness consists dually in the historical position of Borchardt's innovation—that is, in the development of poetic material in the period between Hölderlin and Borchardt—and in the resulting altered range of possible effects of this innovation. That is, Borchardt's use of the resounding echo contained in the variations on 'Zwischen Greif und Sphinge schreitend' works against the dominance of what Adorno terms the primacy of sense, which consists not only of the sign character of language, the conceptual impulse to stand for something else, but also of the tendency to judge language, including in poetry, according to its capacity to communicate. It is not so much that Borchardt is the only writer to have moved toward 'absolute poetry', a conception of poetic writing in which words exist in and for themselves, as that his particular use of reprise was necessary to make this move out of the state of material as it was available to him.

This is consonant with Adorno's emphasis in his essay on Goethe's *Iphigenie*, in which he asserts that '[e]ven for artists of the highest rank, it is necessary to take into consideration the closeness to or distance from the materials in which and about which they expressed themselves' (NzL 496/NtL 2: 154). Material, that is, is both the means of expression and its subject matter, both the words used and the referents of their concepts. Indeed, this second meaning is not always entirely positive, Adorno referring in his discussion of Hölderlin to poetry's 'contamination with the material of thought' (NzL 463/NtL 2: 123). It would be wrong to conceive of the mastery of artistic material as a process that has been completely carried out: the material is not completely subordinated into the artwork, but remains visible, and continues to exert an influence—even when, as in this case, it is a contaminating influence. At no point in Adorno's œuvre does this become clearer than in his discussion of what he terms Valéry's deviations:

> In the idea of the integral artwork, tightly closed within itself and committed only to its immanent logic, which follows from the tendency of western art as a whole toward the progressive mastery of nature—concretely, to complete disposal over its material—there is something left out. (NzL 170/NtL 1: 147)

For Adorno, that is, the tendency toward progress in the mastery of artistic material—in technique—cannot be thought of as absolute, as a process that can be brought to some sort of end. It might perhaps be more helpful to consider it a tendency rather than a law, a tendency that must not be hypostatized, but rather exists in relation to the other moments that manifest themselves within the artwork, including the conceptual traces, introduced by the material, that remain visible within it.

Indeed, for Adorno's Valéry, it is not the material that is supposed to disappear, subsumed into the form of the artwork, but the artist himself—Adorno insists that the 'force of artistic production is that of self-effacement' (NzL 187/NtL 1: 161). Here it is important to differentiate the deletion of the individual artist from the deletion of all traces of the subjective process of forming—and it is the former, and by no means the latter, that takes place here. Rather, Adorno insists that successful artworks are able in some way to break free not from the subjective moment, but from the ownership of the artists who have created them: I return in more depth to this topic in the following chapter on the conceptual and social relationships that can be seen between the artwork and the commodity. This is of course not to deny any sort of link between artist and artwork—Adorno's claim is that artworks 'do not belong to their author, are not essentially his image, but that he is bound to them and to his material by the first move of conception, and becomes the organ of implementation of that which the image wants' (NzL 186–87/NtL 1: 161). The link between artwork and artist is not so much denied as inverted: rather than creating something which is obedient to himself, the artist becomes the vehicle of the work, subservient to the artwork's formal law.

But not everything within the artwork can be attributed to the subjective intervention on the part of the artist: the material leaves its undeniable trace within the work. Indeed, the mastery of material that is artistic technique does not aim at the deletion of this material, but rather at its fulfilment. Technique consists in the mastery not only of the material, but also of the impulse to expression that has its origin in subjective experience. In Adorno's terms, artistic technique 'has command over both involuntary emotion and the heteronomous material at once' (NzL 188/NtL 1: 162). He writes of Valéry's 'mistrust of the immediate contingency of the process of artistic production', insisting that '[t]he impression which it leaves on the reluctant materials, which carry contingency into the artwork, stems from just this distrust of the accident of mere subjectivity' (NzL 172/ NtL 1: 149). The contingency of the material stands opposed to the subjective rationality inherent in the process of forming. An artwork's success consists not in the domination of one of these over the other, but in their productive encounter with one another, as rationality and coincidence, subject and object, are brought together in the process of forming. In the concluding section to this chapter, I now turn to discuss the consequences of this relationship for the theory of form.

Consequences for the Theory of Form

In his radio discussion with Peter von Haselberg on the fragment, Adorno makes the conceptual distinction between form and accident or contingency.[20] Fragments are defined as 'artworks, which have the character of the unfinished, the incomplete, regardless of whether this is intentional'; Adorno speaks of the fragmentary character as something that can be brought about, for example, by destruction in war or through water damage:

> The more time has passed, the more this moment of historical contingency takes possession of all the traditions, and the deeper the fragmentary character permeates. One could say that history itself has in relation to the image of spirit a moment of discontinuity, that history itself has something fragmentary, if one wants to put it in those terms.[21]

Form and contingency are here placed in opposition to one another. One could think of form as the result—perhaps better, the manifestation—of all the deliberate subjective acts on the work—that is, of the process of forming—while its contingency comes both from the material and from influences or interruptions from external factors. The situation is however complicated to a considerable extent by the Romantic period, in which Novalis and Schlegel 'named their works fragments themselves, conceived them as fragments, and—and this is particularly true for Schlegel—executed them most carefully in fragmentary form'.[22] There is, that is, at the very least a certain overlap between the moments of composition and of contingency within the artwork.

In discussions of form and material, however, Adorno accentuates the status of the action and choices of the individual artist. The conscious presence accorded to the author in Adorno's discussion of foreign words—as discussed above, for example, or the further personalization in the insistence that 'Gottfried Benn was the first of the German authors to use this aspect of foreign words, the scientific, as a literary artistic device' (NzL 222/NtL 1: 190)—is perhaps no accident. For if Heidegger's rejection of the concept of form consists in the fact that it attributes a certain madness to everything to which it is applied, the emphasis Adorno places, through the concept of artistic technique, on precisely this madeness in the ontology of the artwork is a more than adequate response to Heidegger's intervention against the term.[23] Indeed, Jarvis has specifically attributed Adorno's persistence 'with many of those concepts from aesthetics which Heidegger sets aside, and particularly the concept of "form"' to the fact that Adorno 'is convinced that technique is the way art thinks'.[24] As the mark of artworks' making, form is the objective manifestation of the exercise this technique.

It is, however, notable that the two concepts do not always go hand-in-hand. In the Eichendorff essay, for example, although the word *Technik* and its cognates do not appear, it clearly forms a central topic of the discussion of Eichendorff's manipulation and working of language. The terms *Form* and *Konstruktion*, however, make their first appearance in the coda on Schumann's settings of Eichendorff's texts: no such discussion takes place in relation to Eichendorff's poetic work. At other times, however, the relationship is foregrounded. In his discussion of *Iphigenie*, Adorno considers the dialectic of civilization and barbarism:

> In that dialectic, form shifts into the centre: as construction of whole and part, just as in the linguistic heights completely new to German poetry. The style of the work is the ether of his language that penetrates everything. Such primacy of form carries the civilizing moment, the material reproach, into what is composed. (NzL 500–01/NtL 2: 158)

In this discussion, form is not so much the result of agency as the agency itself—this is perhaps the best way to understand the insistence that the artist should be obedient to the work, and not the other way round. Form here consists explicitly both in the work's construction, the relationship of its parts to its whole, and in the particular way in which language is crafted through technique, in this case to levels previously unattained. Form is not imposed on material, and nor is material shaped into form: rather, form is able to permeate the work, and with it the material, through the subjective process of composition.

And it is abundantly clear that the subject plays a central role in this process. Adorno describes formalizing as an 'act of subjective reason' (ÄT 248/AT 166), even when this subjective act may not be thought of, at least in relation to the successful work, as arbitrary: 'The subjective domination of forming does not condition indifferent materials, but is read out of them' (ÄT 80/AT 50). The subjective act of forming is directed, constrained by the materials, rather than reigning completely freely and arbitrarily over them. And even in this case, the manifestations and results of this subjective process can themselves turn into artistic material:

> Every step toward the perfection of artworks is one toward their self-alienation, and that always dialectically produces anew those revolts which are characterized, too superficially, as uprisings of subjectivity against formalism of whatever kind. (ÄT 261/AT 175)

While it is important to note that Adorno's relation to the conception of formalism deployed in this quotation is not unproblematic, it is clear that the revolt of which he writes takes place against the results of the development of technique—that is, of the developing ability to form material. What is handed down from one artist to another becomes not only an addition to the available means of working the material, but also a constraint, something that is itself to be worked. Form, that is, becomes material which is itself to be dominated in future artistic production. This is further evidence that artistic material cannot be thought of as wholly object, but in this case as subjective expression, against which subjective reason turns in order to objectify it:

> Observing subjectivity is to be strictly differentiated from the subjective moment in the object, from its expression just as from its subjectively mediated form. (ÄT 246/AT 164)

The separation of subject from object is not and cannot be absolute—even the object contains a moment of subjective expression, the subject's attempt to speak through the object. It is with this in mind that I now turn to discuss the significance of the concept of form in its different constellations in understanding the relationship between art and society.

5

Artistic Form and the Commodity Form

> In poems, the rudiments of meanings from outside are the inalienably nonartistic in art. Art's law of form is not to be derived from them, but from the dialectic of both moments.
>
> —NzL 411/NtL 77–78

At the end of the second chapter, I offered a defense of Adorno's use of a concept of form as a conceptually necessary reflection of the unreconciledness of subject and object, universal and particular, under capitalist social relations. My argument at that point was that the concept of form is an attempt to reconcile universal and particular, an attempt that is made necessary by unreconciled society, and that fails just as necessarily because material antagonism cannot be resolved at the level of the concept, which itself exerts a domination that is betrayed by its refusal to tolerate particularity (cf. ND 311/Ashton 317). The contradictions and tensions that exist within the concept of form can be seen as constituting a reflection or encapsulation of the antagonisms that permeate bourgeois society, antagonisms in which the concept's claim to stand for its object plays an integral part. These contradictions include, for example, the fact that on the one hand form appears as the subjective arrangement of the work's material; and on the other hand that form is experienced as an objective compulsion that limits the subjective (negative) freedom of the artist and mediates subjective expression (in relation to which form appears at once as a restriction of expression and as the condition of its possibility).

In addition to these contradictions whereby form appears to carry out two complementary tasks or work in two opposed directions, or in which (depending on the perspective from which it is approached) it is used to refer to two distinct or even mutually incompatible phenomena, the processes referred to by or embedded within the concept imply further complex relationships. Adorno's account of emergence of form out of content, for example, reveals an otherwise hidden affinity between two moments that are thought in opposition to one another. The case is more complex still in the examination of form through the optic of its relationship to material: the form and forms that crystallize out of the shaping of material, the subjective mastery of material in accordance with its own requirements, themselves enter the repertoire of available material. Material becomes form, which in turn becomes material, in a recursive process within which form is experienced—at the same time—as the consequence of the subjective forming of material, as the resulting objective material repertoire.

The constellation within which I have examined form over the first four chapters reveals that the concept is able to contain within itself at least two distinct diachronic shifts. One is the emergence of form out of content, out of the domination of material, and—as became clear in the discussion of musical expressionism—this form can in turn become content. The other consists in the changes that take place within form over time, the history of form's development—here I mean not only the crystallization or coming-together of new forms and genres, but also what appear as formal developments within particular forms. Form is the index of art's madness, the diverse range of ways in which we experience the result of its making. Its emergence as form, the becoming-form of content and of material, is coterminous with the coming-into-being of the artwork as we understand it. What we experience and conceive of as form only comes to appear as form in the completed work: form in this sense appears not merely as the arrangement of the material within the work, but also (and as a result) as the property, however indistinct, that characterizes and distinguishes artworks as such. Before the individual work is complete it is unformed; before there is a work of art there is no form. The adaptability of form—its ability to refer at once to the manner of the work's arrangement and to this ineffable artistic quality without needing to specify the distinction or accounting for this combination or for the relationship between them—is one aspect not only of the complexity of the concept, but also of its ability to mask or displace this complexity.

Artistic form is thus intertwined with social and political processes in two ways that diverge from Adorno's famous account of the relationship between art and politics in the 'Commitment' essay, according to which the political potency of art consists in the ideal of the autonomous artwork—

of art for its own sake—which exhibits a radical potential because of the autonomous work's refusal to submit to the logic of commodity society, in which goods are produced for the sake of what they can be exchanged for, and thus, in the formulation used in *Aesthetic Theory*, 'wants to interrupt the eternal exchange of need and satisfaction, and not to offend by providing ersatz-satisfaction of unmet needs' (ÄT 362/AT 244). The first of these processes is the emergence of form out of social practice, and in particular ritual, as the secularization of cultic practice in the sedimentation of content. And although artworks, originally 'elements of a praxis which wanted to influence nature, separated themselves from it in the beginnings of rationality, and gave up the deception of real influence' (ÄT 210/AT 139), they sustain a connection to or promise of an as-yet-undefined and unknowable practice of the future: 'Artworks draw credit on a praxis which has not yet begun, and of which no one can say whether it will honor its exchange' (ÄT 129/AT 83). While the particular social critique of the ideal of the autonomous work of art is specific to commodity society, this critique is sustained by its connections both before and beyond the temporal horizon of the commodity form.

The second process is in the history of what Adorno describes as the 'collectively honed aesthetic forms' (ÄT 210/AT 139), with respect both to their coming into being (since the constitution of forms such as the novel or the sonata as forms depends on their plurality) and to the experiments within and against these forms and traditions—experiments that include the kinds of works that carry out the fraying or dissolution of borders between genres and forms, formal hybrids that merge multiple traditions, and complex cases of inclusion and containment, such as eruptions of a lyrical mode within a play or novel, or moments of the tragic within a comedy. Even in cases that do not appear as experiments or hybrids, forms nonetheless rely on this collective process of honing, as, for example, in the case of the innovations—again, Proust is one of Adorno's favorite examples—that seem to shift or reconfigure the genre rather than abandoning it. A collectively honed form can thus be seen as a tradition that comes into being and develops and as it works and is worked on in response to the particular social conditions and the demands they exact—in terms not only of the content of what is to be expressed but also of the mode of address required by the moment of the artwork that seeks to oppose social domination. And as the aspect of artworks that distinguishes them from what they are not, this moment continues to have a determinant effect on the future development of artistic forms.

In this chapter I examine these contradictory relations by means of a comparison of the account of form developed so far in this book with another account of form, bringing Adorno's understanding of artistic form into confrontation with the analysis of what Adorno refers to exclusively as the commodity form, and which Marx and others have referred to interchangeably as the commodity form and the value form, examining the implications of Adorno's enigmatic assertion that artworks are 'products of social labor' (ÄT 15, 335, 337, 393/AT 5, 225, 227, 263). I begin by examining some of the different ways in which Marx and his successors have conceived of social labor, and specifically its relationship to the abstract value of commodity-producing labor. In the chapter's second section I discuss the character of this abstraction in more detail, relating it to social acts of exchange. In its third section I address artworks' capacity to offer an alternative to the coercive sociality of mediation through the value form, and the role of form in theorizing this resistance, thereby opening up alternative modes of social life. I then return to Adorno's reading of Kant's purposiveness without purpose, elucidating in particular the consequences for an emancipated sociality of its focus on its implications for language and communication, implications which I explore in further detail in the fifth section, on poetry and reconciliation. In the sixth I consider Adorno's account of the relationship between art beauty and natural beauty and what it reveals about the mediation of art and nature, showing how form renders thinkable a conceptual bridge or portal from our state of unfreedom to the world free from domination that is posited by the work of art. In the final section of the chapter I examine the consequences of this relationship for the theory of the priority of the object, setting out the aesthetic, intellectual and social challenges of the poetics of form.

Social and Abstract Labor

The problem posed by Adorno's designation of artworks as 'products of social labor' is brought sharply into focus when this designation is placed in the context of Marx's identification in *Toward a Critique of Political Economy* of social labor with commodity-producing labor.[1] Labor is described as social insofar as the labor of distinct individuals is presented 'through the actual reduction of all labors to homogeneous labor' as identical, exchangeable.[2] According to this conception the social character of this labor consists in its abstraction: the elision of differences of quality and kind to render labor exchangeable. This definition is endorsed by the claim in *Dialectic of Enlightenment* that 'the social labor of each individual in the bourgeois economy' provides some people with increased capital, others with the continued capacity to labor (DA 46/DE 23). Here Horkheimer and Adorno emphasize the production and appropriation of a surplus—and the ensuing perpetuation and exacerbation of material and social inequality—over the fungibility and exchangeability that represent the condition of their possibility. The sociality of this labor thus consists in its commodity-producing character—and more specifically, in the social relations under which it is carried out.

However, for Marx labor is not social only to the extent that it is commodity-producing.[3] Labor can also be social on the basis of social relations other than those of capital. Marx provides an example from rural, patriarchal industry of social labor that is not mediated through commodity exchange, in which spinning and weaving are carried out within a single household according to a gender-based division of labor, in which yarn and linen were 'social products', and spinning and weaving 'social labors within the limits of the family'.[4] The sociality presupposed and represented by the commodity form differs from this in that its idealized form is a collection of atomized individuals: 'The labor that is presented in exchange value is presupposed as labor of individualized individuals'.[5] This, however, does not mean that the only sociality within a society based on the social relations of commodity production is that of the economic relationships of exchange and employment, but rather that the idealized form of the particular social relations presumed and furthered by commodity production is that of atomization and reification—processes which, as Castoriadis observes, can never be fully realized without putting a stop to industrial production and therefore not only to the production of surplus value but also to the social metabolism that it both depends on and enables.[6]

Indeed, the kinds of sociality that are not encapsulated by (and indeed that precede) that of solely economic relationships serve to enable increased economic efficiency. In the first volume of *Capital*—a work in which the exchange commodity–money–commodity is presented as the 'metabolism of social labor')—Marx discusses the consequences of the fact that 'the production of a workshop for twenty people costs less labor than that of ten workshops each for two people', leading to a tendency to the concentration of the means of production disproportionately to their utility.[7] This concentration enables savings to be made by more efficient use of the means of production—in Marxian terms, the organic composition of capital is altered and the proportion of variable capital increases such that less constant capital is required for the production of each commodity, leading to an increase in the rate of profit even if the rate of surplus value remains constant. But in this process of concentration, the means of production take on the character of being a necessary 'condition of social labor' even when the workers merely work in the same space, without actually cooperating.[8] While the increased sociality of labor enables the generation of higher profits, its social character consists less in the fact that it involves cooperation or even human interaction than in the developments in the relations of production that arise as a result of the compulsion to maximize economic efficiency.[9] In this respect, when Castoriadis remarks that capitalism 'can function only by continually drawing upon the genuinely *human* activity of those subject to it', he is emphasizing something already present within Marx's account of the development of the capitalist mode of production.[10] Capital relies on this activity, which it then transforms in the process of its real subsumption.

Social labor, that is, is characterized as much by its product (and the uses to which it is put) as by the manner in which it is carried out. This becomes clearer when Marx insists that when cooperation brings about increased productivity, 'the specific productivity of the combined working day is the social productivity of labor or the productivity of social labor', regardless of how this increase in productivity is brought about.[11] Marx's concept of social labor thus contains a tension between two different kinds of sociality: that of the cooperation inherent in what Castoriadis refers to as 'genuinely *human* activity', and that of the organization of society on the basis of production of commodities for sale to anonymous others into which this human activity is transformed, and to which it gives way. This tension is not merely an ambiguity or fuzziness within the concept, but rather corresponds to or reflects a tension within the world, and more specifically the distinction and conflict between the sociality of human interaction and cooperation, the economic advantages to which this interaction can be put in industrial production, and the as it were asocial sociality of a society founded on production of goods by individuals for sale on a market to people they do not know. It is not so much the case that the concept of social labor conflates these multiple kinds of sociality as that it reflects the relationships between them, according to which there is a tendency for the replacement of one with another.

According to this conception, social labor need not be understood as identical with commodity-producing labor. All commodity-producing labor is by necessity social—production for the purpose of exchange by means of sale on an anonymous market is by definition not production of goods for the satisfaction of the needs of the individual producer, but for others within society. In describing artworks as products of social labor, that is, Adorno is not necessarily professing the identity of the activity by means of which artworks are constituted with the abstract, socially necessarily labor that is constitutive of exchange value. Indeed, at times Adorno appears to be working with a transhistorical concept of social labor as the condition of the possibility of human existence, such as in this claim from the *Introduction to the Sociology of Music*:

> There is no life without social labor, which first brings enjoyment into the world; however, social order reduces the use of the goods that are produced [. . .] to a means of sustaining the apparatus of production for the sake of profit. (EM 399/ISM 198)

Here social labor refers to deliberate human activity for the purpose of improving human existence, which is only transformed into a social power relationship with the progressive development of social domination. Similarly, in *Negative Dialectics*, Adorno follows Alfred Sohn-Rethel in arguing that within that which exists—'the universal and necessary activity of spirit'—there 'is harbored inalienably social labor' (ND 178/Ashton 177).[12] The verb Adorno uses is *sich bergen*, an uncommon reflexive usage of a verb that means to salvage, hide, rescue, or contain, the implication being that social labor rescues and preserves itself within empirical reality. He insists that social labor must be 'labor directed at Something', a cognition he attributes to Kant's claim that the functionality of the subject 'would be empty without the material that it encounters' (ND 179/Ashton 178). Even in a world in which the 'universal domination of exchange value over humans, domination which a priori prevents subjects from being subjects, demeans subjectivity itself to a mere object' (ND 178/Ashton 180), the possibility of differentiation remains within Adorno's concept of social labor, which cannot simply be reduced to abstract labor, wage labor, commodity-producing labor. That the labor harbored within activity of spirit is described as inalienably social indicates that its sociality differs from that of commodity-producing labor, which is social precisely because of the fact that it is alienated.[13]

However, this specifically capitalist form of abstract, commodity-producing labor is not only an epiphenomenon of the capitalist relations of production under which it exists, but is also, as Adorno insists in 'Aspects', the first of the three studies on Hegel, central to the constitution and mediation of that society. He argues that 'the principle of the equivalence of social labor turns society in the modern, bourgeois sense into the abstract' (3SH 267/H3S 20), that 'the world, integrated through "production", through social labor arranged according to the exchange relationship, depends in all its moments on the social conditions of its production' (3SH 273–74/H3S 27). Wage labor, commodity-producing labor, reinforces and continually reproduces the conditions of its own possibility—the possibility of the exchange and sale of the commodity labor power. At the same time, his characterization of bourgeois society as one mediated by the principle of the equivalence of social labor arranged according to the exchange relationship admits the possibility that there are other kinds of social organization. Exchangeability is not the only possible basis for the sociality of labor. To describe an activity as social labor is not to identify it with abstract, commodity-producing labor. Moreover, even in a society in which wage labor is the predominant form of social labor, in which social relations are primarily mediated through the commodity form—in which capitalist production is the dominant mode of production—there exist kinds of making, of productive activity, that are not and do not take the form of wage labor, and that are themselves grounded in a different kind of sociality.

Abstraction and Exchange

Artworks stand opposed to commodities and the relationships of fungibility that they imply, encapsulate, and perpetuate. At the same time, and precisely by virtue of this opposition, they and their making are not wholly separate from or unaffected by the commodity and the abstract labor by means of which it is produced, and the conditions of the possibility of which it reproduces. Moreover, the connection between artwork and the commodity and the labor by means of which they are made is not solely a matter of the negative determination that results from their opposition to one another. In *Aesthetic Theory* Adorno modifies somewhat his famous account of the autonomous artwork's resistance to the instrumental logic into which the committed artwork seeks to intervene as set out in the 'Commitment' essay:

> That which appears is not exchangeable because it remains neither blunt particularity which allows itself to be replaced by others, nor an empty universal that would, as a unity of characteristics, equalize everything specific that is subsumed under it. If everything

in reality has become fungible, art holds out toward everything that exists for another images of that which it would itself be, emancipated from the schemata of superimposed identification. Art, however, dallies into ideology by suggesting, as the imago of what is not exchangeable, that not everything in the world is exchangeable. Through its form, art must restrain what is exchangeable to critical self-consciousness for the sake of what is not exchangeable. Artworks have their telos in a language whose words the spectrum does not know, that are not captured by preestablished universality. (ÄT 128–29/AT 83)

Here Adorno rejects the false alternatives of general and particular as they appear in opposition to one another. Both are exchangeable: the blunt particular that emphasizes its own particularity to the extent that it is no longer relevant which particular is at stake, the empty universal because it displays an indifference to the particularity which is subsumed under it, which can then be substituted for anything else. This is a rejection both of the tendency within idealist aesthetics to 'make art swear an oath on that which it symbolizes' (a tendency which 'offends the spirit within the artwork itself') and of what Adorno describes as the romanticist attempt to equate art with the content that appears, reducing it to a mere particular (ÄT 128/AT 82). Art does not so much resist the fungibility of the objects that constitute a world which is mediated through production for the sake of exchange as present the image of what it would itself like to be, if only it could exist solely for its own sake—to this extent the aestheticist ideal is an aspiration that is never fully realized rather than a complete achievement. That art can only present this image—that is to say, that it is not, at present, able to exist solely for its own sake—is an indication of Adorno's understanding of the depth to which society is mediated through commodity exchange. Artworks cannot offer a blueprint for an alternative to unfree society, but rather express their desire to be free from mediation through exchange that is predicated on identity.

Moreover, the contemporary making of artworks has certain affinities with or at least resemblances to the abstract, commodity-producing labor through which the reproduction of contemporary society is mediated. In a manner analogous to the discussion of technique and its relationship to the relations of production in the fourth chapter, the making of artworks draws on processes that are developed within the production of commodities. The deployment in artistic making of processes that derive from and that are used within industry means that particular activities of making (if not the social relations and economic conditions under which they take place) resemble those of the workplace. And even though this labor takes place in circumstances that are not (and indeed that are frequently radically different from) those of the wage relation, the activities themselves—the means of production themselves, but also the processes of making, and the relationship to tools in that making—are to an extent mediated by the relations of production under which they were developed, an extent that increases with the development of what Marx terms real subsumption. Tools, techniques and processes used in the making of art have frequently emerged and developed within industrial or even military contexts.

This is not to efface the artwork's claim that by asserting its existence for its own sake it is radically distinct from the commodity that is produced for the sake of exchange. But nor is it to rely on a diffuse, transhistorical, or hypothetical concept of making or production or activity into which both abstract, commodity-producing labor and the making of artworks might fit: such a concept would involve further abstraction not only from the sensuous, particular, qualitatively distinctive character of the activities that are subsumed under it, but also from the specific economic and social conditions under which they take place. For the distinction between artistic making and abstract labor consists in the fact that artistic making retains and depends on the specificity of the making of a sensuous particular. Abstract labor, in contrast, is indifferent to the tangible features of the commodities that it produces, which are produced for the sake of their exchangeability. That is, the process of abstract labor is one from which all the particular, qualitatively distinct details of that labor have been erased. In contrast, as long as the artwork is not exchangeable—as long, that is, as its claim to exist solely for its own sake continues to cherish and draw attention to both its own sensuous particularity and that of the purposive human activity by means of which it comes into being—the making of art does not undergo this kind of abstraction.

It is fundamentally important to distinguish between, on the one hand, the resemblances of the processes and products of artistic making to those of commodity production, and, on the other hand, these radical differences between artistic making and wage labor, between the artwork and the commodity. The former consists in the as it were surface resemblance between the activities, physical and mental, that go into the two processes, despite the radical structural difference that determines the latter: the difference between the economic and social relations under which they take place. And this surface resemblance is not a particularly new phenomenon, although it is perhaps one that can always appear to be new, because it always involves the relationship between art and the technologies that exert the strongest claim to define the contemporary age. It is the failure to recognize this distinction between artistic making's surface resemblance or similarity with wage labor and the exchangeability and abstraction that distinguish the two as the result of the this structural difference that leads to the misrecognition of the coincidence between capitalist production and the state of creative, technological advances at any given time.[14]

There is thus a fundamental distinction between comparability or resemblance (on the level of the sensuous particular activity or result) and the equivalence (on the level of social and economic relations) that derives from the social reality that wage labor is by definition exchangeable. This equivalence is what Sohn-Rethel terms a '*real abstraction* resulting from spatio-temporal activity', and thus an abstraction which 'does not originate in men's minds but in their actions'—in Adorno's words in *Negative Dialectics*, actions that have taken place therefore 'have real objectivity, but are at the same objectively untrue' (ND 190/Ashton 190).[15] The force of the critique of the real abstraction of labor and the commodity is threefold. First, it subsumes under itself a range of activities that are incomparably different from one another. Second, and more poisonously, it does so by means of its utter indifference to particularity. And third, as a result of this indifference it renders the question of comparability with respect to sensuous particulars immaterial.

And yet there nonetheless remains within the particularity of artworks and their making an element that is influenced by and that comes to resemble the labor process, an element which becomes most visible in response to changes and developments in industrial production, and in particular as artists draw on and incorporate the most recent industrial processes into the making of artworks. This has the capacity to foreground and perhaps even transform the sensuous particularity of activities that were developed in the service of the production of abstract value—that is to say, the capacity as it were to counteract the abstractness of activities that previously existed precisely and solely because of their abstract character, because they form part of a process of production for the sake of exchange. Artworks thus have a dual character that exists in parallel to that of the commodity: but rather than being sensuous particulars as use values and abstract as the bearers of exchange value—the manifestation of the socially necessary (abstract) labor time that went into their production—artworks are sensuous particulars which assert that they are not useful (this is the force of Kant's insistence on disinterested delight and on the radical separation of what is pleasing from what is useful or what is good for something), and which as sensuous particulars bear the trace of their making as the result a particular, deliberate activity.[16] And they do so even—and indeed especially—when the social manifestation of production that resembles that making (more accurately, perhaps, of production that that making resembles) within the commodity-producing economy exists only because of its abstract character.

At the same time, there exists a thinkable category of activity that includes both artistic making and commodity-producing labor. However, this category does not represent a further abstraction from both of these categories, but rather an abstraction of a different kind. For the real abstraction of wage labor already subsumes myriad labors in their particularity under its universal concept. Artistic making is another particular activity—but one that resists the process of real abstraction because it refuses the logic of equivalence. It is nonetheless thinkable within a category that also subsumes its particularity—but this category comes about by means of an abstraction that is thought rather than by a real abstraction that results from social practices that are carried out in space and time. And the real abstraction of commodity-producing labor is such that it empowers and encourages the thought abstraction to assert a further claim over an expanded set of particulars, and in such a way that this distinction between real and thought abstraction is obscured, as all activity becomes construable in terms of a timeless, transhistorical expenditure of abstract labor. The indifference that constitutes the logic of identity—the indifference to the particularity of the object on the part of the concept into which it will never go without leaving a remainder—is thus bound up with the compulsory structure of real domination according to which people are compelled to subjugate themselves to the heteronomous logic of production for the sake of exchange. The real abstraction of commodity-producing labor leads us to overestimate the scope of its implications, to conclude that the sensuously particular making of an artwork can also be subsumed under the abstract concept of labor.

Artworks are not commodities—by asserting their claim to exist only for their own sake they are radically opposed to production for the sake of exchange—and are not made by means of commodity-producing, abstract social labor. And yet they are products of social labor. Adorno thus sites the making of artworks within the context of a history of social production (in fact several histories of social production) that are not founded on the exchange of abstract equivalence. The insistence that artworks are products of social labor thus emphasizes that abstract labor is not the only kind of social labor, that it is not purposeful human activity *tout court*; and as Ernst Lohoff argues in one of the founding texts of the critique of value that emerged in the Federal Republic of Germany in the 1980s, the category of abstract labor is not so much a prerequisite of capitalist production as its product.[17] Adorno thus recognizes that wage labor is not the only possible kind of social labor, and provides a critique of the attempt to expand its abstraction beyond the kinds of making that become exchangeable as a result of the real abstraction of the wage relation, to all other kinds of making that can potentially be included under this concept by means of the thought abstraction.

Moreover, his insistence that artworks are products of social labor not only refutes abstract labor's transhistorical claim to be the source of all social wealth, and the only such source that there has ever been, but also insists on the concrete and actual existence of a kind of social labor that is not that of abstract, commodity-producing labor governed by the wage relation. That is to say, Adorno's claim serves as a reminder not only that there have (despite the political economists' attempts to project their categories back onto noncapitalist societies in order to provide a natural, scientific, and nonideological justification for bourgeois economics) been societies in which the sociality of labor is founded on something other than the exchange of abstract equivalents, but also that artistic making represents a kind of social labor in the here and now that asserts its aspiration not to be subject to the principle of the exchangeability of abstract equivalents. The sociality of this labor does not depend on—and is indeed opposed to—the abstract exchangeability that is indifferent to the particular characteristics of what is made. Moreover, this sociality promises to rescue particularity from abstraction—including, as a result of the dual character that artistic making takes on by virtue of its incorporation of techniques and technologies taken from commodity production, techniques and technologies that are thus thoroughly mediated through the commodity form and the wage relation—the particularity that comes about precisely because of the abstraction of the labor process.

Mediation and Form

Artworks thus testify not only to an individual activity but also to a sociality or social mediation that is not that of the value form—and their testimony is not confined to a past to which we can never return, or to the possibility of a future that is yet to come in such a radical sense that any attempt to imagine it from within the damaged present would damage it as if by contamination, but within the here and the now.[18] Artworks, that is, exemplify the actuality of a social labor that is liberated from compulsory abstraction, an actuality that is more present than the negative utopianism of the claim that things (in the more pessimistic version) ought to or (more optimistically) could be different—as James Gordon Finlayson argues, artworks make the promise of happiness not as its prefiguration, but in their revealing of 'the social world as one that is unworthy of affirmation'.[19] But in doing so they not only serve as a reminder that it is possible to resist the totalizing claims of abstract value and its logic of exchangeability, but also present a kind of social labor that does not efface the particularity of the activities that constitute it. The sociality of this labor, rather than being indifferent to particularity, would be founded on it. This involves the replacement of the material social actions relations that efface particularity—those that imply the substitutability and exchangeability not only of individual objects but also of individual persons, activities, even quanta of time—with practices and relationships that cherish the particularity of activities carried out for their own sake.

This is not an argument in favor of a society founded on the production of artworks rather than of commodities—and not merely because of the practical difficulty of reproducing one's life solely through art. For whereas commodity production, and in particular the increasing commodification of more and more aspects of social and individual life, reproduces the economic conditions in which proletarians have nothing except labor power to exchange in return for the means of subsistence, the precondition for the continued relationship between capital and the commodity labor power, the making of artworks does not reinforce the social conditions of the possibility of their making. The elusive sociality founded on particularity, that is, must not only enable the reproduction of human life, but also and at the same time reproduce itself. Moreover, our conception of the artwork depends on its position within commodity society. Our encounters with artworks as distinct from and opposed to commodities is contingent on their taking place within a society founded on (in which sociality is mediated through) the production of commodities: these encounters can take the forms they do within commodity society, which conditions (while not determining) our conception and experience of the artwork. The artwork as we encounter, experience, and conceive it, that is, is a consequence and a phenomenon (if by no means a wholly incidental epiphenomenon) of capitalist society. Absent this coercive, violent sociality, the artwork ceases to be thinkable as we think it, as both a mode of resistance and a promise of something better.

So while the artwork as we encounter it is conceived in opposition to the commodity, it does not itself constitute an alternative form on which a noncoercive sociality of human life could be based. That is to say, the form that is the focus of discussion in this book is not a candidate for the replacement of the value form as the elementary form of a kind of sociality that is not mediated through commodity production. Nor could artistic making as it subsists within commodity society constitute basis of a noncoercive sociality that reproduces the conditions of its own possibility. Artworks and their making point rather to the possibility of such a sociality, without instituting or instantiating it. Their relationship to this indeterminate future is gestural: they point toward such a state of freedom, rather than representing it (either in the sense of depicting it or of standing for it as a token). This gestural logic is neither that of sign nor that of image: it functions neither by signification nor by imitation. Rather, by calling into question the claims of the commodity and its abstract labor to stand for and represent all objects and all kinds of human activity, artworks serve to open up a space for thinking beyond the horizon of commodity society, and in doing so open up an alternative to the two competing logics of sign and image, of classification and resemblance.

This alternative consists in a gestural pointing-toward predicated on negation. For by distancing themselves from the constraints and coercions to which everyday life is subject—by asserting their otherness, by laying claim to a distinction from everyday life, and specifically from the lived reality of instrumental reason and abstract exchange that permeate it—artworks gesture toward the possibility of life lived without these constraints. Artworks are thus a kind of clearing within a world dominated by instrumental reason, opening the way for emancipation from it. It is not simply that artworks serve as a reminder that there could be something beyond the logic of fungibility and subservience that is the world of commodity exchange (that they allow us to think beyond the horizon of the commodity), but that they constitute a kind of social praxis that resists the logic of the commodity form. This social praxis consists not only in the fact that, as Adorno reminds us, artworks testify by the diverse histories and realities of their making to the presence of a social labor that is not founded on the abstract and violent sociality of commodity-producing society, but also in the equally diverse set of ways in which we interact with them, whether these interactions are imbued with reverence, play, outrage, indifference, or indeed any of countless other attitudes.

To acknowledge this plurality, however, is not to lose sight of the critical force of Adorno's modernist aesthetics. As Hammer has observed, he 'conceives of modern art as the antidote to industrial late capitalism and its incessant transformation of every entity and every body into fungible means of production and profit-extraction', and while the specificity of his analyses is embedded within its historical moment, the alternative to the social and political seriousness that underlies his normative claims is 'trivialization and nihilism'.[20] In this respect the precise details of the complex and ambiguous relationships between these attitudes depend themselves on an urgency that is closely related to the relationship between art and society. Adorno accounts for his formulation of the dialectic according to which art oscillates between seriousness and lightheartedness (albeit not in the synthetic form in which it is found within the culture industry) by means of the constitutive tension that results from the fact that art is 'something which has escaped from reality and is permeated by it all the same' (NzL 601/NtL 2: 249). In this respect artworks are elements of social reality that come to define themselves in opposition to that reality, and yet sustain that connection to that of which they used to be a part. This becomes particularly clear in Adorno's discussion of art's artifactual moment, the accent on which 'pertains less to their manufacturedness than to its constitution, regardless of how it came into being' (ÄT 14/AT 4–5). As was the case in the discussion of the relationship between form and material, Adorno considers the details of the process of making to be of less significance than the fact of their being made. What he terms the works' constitution takes on a double meaning here, referring not only to the internal arrangement and composition of artworks, but also, and perhaps even primarily, to their status as made objects, a status which is fundamental to the way in which they relate to society:

> But it is precisely as artifacts, as products of social labor, that [artworks] also communicate with the empirical reality that they reject, and they draw their content from this reality. Art negates the determinations that are stamped categorically onto empirical reality, and at the same time conserves that which empirically is within its own substance. If art opposes empirical reality through the moment of form—and the mediation of form and content cannot be construed without their distinction—this mediation is somewhat generally to be sought in the fact that aesthetic form is sedimented content. (ÄT 15/AT 5)

Artworks' rejection of the reality of the domination of the principles of identity and exchange cannot be construed independently of the fact that they are created out of elements of this reality. In considering the claim that art conserves within itself that which empirically is while at the same time rejecting the determinations to which it is subject, one might think of Duchamp's *Fountain*, in which a Bedfordshire-model urinal, ripped out of its context by the two acts of rotation and displacement, is as it were freed from the functional logic of means and ends in which it would otherwise have been found. According to Adorno's conception, this act of reframing or transposing could be thought of as an accentuated version of something that takes place within every artwork. A poetic analogue to this process can be found in the discussion in the first chapter of the incorporation of the subject into language. Within a poem, natural language of the empirical world is freed from the demands and determinations of conceptual and predicative logic, conserved within the poem such that the 'communication of what is differentiated' begins to become imaginable (S 743/CM 247).

In the claim that the moment of form is what enables to oppose the reality of labor and the commodity, form is thus deployed as a means of expressing art's suspension of the reality that it at once preserves and rejects. And once again, this form is being used in two senses at the same time. In one sense form is the moment by which the elements of this reality—that is, the content—are sedimented—as it were transposed, arranged, and transformed—into the artwork: form wrests the content from reality and does something with and to it in the making of the artwork. In the other sense form is what enables and compels art to oppose the reality from which its content is taken—a power and obligation which are the result of that sedimentation. Adorno thus advances an argument in which form, apparently rather confusingly, is also used to refer to the mediation of form and content: it refers both to that which enters into mediation with content, and to the result of that process of mediation.

This, however, is neither a merely terminological nor a conceptual slippage: the concept of form that becomes apparent through close analysis of Adorno's writings on literary artworks in particular reflects (and, indeed, results from) the peculiar nature of these works' connection to the reality from which their content and material are taken and which they oppose. The apparent conceptual looseness mirrors the recursive nature of the artwork's relationship to reality. Form thus helps render this complex relationship thinkable, and what appear as inconsistencies within the concept reveal something of its intricacy. Form makes explicit the tension inherent in the claim that artworks distance themselves from empirical reality of which they are constructed—for the sake of the richer experience of a richer reality that is not constrained by the relations of power and domination that saturate the reality of our experience. Empirical reality is to be rejected not because of any kind of downplaying of the significance of experience with respect to theoretical a priori cognition, but rather because in this reality experience is debased. It is rejected in the name of a reality to come in which there is more experience, a much wider range of experience, than there is within what presents itself as empirical reality. Artworks reject this empirical reality not by negating or even by offering a positive alternative to the instrumental logic of ends and means, but rather by negating the assertion that this logic is all-encompassing, by denying its claim to represent the totality of human interactions. In this respect art's distancing itself or setting itself apart from empirical reality is itself an aspiration rather than an observation or constative declaration; art's rejection of empirical reality is programmatic, and the analysis of that rejection is that of a moment within artworks, rather than of their entirety.

Purposiveness, Communication, Language

It thus becomes possible to offer a complementary contemporary account that further complicates somewhat Adorno's historicization of the Kantian purposiveness in general without any particular purpose as discussed in the first chapter. Central to Adorno's narrative is the artwork's abrogation of the claim to exert a direct effect into the world—this abrogation is the secularization or disenchantment of the mythical practice from which artworks originate. He insists that the purposiveness of artworks consists in the organic unity of their individual moments, and their 'without purpose' in the fact that they 'have stepped outside the ends–means relation of empirical reality' (ÄT 210/AT 139). But, as the previous discussions reveal, this stepping outside of the instrumental logic of means and ends does not pertain only to the historical origin of art as the secularization of cultic praxis: the empirical reality to which Adorno refers is not only that of the ritual that seeks to exert a direct influence in the world, but also that of the instrumental rationality of commodity production.

There are two significant tensions within this account. The first is the conflict between continuity and specificity. For on the one hand this account places artworks within a tradition of resistance to and rejection of heteronomy that long predates the emergence of the abstract equivalence of the value form—art's rejection of this abstract equivalence is thus the contemporary manifestation of 'without purpose', the historical form proper to bourgeois society of a phenomenon that began with the secularization of magic ritual. On the other hand, there is something jarring about the subsumption under a single concept of the rejection of instrumentality both art's emergence out of cultic praxis in the process of its secularization and its as it were epiphenomenal existence alongside an economy based on commodity exchange. The analogical counterpart in commodity society to the emergence of artworks from ritual is the making of artworks by means of the techniques used in industrial production—and while this represents a stepping away from instrumental rationality, it does not seem to go hand-in-hand with the decline of that rationality from which it emerges.

The second tension within the translation of this account of purposiveness without purpose onto modern and contemporary artworks is Adorno's acknowledgment of the extent to which artistic purposiveness is bound up with notions of organic wholeness:

> Artworks were purposive as a dynamic totality, in which all individual moments are present for their purpose, the whole, and in the same way the whole for its purpose, the fulfilment or negative redemption of the moments. (ÄT 210/AT 139)

This emphasis on the organic unity of parts and whole might seem to suggest an understanding of aesthetic purposiveness that is predicated on harmony, that would thus exclude the twentieth-century works of art for which Adorno reserves his highest praise. Here it is important to understand that for Adorno dissonance is not defined in straightforward opposition to harmony.[21] Organic wholeness is not automatically identifiable with harmony and consonance, especially if the latter is taken to constitute endorsement of unfreedom. Observing the tensions in Adorno's writings on aesthetic harmony and wholeness, Finlayson notes that 'there is more than one notion of the whole, and of totality, in play in Adorno's philosophy', and draws attention to a certain inconsistency in Adorno's distinction between them in the acknowledgment that he 'at least some of the time, is keen to distinguish the ideal of organic wholeness from the more coercive notion of system totality'.[22] An account of the current social and political resonance of Adorno's poetics of form requires an attentiveness to these distinctions, even where Adorno does not make them himself.

His discussion is more nuanced when he brings his account of purposiveness without purpose into closer relation to the language-like character of art, arguing that art's 'purposiveness externalized from practical purposes is that which resembles language' while its being without purpose 'is its aconceptuality, its distinction from significative language' (ÄT 211/AT 140). In this account purposiveness is presented as already distinguished from practical purposes—that is to say, purposiveness is neither identified with nor viewed in strict opposition to the service of particular purposes, but rather seen as emerging out of such service. Artworks are language-like without signifying. Art's resemblance to language does not consist in the composition of poetry out of elements of significative language (this, instead, can be characterized as the composition of works out of elements of the empirical world of means and ends) but rather in the moments in which it tends toward the universal—however, unlike significative language, which is hostile to the particular, art attains universality 'by means of its tendency toward radical particularization' (ÄT 305/AT 205). The work of art seeks to link the particular to the universal not by abstracting away from and therefore turning against particularity, but rather by preserving and intensifying the particular.

This nonsignifying, mimetic universality is a helpful way of construing Adorno's interpretation of purposiveness without purpose: artworks have something about them that resembles the universalizing moment of signification, but without either abandoning particularity or signifying anything in particular. And artworks' affinity with language is closely related to their internal organization:

> Artworks approach the idea of a language of things only through their own language, through organization of their disparate moments; the more it is syntactically articulated in itself, the more it comes to speak along with its moments. (ÄT 211/AT 140)

Here the organization of artworks is explicitly described as a language—albeit one proper to artworks. This notion of the language of things and the language of artworks is of course taken from Benjamin's enigmatic, posthumously published essay 'On Language as Such and on the Language of Humans', in which he not only distinguishes the language of things from the significative language of cognition, but also insists that it is both silent and nameless.[23] Indeed, this language of things and artworks' own language are so far removed from the conceptual and predicative language that stands opposed to subjective expression that even to call it language is potentially misleading. Nonetheless, Adorno locates this as it were non-linguistic language in the relationships between the elements out of which artworks are composed.

Artistic Form and the Commodity Form

He offers what is in many respects an interpretation or reading of Benjamin's elusive argument. Indeed, Benjamin's own account contains many elements that are recognizable in the more comprehensive account of literary and poetic form of Adorno's later writings that is the focus of the first four chapters of this book:

> There is a language of sculpture, of painting, of poetry. Just as the language of poetry is founded if not solely then partly on the name-language of humans, it is very conceivable that the language of sculpture or painting is founded on certain kinds of thing-languages, that in them there is manifest a translation of the language of things into an infinitely higher language, but perhaps even a language of the same sphere. What is under discussion here are nameless, nonacoustic languages, languages out of material; here it is important to think of the material community of things in their communication.[24]

In many respects this extract can be viewed as if retrospectively through Adorno's later contention as if it is a text of which Adorno seeks to provide an interpretation or account (in a manner that is in a sense comparable to what I have sought to do more explicitly in explicating some of Adorno's denser or more allusive passages within this book). So when Adorno equates artworks' own language and their proximity to the language of things to the 'organization of their disparate moments', he is providing a kind of explanation of how the process to which Benjamin refers can take place, an account of the aspects in which artworks come to resemble the language of things, and the means by which they do so. And indeed, Benjamin's insistence that the nonsignifying, nameless, as it were second-order languages of artworks are derived from and thus have an affinity with the material out of which they are constructed finds its echo in Adorno's more detailed schematic conception of the influence of the material on the work's form, and thus on its expression. Adorno's siting of the development of this second-order language in the organization or arrangement of this material thus presents an account in which Benjamin's claim is made more tangible.

However, there is another sense in which the mystical, unknowable element of Benjamin's account that insists on the importance of thinking the 'material community of things in their communication'—of thinking that which the conceptual resources of the human language of names is unable to think—goes missing in Adorno's more process-oriented account. That is, there contains within Adorno's interpretation or rethinking of Benjamin a kind of secularization, that is perhaps the price paid for the more detailed and conceptually nuanced formulation of the later account. It is however the case not only that there is a considerable degree of common ground between the two positions, but also that the enigmatic and aporetic moments in Adorno's own account of the artwork's resistance to domination offer a point at which this Adornian secularization can be challenged. And one of these points is the consensus between Benjamin and Adorno that the human, conceptual, predicative, signifying language of names is the material out of which poetry is made. This is poetry's link to the empirical world of means and ends, the instrumental impulse to classify and master the world to which conceptual language refers—an impulse that ignores the discrepancy between an object in the world and the concept into which it will not go without leaving a remainder.[25] To this extent the secularizing moment of Adorno's explication is thus a kind of conflation of the unknowable language of things not only with the knowing, classifying aspect of human language, but also with the tendency to transform and simplify this human language to render it more easily and more completely knowable.

Poetry and Reconciliation

The language of things and its close counterpart the language of artworks are themselves to be distinguished from the human language of signs—as Adorno acknowledges in his 'Fragment on Music and Language', music 'does not form a system of signs' (QF 251/Livingstone 1). They are described as languages in the sense that what they do is communicate—only once again, the term communication as it is commonly used and understood is inadequate to the process that is being described. For what is at issue here is the ability of things (and, a fortiori, of artworks) to express, to share, to commune with one another—to do all the things that secular, disenchanted Enlightenment reason tells us that things don't do. Indeed, in his essay 'On Subject and Object' Adorno holds up the possibility of such a reconfiguration of communication beyond the limits of the ways in which we are currently able to understand it for the world to come:

> If speculation as to the state of reconciliation were permitted, in it could be imagined neither the undifferentiated unity of subject and object nor their antagonistic antithesis; rather the

communication of what is differentiated. Only then would the concept of communication, as objective, take up its place. (S 743/CM 247)

This communication of what is differentiated is fundamentally different from the commonsense understanding of communication (and all the more so from communication as conceived semiotically). In particular, it is not mediated through concepts. It is thus a kind of communication that does not level down whatever is communicated to something already pre-given and known, but rather preserves the differentiation that is erased by the mediation of its transformation into the object of a subject that is not only other than but also hostile to it. Such a nonconceptual, nonsubjective communication of things remains present in Adorno's ambivalent and almost-prohibited vision of reconciliation, his secularization of the prohibition on graven images into a 'refusal to allow positive depictions of utopia' (ND 207/Ashton 207) to which he frequently fails wholly to adhere.

The distinction between signifying language and the language of artworks helps to account for the tension between the poem's substantive and its propositional content, between what the work of art says and what its words say. This tension between the nonsignifying, thingly language of poetry and the signifying everyday language out of which it is composed—comparable to the tension between a sensuous particular and the commodity form, and between the object and its concept—is the particular site at which poetry not only contains a link to the empirical world of means and ends, but also comes to resist it. The peculiarity of the poem or linguistic artwork consists in the fact that the thingly language of the artwork coexists with the human, signifying language of names, and that as a result the tension between the artwork and the empirical world from which its material is taken and which it at the same time rejects becomes most manifest (even if at the same time and for the same reason the distinction is also in the greatest danger of being overlooked). That is to say, the transformation of conceptual language into the material of poetry—and thus into something that stands opposed to the heteronomy of this language—serves as a stark reminder that even out of this language of names there can be made a silent language of things that calls into question the claim of conceptual language to stand for sociality in its entirety. The transformation of language as poetic material such that the language of the artwork comes to the fore constitutes a challenge to the accommodationist conflation of sociality as it is, mediated through the concept, through the commodity, with social life as it could be and ought to be, in its as yet unrealized fullness.

This lays the ground for something of a clarification of Adorno's demand that life imitate art. For as Adorno's formulation makes clear, this demand is an insistence at once on the radical otherness of any kind of state of reconciliation from the coercive sociality of the commodity form, and on the longing for such a state from within the wrong state of things:[26]

> Ultimately the theory of imitation ought to be inverted: in a sublimated sense it is reality that should imitate artworks. But the fact that artworks exist indicates that that which is not could nonetheless be. The reality of artworks testifies to the possibility of the possible. What artworks' longing aspires to—the reality of that which is not—is transformed in longing's memory. In memory that which is, as something that has been, espouses that which is not, because that which has been no longer is. (ÄT 199–200/AT 132)

This difficult and condensed formulation of the itself elusively complex configuration of the relationship between possibility and actuality within the artwork relies on and follows from Adorno's account of the transformation of elements of the empirical world into the artwork, an account the complexity of which is to a great extent derived from the way in which the work of art constitutes a nexus of interrelating modalities. For artworks stand as it were at the threshold between the instrumental logic of empirical reality, the wrong state of things—out of elements of which they are composed—and the unreality of the world for which they yearn. The reality of artworks consists in no more than the fact that they are: the term is thus potentially misleading, because it is distinct from the empirical reality that artworks reject. However, to the extent that this is misleading it is necessarily so: it is misleading precisely because the reality of artworks points toward (without effecting) the actualization of the possibility of that which is not—it serves as a reminder that the unreality of that which is not is a temporary state of affairs, that the observation that it is not should not be mistaken for the claim that it ought not to be.

In testifying to the possibility of the possible, artworks thus go beyond the recognition of critical thought that social antagonism is contingent, as formulated in his discussion of world spirit and natural history, the second of the three models that conclude *Negative Dialectics*:

Only if things could have turned out differently—if totality's claim to absoluteness, the socially necessary semblance as hypostasis of the universal that has been extracted from individual human beings, is broken—can critical social consciousness preserve the freedom to think that things could one day be different. Theory can only shift the inordinate burden of historical necessity if this necessity is recognized as semblance that has become reality, if historical determination is recognized as metaphysically accidental. (ND 317/Ashton 323)

While this claim emphasizes the importance of thinking this contingency in order to be able to conceive of the possibility of such an alternative, the account in *Aesthetic Theory* of the implications of the reality of artworks gestures toward a primitive conception of the possibility of freedom might come to be actualized from within our unfreedom.[27] By focusing on the mingling within the work's sensuous particularity of reality and unreality, present and future, rejection (of the wrong state of things) and affirmation (of their—still absent—rectification), Adorno opens up the possibility of the emergence of a transformation out of the existing order. Artworks thus constitute a kind of bridge or portal toward a state of reconciliation beyond its merely negative conception as the rejection of that which is—of the state of unfreedom. They are not merely the thought that things could conceivably, imaginably (if not actually) be otherwise—Adorno's stark rejoinder to any pronouncement that there is no alternative, a deeply ideological attempt to disguise contingency as necessity—but themselves reality, a reality that promises, longs for, aspires to freedom from the heteronomy of empirical reality of which it is constructed, and that by virtue of this construction promises to consign this empirical reality to obsolescence.

The insistence that life should imitate art is thus not only an exhortation that the sensuous particularity of the richness of life lived to its fullest extent be set free from the strictures of the commodity form, but also if not an account of the work required in order to effect this liberation then perhaps an incipient formulation of the complexity of the relationship between commodity society and a successor to it that is worth wishing for. And in this relationship artworks are the longing for such a future society—and more specifically, the longing for what is not, expressed in the material composed out of that which is. Bringing the insistence that life should imitate art into closer relation with the economic relations of domination that mediate the production of goods suggests an interpretation of the combination of continuity and radical distinction in the mingling of that which is and that which is not: the continuity consists in the preservation of the human and nonhuman resources and potentials of creativity and ingenuity, the radical difference in their liberation from the constraints of the value form. This interpretation enables the sublimation to which Adorno refers to be characterized a little more precisely. For it implies that such a future would consist not in a more equitable (less still a more efficient) distribution of the 'monstrous collection of commodities' that represents wealth as it is accumulated in bourgeois society but rather in the freedom of material wealth from the constraints of this form and its oppressive sociality—not only the affirmation of the sensuous particularity of life lived in all its richness, but a life of sensuous, material, bodily pleasure (where bodily is understood not in opposition to intellectual, but as incorporating it).[28]

This emancipation from the strictures of the commodity form, moreover, is not simply a matter of developing a cooperative or noncommercial deployment of existing technologies, less still organizations, which would persist unchanged, for these technologies and organizations are enabled by and mediated through and permeated with the repressive, atomizing sociality of the economic relations under which they are subsumed. Indeed, the transition from formal to real subsumption as the economic imperative of the logic of capital leads to reorganizations and reconfigurations of social life in pursuit of higher efficiency in order to maximize profit by increasing the amount produced during the working day (by means of an increase in relative surplus value), a tendency that has been described as capital's drive to 'reshape that process in its own image'.[29] That is to say, it is not only the case that the productive forces are constrained and restricted by the relations of production, but also that that with the advent of real subsumption, the evolution of these forces is motivated by and take place in accordance with the logic of the economic imperative, as an ever wider range of technologies develops and is developed in order to serve the autotelic end of the self-valorization of value.

The empirical social reality out of which the material of artworks is taken and with the technologies of which it is worked is thus not only thoroughly mediated by the relations of production, but also to a great extent shaped, designed, and developed in accordance with the imperative to produce abstract value for its own sake. And here the demand that life should imitate art can helpfully be brought into closer relation to Adorno's rethinking of technique and its relationship to the forces of the production as discussed in the fourth chapter of this book. In that chapter I examined the implications of Adorno's claim that the artist 'embodies the social productive forces, without necessarily being bound to the judgments dictated by the relations of production, judgments which he always criticizes through the consistency of his *métier*' (ÄT 71/AT 43–44): the artist works the material in a way that is sensitive to its requirements or needs, requirements which are different in kind from the externally imposed constraints of the relations of production and the imperative to maximize valorization.

Art Beauty and Natural Beauty

The consistency of the artistic *métier* consists precisely in the responsiveness to the material, a responsiveness that is not slavishly obedient or constrained by what has been done before within the same medium, but that perpetually seeks new ways to work within it—a novelty which in retrospect so often seems indispensable or even inevitable. This consistency thus consists in a comportment that is neither fully active nor fully passive, the attunement of an artist who is never wholly subject to the requirements of material that is never wholly objective. Such an attuned comportment criticizes the terms imposed by the relations of production precisely because it rejects and presents an alternative to the indifference of abstract value to the specificity of what is made. That is to say, Adorno's account of the artwork's rejection of the logic of exchange and the abstract equivalence on which it is based finds a counterpart in the insistence not only on the sensuous particularity of the artwork, but also on a process of making that is anything but indifferent to the material of the artwork. This making is made manifest in form. As the index or mark of this making, form is what distinguishes artistic from natural beauty, within which Adorno locates an emancipatory promise, arguing that it 'remains as dispersed and uncertain as that which it promises, that which surpasses everything that is intrapersonal' (ÄT 114/AT 73). That is to say, its emancipatory character or promise consists to a great extent in its refusal to be constrained within the concept that can be applied to it.[30]

But this promise of the nonidentical is by no means confined to natural beauty. Adorno explicitly links art to a nature that is free from oppression, locating within the experience of artworks something that goes beyond the narrow confines of human, subjective experience, narrowly construed:

> It is not aesthetic trepidation that is semblance, but the position it takes with relation to objectivity: in its immediacy it feels potential as if it were actualized. The I is seized by the unmetaphorical consciousness that shatters aesthetic semblance: the consciousness that it itself is not ultimate, but semblant. This transforms art for the subject into that which it is in itself, the historical advocate of oppressed nature, ultimately critical of the principle of the I, the inner agent of oppression. The subjective experience of art opposed to the I is a moment of the objective truth of art. Whoever, in contrast, experiences artworks by relating them to himself, does not experience them at all; what is taken to be experience is in fact a surrogate that is culturally palmed off in its place. (ÄT 364–65/AT 245–46)

Art is not identified with nature, but becomes able to speak for it. It does so by virtue of its opposition to the principle of subjective reason, by calling subjective experience into question. This is the reason for Adorno's insistence that what he at different points within his œuvre refers to as aesthetic or artistic experience does not involve simply relating the artwork to oneself: such an act of relating is necessarily preformed in accordance with the constraints of identity thinking.[31] The experience of art in its fullest, emphatic sense is opposed to the I insofar as it calls into question—that is to say, forces the subject to call into question—the primacy of conceptual thought. Hence the emphasis Adorno places on the nonsubjective character of the experience of art, nonsubjective insofar as it is something that happens to the subject rather than being in the strict sense of the subject's own making.[32] Form is thus not only the location and ground of the distinction between the beauty of the artwork that of nature, but also of their profound connection. For form is the index of a specific kind of making, a making through technique that is attuned to the requirements of the material. It is the mark of a madeness through which nature speaks.

This conception of form thus provides a resolution to what seems to be a contradiction that arises within this understanding of the emancipatory promise of art, and particularly within the ability of art to speak for and on behalf of oppressed nature. For if the idea of nature is what is free from (or more strongly, opposed to) the mediation of the human will, the question arises as to how it is that art, which, as was made clear in the previous chapter, depends on the human mastery of artistic material, can come to speak for it. How, in other words, can an act of domination plausibly claim to speak for the oppressed? Form is the mark of a domination which is not the willful exercise of subjective power, but in which objectivity exerts a hold over the subject. This interpretation sheds light on Adorno's account of the transition from natural beauty to art beauty, which he describes as dialectical insofar as it is 'a transition of domination'. 'Artistically beautiful is that in the image which is objectively mastered which can transcend mastery on account of its objectivity' (ÄT 120/AT 77). The significance—one could perhaps even say the end—of the process of mastery of artistic material discussed in the previous chapter thus comes into sharper focus. It is not an end in itself, it does not work toward an attitude in the recipient, like the committed work, but rather seeks to 'transform the aesthetic comportment which receives the naturally beautiful into a form of productive labor modelled on material labor' (ÄT 120/AT 77). The experience of art, that is, is presented as far removed from the leisure associated with the experience of nature, but as an activity that involves something akin to labor.[33] And yet it remains radically different from the abstract labor of the value form, which remains indifferent to the particularity of that on which it is expended.

The link between art and nature thus goes beyond the shared aesthetic comportment that is at work in the experience of both, and consists in art's desire 'once again to reach that which becomes more obscure to humans in the language of nature' (ÄT 120/AT 77). The apparent paradox lies in the fact that art's attempt to realize this desire consists not in striving to restrict the scope of human domination, but rather, conversely, in the 'extension of the field of human domination to the extreme' (ÄT 120/AT 77). Artworks posit the existence of a sphere that is free from domination, that exists in and for itself. And they do so as the result or manifestation of domination themselves—of a subjective human making over which the objective material nonetheless holds sway. Form testifies to the fact that such a making need not be the subordination of nature to the logic of means and ends, but can result in an artifact that calls into question the illusion of enlightenment subjectivity. Form thus sheds light on Adorno's oblique claim that the artwork's act of positing of a sphere that is free from domination 'separates itself from real domination precisely through its posited immanence, and thereby negates this domination in its heteronomy' (ÄT 120/AT 77). Form is the mark of a domination that by its attunement to what it dominates is oriented toward the suspension of domination.

Form thus offers reflects and condenses Adorno's understanding of the dual character of artworks as autonomous structures and social phenomena—on the one hand they consist in 'unconscious writing of history, anamnesis of the defeated, of the repressed, perhaps of the possible' (ÄT 384/AT 259), on the other they have a 'monadological constitution' (ÄT 269/AT 180). As the writing of history, artworks, by virtue of their 'inner historicity, sedimented memorized history' (ÄT 133/AT 86), display an undeniable and indelible link to the society in which they are created. As monads—'forcefield and thing in one'—they present themselves as self-sufficient and closed off from this external world, which they nonetheless represent (ÄT 268/AT 179). Their monadological character asserts its isolation from the world, its existence for its own sake, its refusal to comply with the logic of validation according to externally defined, heteronomous criteria. They stand opposed to the functional, instrumental rationality of means and ends. This is the posited sphere that is free from domination. At the same time, their historical character foregrounds not only a link to the social relations in which they exist, but also their madness—that is to say, the fact that they are a result of human domination.

Form brings together these two aspects, rendering them thinkable together. As the unique form of the singular work it reflects the monadological constitution; as something that is stretched out across multiple works (whether in formal properties that subsist across multiple works or in the collectively honed forms in which they are grouped together) it reflects art's sociality. It is the mark of a making that exhibits an unbreakable connection to the social production of goods, but at the same time opens up a clearing that is set apart from the instrumental rationality of this very production. This is the sense in which the extension of this field of domination can at the same time negate heteronomy: for the domination that is extended, a domination attuned to the requirements of the material, culminates in a form that offers resistance to domination. This further develops the discussion in the second chapter of Adorno's suspension of the opposition of mimesis and technique by means of the insistence that the mimetic comportment of artworks consists in their attempt, realized via technique, to make themselves similar to nature. Form is the manifestation of this technique.

Form thus represents a reconfiguration of spirit or mind with nature, a transformation of the damaged reality in which they are thought of as fundamentally opposed to one another:

> In artworks spirit is no longer the old enemy of nature. Spirit mellows until it is able to reconcile. Nature does not signify reconciliation in the classicist sense: reconciliation is its mode of behavior that becomes aware of the nonidentical. Spirit does

not identify the nonidentical, it uses it to identify itself. By pursuing its own identity with itself, art makes itself the same as the nonidentical: that is the contemporary stage of its mimetic essence. (ÄT 202/AT 134)

Human spirit is initially defined as radically opposed to nature. The argument of *Dialectic of Enlightenment* charts its development into a godlike 'ruler of nature' (DA 25/DE 6), a development which is further disenchanted when this spirit is construed as intelligence or intellect. Artworks call this opposition into question by virtue of the status of their material as 'sedimented subject' (ÄT 248/AT 166) which as art seeks not to dominate nature but to become like it. Indeed, Adorno insists that artistic spirit is not only radically opposed to but even the 'negation of the spirit that dominates nature'. As such it 'does not appear as spirit', but 'ignites in what is opposed to it', in materiality or prespiritual mimesis (ÄT 180/AT 118). This ignition—the process whereby spirit comes to appear as something other than what it is—consists in its adapting to that which it works, the apparent necessity of artistic form discussed in the second and third chapters. The origin of form in content and material is the mark of this adaptation.

Art's resemblance of nature is thus founded on anything but an attempt to become a sort of surrogate for or slavish imitation of the natural world, the 'pseudomorphosis of art into nature' in Adorno's terms (ÄT 120/AT 77). Indeed, artworks attain their proximity to nature by refusing precisely this:

> The more strictly artworks abstain from *Naturwüchsigkeit* and the illustration of nature, the more closely successful artworks approach nature. Aesthetic objectivity, the reflection of nature's being-in-itself, merely implements the subjectively teleological moment of unity; it is only in this way that artworks come to resemble nature. (ÄT 120/AT 77)

Aesthetic objectivity is used here as a synonym for the appearance of necessity within the artwork. This accounts for the peculiar relationship between subjectivity and objectivity. Artistic subjectivity appears to be governed by a predefined teleology. The 'moment of unity' refers to that which is expressed by 'the identity of the linguistic form' (ME 228/AE 227), that is to say the identity of the subjective and the objective (ÄT 245/AT 164). Its implementation within the artwork consists in the fact that that which appears as necessary is at the same time entirely subjective. Hence the ability of something apparently radically other to nature to resemble it: the freedom of the will appears as no less necessary than nature, as in the discussion of mimesis in the second chapter. By resembling nature precisely by virtue of their human madeness—as sedimented in their form—artworks are thus products of human creation that refuse the radical separation of the human from nature, the hard distinction between subject and object.

Priority of the Object

This overcoming of the hard separation of subject and object is of course at the heart of Adorno's philosophical project, and particularly in the account of the priority of the object as set out in particular in *Negative Dialectics* and in the oblique, enigmatic, and highly condensed late essay 'On Subject and Object'. As Adorno makes clear, in this essay, the priority of the object is not the restoration of 'the old *intentio recta*, the slavish faith in the external world that as is such as it appears this side of critique' (S 746/CM 249). This priority is, as Brian O'Connor observes, 'not a matter of giving to the object what the idealist tradition par excellence had given to the subject', but rather means 'the progressive qualitative differentiation of that which is mediated in itself, a moment in the dialectic, not beyond it, but articulating itself within it' (ND 185/Ashton 184), and is 'only attainable by means of subjective reflection, and reflection on the subject' (ND 186/Ashton 185).[34] This dual reflection that lies at the heart of Adorno's immanent critique of metaphysics, a reflection that is both on the subject and on the part of the subject, strongly resembles the making that is embodied in artistic form. Much like the comportment that characterizes the consistency of aesthetic *métier*, this reflection is neither active nor passive, but takes place as it were within the middle voice, all the time both reflecting and reflected upon.[35]

The theory of the priority of the object makes explicit and further develops something that Adorno identifies in Marx's critique of political economy, and in particular in the analysis of the commodity with which he opens the first chapter of *Capital*, in which 'is expressed the difference between the priority of the object as something that is to be produced critically, and its grimace in that which is, its distortion through the commodity character' (ND 190/Ashton 190). The theory of the priority of the object is thus the correlate within the critique of actually existing metaphysics of Marx's critique of the violence done to reality by the imposition onto it of economic categories. Moreover, this metaphysics is that of an illusory and deceptive semblance: 'Strictly speaking priority of the object would mean that there is no object as something that is abstractly opposed to the subject, but that it necessarily appears as such; the necessity of this appearance ought to be removed' (S 754/CM 255). The account of the priority of the object sets its sights on this necessity.

However, as an account of the relationship between subject and object, it remains bound to the dialectical relationship between subject and object:

> The priority of the object, of something that is nevertheless itself mediated, does not break off the subject–object dialectic. Immediacy is no more beyond dialectic than mediation. (ND 187/Ashton 186)

Rather than putting a stop to the subject–object dialectic, the priority of the object at once enables and results from its immanent critique. In Adorno's terms, 'it is through the transition to the priority of the object that dialectic becomes materialist' (ND 193/Ashton 192). And as immanent critique it is committed to investigating the implications of the distinction between the concepts of subject and object and the realities that they obscure: as Adorno recognizes, even in its most materialist, dialectical conception, object 'is a terminological mask' for the nonidentical of which it is the positive expression (ND 193/Ashton 192). As such the priority of the object is a formulation of the limits of what can be thought by means of the concepts of metaphysics, even after they have gone through their most thorough critical rethinking.

Even (or indeed especially) after this critique, the theory of the priority of the object is presented in highly enigmatic and cryptic formulations such as the assertion that it is 'the *intentio obliqua* of *intentio obliqua*' (S 747/CM 250)—that is to say, that the focus of cognition on the image of the object as it is construed the understanding (rather than in itself) is itself contemplated in the form of the image in which it is construed by the understanding. In this respect the priority of the object is not so much its unveiling as the recognition that it is doubly veiled; mediation is not removed to reveal immediacy, but recognized as itself subject to mediation. So when Rose criticizes Adorno for being 'under the spell' of the dialectic, unable to make the transition from dialectical to speculative thinking, she is in danger of mistaking Adorno's immanent critique of metaphysics, the attempt to prove the limits of the concepts of metaphysics, for their uncritical endorsement.[36] In doing so she neglects the fact that, as Jarvis argues, the most condensed and enigmatic formulations of Adorno's materialism 'do not solve a problem, but define a task'.[37]

This task involves dismantling the apparent power of the constitutive subject, and in particular breaking down its sense of the necessity of its classification of everything that it itself is not under the rubric of object. In Adorno's terms, 'the priority of the object gleams through at the points where subjective reason senses subjective contingency' (S 752/CM254)—at the points, that is, where the subject recognizes the illusory character of what it otherwise conceives of as its own necessity as such. And one such point is in the experience of nature:

> What is beautiful in nature is what appears as more than what it literally is. Without receptivity there would be no such objective expression, but it does not reduce itself to the subject; what is beautiful in nature points toward the priority of the object in subjective experience. It is perceived at once as something necessarily binding and as something incomprehensible that quizzically awaits its resolution. (ÄT 111/AT 70-71)

In this account natural beauty is experienced by the subject, but in such a way that is neither reduced to nor incorporated into the subject: it is experienced by the subject, as foreign to the subject. This presence of something foreign within subjective experience, in such a way that its foreignness is preserved, even accentuated, serves as a nonconceptual gesture that discloses to the subject the limits of its own power. Specifically, the combination within natural beauty of the known and the unknowable, the logical coherence of necessity and the incomprehensibility of something that seeks resolution but never finds it. This is consistent with the Kantian relation of aesthetic judgment to the powers of cognition, and in particular with the account of the judgment of taste whereby instead of the resolution attained when a reflective judgment of cognition finds the universal from a given particular, the forces of cognition are set into play, and the state of disposition in the experience of beauty 'must be that of a feeling of the free play of the forces of imagination'.[38]

This subjective experience of something nonsubjective is not itself the priority of the object, but points toward it. In doing so it also points beyond the obliquity that results from the attempt to probe the limits of metaphysics within its very own terms. Moreover, Adorno insists that the combination of logicality and incomprehensibility within the beauty of nature is the respect in which art beauty has most in common with the beauty of nature. In his continuation, he identifies the complication of the relationship between subject and object as one of the sites of closest connection between art and nature:

> Very little of the beautiful in nature has been transposed onto artworks as completely as this double character. In its terms, art is, rather than imitation of nature, imitation of what is beautiful in nature. It grows with the allegorical intention that it evinces without decoding it; with meanings which—unlike in intentional language—do not objectify themselves. (ÄT 111/AT 71)

Artworks are thus human-made objects—products of a kind of social labor—that have in common with natural beauty that they are experienced as logical and inexplicable, and therefore as subjective and nonsubjective. They thus appear as human creations that have—not completely, but to an extent—escaped the instrumental logic of ends and means (and with it both the logic of exchange that pertains to the commodity and the significative, classifying logic of the concept) and attained a kind of independence from the subjective human endeavor by means of which they are made. As such the ontology of the artwork offers an alternative to and thus gestures to a way past the strictures of metaphysics (strictures in which the immanent critique of metaphysics so often appears to remain confined), toward an interaction with the world that is not based on the subjective mastery of everything that is external to and (therefore) other than itself.

This challenge to the hypostatization of subject and object resonates with my description of the consistency of artistic *métier* at the beginning of the previous section as a comportment that is attuned to the requirements of the material that is worked. Artworks are products of an endeavor that is not wholly subjective, a working of artistic material that is in no sense indifferent to its demands, but rather characterized by middle-voiced attunement of the artist who is not fully subject to a material that is never solely object. In the making of the artwork its material exerts its priority over its creator, who creates, hones in a manner in accordance with what is experienced not only as the objective necessity of the law of form, but also as the requirements or demands of the material that is being worked. And then, as if imbued with some mystical property as a result of this making, it continues to express its priority over the person who experiences it as artwork, as agency, as power. The artwork is an object, that is, that—from before the moment of its completion, before its consummation as an object, perhaps even from before its conception as an object—is never experienced solely or wholly as object. It thus reveals the falsity both of artworks' categorization as object, and of the category of object as such, as defined in abstract opposition to the subject.

This dual priority of the artwork over the subject lies at the heart of the web of conceptual recursions and reciprocal interactions that lie at the heart of the constellation of form as explored in the first four chapters of this book, and brought together within this chapter. Form contains within itself the contrast discussed in the introduction to this chapter between the account of form's origin as the sedimentation of content in the first chapter, and that of the recursive process that emerges from the discussion of material in the fourth, according to which material becomes form which in turn becomes material, and in which material is the object to be worked by the subject, but nonetheless exerts power over the subject. Moreover, as discussed in the account of the mediation of form in the third section of this chapter, form contains such a recursion within itself, insofar as it is both that which mediates content, and the result of that process of mediation within the form of the individual work: in the words of the claim that was quoted in the discussion of the relationship between form and content in the first chapter, 'the form which befalls content is itself sedimented content; it is this, and not the regression to preartistic ideas of content, that makes the priority of the object in art what it is' (ÄT 217/AT 144-45). The complexities and apparent slippages within the concept of form reveal something of the way in which the experience of the artwork (both in its making and in its reception) eludes the concepts with which we might usually attempt to grasp it; these slippages are examples of Jameson's claim that the categories of aesthetics 'carry within themselves, and within their empty conceptuality, the sedimented experience of specific historical works as such'.[39]

The tensions within the concepts of aesthetics reveal something real about the experience of artworks. They appear as conceptual slippages because of the refusal of aesthetic experience to fit neatly into the concepts of traditional metaphysics. This helps account for the fact that form appears to be able to explain the phenomenon that artworks seem to function as kind of vector of power. It is not only the case that works of art appear to transfer or convey the agency of their makers onto those who experience them: their makers' agency is also combined and complicated by the power that the material exerts over the maker in the form of an attuned, consistent technique or *métier*. Form effects this explanation. And it does so in a way that is at once misleading (because it conflates diverse phenomena by subsuming them under a single concept) and true (because their diversity comes about as the result of a process of real abstraction). The urgent question posed by the examination of form, the question of how to make life imitate art, is also the question of how to expand the middle-voiced making that is attuned to the requirements of the material out of a particular sphere that is separated off from the life of social interaction and the mutual satisfaction of needs and that thus appears as epiphenomenal to that life—of how, that is, to generalize this middle-voiced, attuned comportment to all aspects of a fulfilling life of social interaction.

Coda

Lyric, Form, Society

> Critique is an indispensable element of a culture, which is in itself contradictory; in all untruth still as true as culture is untrue.
>
> —P 15/WWN 22

Lyric

In his 1957 talk on lyric and society, Adorno advances the thesis that lyric work, whatever else it is, 'is always also the subjective expression of a social antagonism' (NzL 58/NtL 1: 45). This 'also', missing in Nicholsen's translation, is significant insofar as it emphasizes that Adorno here is not identifying lyric with the expression of social antagonism, but drawing attention to one aspect of the work it carries out. The antagonism expressed is that of the world in which lyric comes to exist. As such, lyric is not identical with 'the expression of subjectivity, to which language grants objectivity' (NzL 58/NtL 1: 45), but also testifies to the objective social conditions of this antagonistic world. Moreover, in lyric this expression is given objective form: the 'specific paradox' of lyric work consists in the fact that it embodies the transformation of subjectivity into objectivity (NzL 56/NtL 1: 43). The cause of this paradox is the 'primacy of the structure of language in lyric' (NzL 56/NtL 1: 43), which Adorno argues is the source from which the primacy of language in all literature stems. Lyric is thus presented as, to a certain extent, exemplary for all literature.[1] The poetic incorporation of the subject and its expression into language discussed in the first chapter is not a reduction of lyric to the expression of a transcendental subject that has been abstracted from individual, living humans (cf. S 744/CM 247), but a transformation of the possibility of what can be done with language.

Adorno emphasizes the consequences for lyric of language's sign character, its tendency that is at once universalizing and social, and its connection to the human language of names and its instrumental logic of signification and identity. Within the linguistic artwork subjective expression comes up against this sign character:

> The highest literary works are thus those in which the subject, with no remains of mere matter, resounds in language until language itself becomes loud. The self-forgetting of the subject that commits itself to language as to something objective, and the immediacy and spontaneity of that subject's expression, are one and the same: language thus mediates lyric and society at their innermost core. (NzL 56/NtL 1: 43)

This argument is familiar from the discussion of the incorporation of subjective expression into language in 'Parataxis'. Here Adorno insists on the social aspect of this process. The erasure of subjectivity by making language into something objective is the flip-side of the illusion of immediate subjective expression. They are equivalent insofar as neither recognizes the extent to which subjectivity and language are bound up with one another. The mediation of lyric and society takes place in its most pronounced form at those points where 'the subject whose expression is successful itself attains parity with language, with the inherent aims of language' (NzL 56/NtL 1: 43). Adorno thus calls into question what Jonathan Culler has identified as 'the dominant pedagogical paradigm that sees lyric as fundamentally dramatic monologues'.[2] Lyric rejects a pragmatic model of communicative language, and in doing so reveals the possibility of a language that is adequate to subjective expression. Adorno insists that subjective expression—which he distinguishes from the 'mere signification of objective contents' (NzL 57/NtL 1: 44)—is not a supplement to linguistic objectivity, but inheres within it. 'Language only comes to speak of its own accord when it no longer speaks as something alien to the subject but as the subject's own voice' (NzL 57/NtL 1: 44).

The talk on lyric and society thus provides as it were a complement to the argument of the essay on commitment, which further develops the discussion of the transformation of linguistic material in the fourth and fifth chapters. While 'Commitment' advances the thesis that artworks resist the logic of means and ends by claiming to stand for themselves, the talk makes an analogous claim for language within lyric poetry:

> Only by virtue of a differentiation that prospered to such an extent that it could no longer tolerate its own difference, that it could no longer tolerate anything other than the universal, freed from the ignominy of individualization, within the particular, does the lyrical word represent language's being-in-itself as opposed to its service in the kingdom of ends. (NzL 67/ NtL 1: 53)

Adorno's argument here is that the kingdom of ends—the Kantian formulation for a world in which people are treated as ends in themselves and not as means to the fulfilment of external ends—is incomplete as long as within it language is instrumentalized.[3] As the incorporation of subjective expression, language must be allowed to stand for itself. Such a freedom of language is necessary for the 'thought of free humanity'. This is the force of Adorno's claim in the closing sentences of the talk on lyric and society that the truth of Stefan George's work lies in the fact that 'his lyric beats down the walls of individuality in its consummation of the particular, in its sensibility of opposition to the banal as much as to the select' (NzL 67–68/ NtL 1: 54). That is, the emphasis on particularity in poetry, the expression of which 'concentrated itself in individual expression', gestures toward the possibility of 'the voice of humans between whom the barriers have fallen' (NzL 68/NtL 1:54).

This is the theoretical framework within which Adorno addresses Baudelaire's writing of lyric at a time when the administered world is in the ascendency over the subject, his 'heroically stylized language' characterizing a lyric that took the anti-lyricism of the modern as its theme, in which 'the contradiction between poetic and communicative language reached an extreme' (NzL 57/NtL 1: 44). In *Aesthetic Theory*, Adorno relates the subjectivity of Baudelaire's work to the status of the artwork within capitalist society. He claims that Baudelaire 'neither rails against nor depicts reification', but rather 'protests against it in the experience of its archetypes, and the medium of this experience is the poetic form' (ÄT 39/AT 21). He continues:

> That raises him imperiously above all late-romantic sentimentality. His work has its moment in its syncopation of the overwhelming objectivity of the commodity character, which sucks up all remains of the human, with the objectivity, prior to the living subject, of the work in itself: the absolute artwork meets the absolute commodity. (ÄT 39/AT 21)

In his discussion of these sentences, Stewart Martin defines the absolute commodity as the commodity from which all use value has been stripped away, a 'pure exchange-value'.[4] This resounds with Adorno's claim that 'under monopoly capitalism, it is largely exchange value that is enjoyed, and no longer use value' (ÄT 39/AT 21).[5] Precursors to this claim can be found in Adorno's work as early as 1938, particularly in the essay on the fetish character of music, in which he argues that in the world of commodities the cultural sphere 'appears to be an exception to the power of exchange', that its goods appear free from mediation. This semblance of freedom from exchange is itself brought about by the very exchange value of cultural goods that it comes to hide: 'The semblance of immediacy usurps what is mediated, exchange value itself' (D 25/CI 34). The enjoyment of exchange value as opposed to use value in culture consists most visibly in the public valuation of singing voices according to which they become 'sacred like a trademark', or of the Stradivarius or Amati (D 23/CI 32–33). 'The consumer worships the money that he has spent on the ticket for the Toscanini concert' (D 24–25/CI 34).

It is notable here that Adorno interprets this phenomenon in terms of the distinction between use value and exchange value. The use value that is no longer enjoyed in art stands for the qualitative character of artworks, that which is thought in opposition to commodity fetishism, regardless of whether it may in any sense be considered useful. This illuminates the claim in *Aesthetic Theory* that 'Baudelaire's poetry was the first to codify that in a fully developed commodity society, art can only look on powerlessly as that society develops' (ÄT 39/AT 21). And it also accounts for the significance of the claim in the draft introduction to *Aesthetic Theory* that art 'relapses into fetishism, becomes a blind end in itself, and exposes itself as untrue' (ÄT 506/AT 340). The relapse consists in art's assumption of a fetish character that it can only take on by virtue of artworks' movement away from their fetishism as ritual objects. Artworks 'were elements of a praxis which wanted to influence nature, separated themselves from it in the beginnings of rationality, and gave up the deception of real influence' (ÄT 210/AT 139). The demise of use value represents the completion of the process of development of art away from cultic ritual—the abandonment of one fetish character gives way to the assumption of another.

At the same time, this second fetish character is central not only to the role of artworks within society, but also to their existence as artworks:

> But on the other hand the truth of all artworks would not exist without that fetishism that proceeds to become their untruth. The quality of artworks essentially depends on the extent of their

fetishism, on the veneration paid by the process of production to what is self-made, to the seriousness that forgets the enjoyment of it. It is only through fetishism, the blinding of the artwork to the reality of which it is itself part, that the work transcends the spell of the reality principle as something spiritual. (ÄT 506/AT 341)

The untruth Adorno invokes here is what he terms a 'collective hallucination' (ÄT 506/AT 340), which arises when art's truth content begins to waver. Such a wavering is presented as the result of a psychoanalytic conception of art as mere sublimation, a 'tool of the psychic economy' according to which it loses its connection to reality, to the world outside the psyche (ÄT 506/AT 340). That is, if art is reduced to nothing other than a quasi-therapeutic attempt to displace and desexualize sexual instincts, it becomes, contra Freud, mere semblance rather than a force for the development of culture.[6] This secondary fetish character of artworks—in Martin's terms, the fact that the artwork 'conceals the extent to which it is actually the product of social labor'—constitutes a close connection between artistic form and the commodity form.[7] Artworks are bound by their form to a reality that is socially mediated through the commodity form and relationships of exchange.

As discussed in the previous chapter, these relationships also imply that this fetish character is bound up with the conceptual character of language: in lyric it takes the particular form of the illusion that poetry is a particular category or example of language in general. While the fetish character hides the status of artworks as products of social labor, the sign character of language within lyric masks its distinction from communicative language. Kaufman's claim that lyric's special role derives from the 'otherwise almost unremarkable fact that, as a formal matter, lyric maintains a special relation to the presumptive medium for significantly communicable conceptuality: language' thus requires further determination.[8] It is less that lyric has a 'special relation' to conceptual language than that conceptual language is a moment within lyric, a moment without which lyric would be impossible. In Caygill's terms, lyric poetry 'is possible because of the process of mutual reflection between subject and object, individual and collective, expressive and communicative language'.[9] The possibility of lyric consists in the tension inherent in giving objective form to subjective expression, in enabling communicative language to do more than communicate.

In the essay on commitment, Adorno famously remarks on a difference between literary language and the language of communication:

> If no word that enters a literary work rids itself entirely of the meanings that it possesses in communicative speech, it is also the case that in no work, even in the traditional novel, does this meaning remain the same as that which the word had outside. Even the simple 'was' in a report of something that was not takes on a new formal quality by means of the fact that it was not. (NzL 410/NtL 2: 77)

Literature—Adorno uses the term *Dichtung* here—is neither identical with nor wholly distinct from language as it is used in communication. The 'new formal quality' that words take on—the German is *Gestaltqualität*, referring at least as much to the shape or form of the word itself as to its contribution to the form of the work as a whole—is inextricably linked to the content of the work, the status of the words and sentences and substantial content of the work rather than the literal meaning. A concrete example can be found in Adorno's remarks on Trakl in *Aesthetic Theory* in which the verb to be is 'alienated in the artwork from its conceptual sense' (ÄT 187/AT 123). As I discussed in chapter 2, Adorno claims that the copula resists the judgment of identification such that it comes to mean its other. But the conceptual, communicative meaning of words does not disappear within artworks:

> In poems, the rudiments of meanings from outside are the inalienably nonartistic in art. Art's law of form is not to be derived from them, but from the dialectic of both moments. (NzL 411/NtL 2: 77–78)

The law of form, that is, comes about as a result of the mediation and reciprocal implication of art and non-art, expression and communication, particular and universal, subject and object. Form is thus a dialectical concept in the strict sense that it both encapsulates and depends on the unreconciled character of the society in which it appears. To this extent Adorno's poetics of form might be thought of as a poetics of the wrong state of things, a poetics that refuses to lose sight of the possibility that things might one day be different.

This is a poetics according to which it is the case not only that artworks distinguish themselves from and reject the instrumental logic of exchangeability of the mediation of social life through the commodity form, but also that the analysis and above all theorization of works of art can point toward a reconfiguring of the ground of social life through an attuned and receptive comportment toward the world. The interrogation of the concept of form begins to reveal the complex ways not only in which we think about, analyze and theorize works of art, but also in which we relate to them, in which they seem to hold sway of us from the beginnings of their making—and it does so by unpicking and making explicit some of the implicit knowledge embedded within works of art. This includes the makers' knowledge of the material that they work and of its requirements (poetics in the long-established sense of the exposition of the principles of poetic composition and artistic making more generally), but also admits the broader questions of what artworks can reveal about the world, and of what the concepts with which we think about artworks reveal about our relation to them and to their worlds.

Engaging Form

In this respect the analyses and arguments I have developed this book have a great deal in common with both the concerns and the aims of the new or strategic formalism. To return to and expand a formulation discussed in the opening section of my introduction, Kornbluh characterizes this formalism as 'a kind of "social close reading" blending deconstructive techniques and the best historicist impulses to explore the intellectual and political force of literary forms that do not reiterate a preexisting world, but rather limn, ironize, and even unmake forms of worlding'.[10] This blend dissents both from 'the historicist's reduction of literature to discourse' and from the deconstructive 'autonomy of language from logic or meaning', instead attending to the manifestations of literary (and specifically realist fictional) technique within the specificity of the nineteenth-century economy in working to 'encounter the material and process of literary thinking'.[11] At the center of Kornbluh's study is the 'contemplative agency leveraged by literature'; her endeavor presents itself as a formalism in the sense that it attends to and offers an account of 'literary form's critical thinking about the historically specific material and conceptual question of finance': it analyzes both 'figurative language' and 'formal structures of literary self-reflexivity such as irony and satire as modes of critical inquiry that convey not just the mechanics of their tropes, but their effects in any world'.[12] This is a formalism in anything but the traditional sense rejected by Wolfson 'of an ideologically toned disciplinary commitment that prioritizes and privileges form in relation to other possible locations of value'.[13]

This concern with the complex ways in which literary form relates to effects in its worlds is what distinguishes Kornbluh's approach not only from this traditional formalism, but also from that of a deconstruction which is unwilling or unable to bridge the gap between the text and its worlds: 'where some versions of deconstructive literary criticism might circumscribe the functions of language within the context of a given reading, or of a text reading itself, it strikes me as necessary, in the case of the realist novel (the aesthetic mode whose specificity is its mediation of realities and of worldliness; the aesthetic mode less commonly studied by deconstructive critics), to attend to the ways that realism strategically reveals the work of tropes in worlds'.[14] In this respect, insofar as this version of formalism is characterized by its commitment to 'close reading', it is committed to a reading that is never only close, that always aspires to trace its implications beyond its starting point, both on a larger literary scale, and beyond the bounds of the literary work.[15] Indeed, Kornbluh conceives of form as the connections 'between the voices, plots, temporalities, and images that are mobilized within one bounded work': it pertains to the single work, but looks and points beyond it.[16] In a phrase that she takes from Wolfson, she argues that form 'wields a conceptual agency—an agency for assembling concepts while simultaneously defamiliarizing them—for relating without reifying, for weaving a loose and gossamer web', but distinguishes her approach in that whereas Wolfson is concerned with 'the way form shapes perceptions and critical thinking', the target of her own investigation is 'the way form thinks'.[17] That is, whereas for Wolfson form is a prompt for us to think differently, for Kornbluh literary form is itself a site where thinking takes place.

I share the concern with both the ways in which form itself thinks and the ways in which it shapes our thinking—and, just as importantly, with the relationship between these two questions. However, my interrogation within this book of Adorno's deployment of form differs from both these undertakings in that what both Wolfson and Kornbluh's characterizations of their investigative concern have in common is a certainty as to what form is, a certainty on which the ability to ask the questions of how it thinks and how it shapes our thinking depends. For as I have argued throughout this book, these questions are in fact bound up with the internal constitution of the concept of form: how form thinks and how form shapes our thinking are functions of the conception of what form is, what distinguishes it as form, how it becomes form, and above all on the particular combination of phenomena that are brought together, combined, condensed, or even conflated under the rubric of this single elusive term. The capacity of the concept of form to describe or explain otherwise apparently inexplicable, even mystical phenomena depends on the particular configuration of the concept that is appealed to.

In particular, the investigation of the constellation of form against the other concepts that exist around it, the concepts from which Adorno distinguishes form and those to which he relates it, reveals that what appears as the agency of form is closely connected if not directly attributable to the complex reciprocal and recursive connections that form makes. Form is thus a token or, better, a deposit for a wide range of connections between us and the worlds to which the work connects us: it lies at the nexus of these connections, frequently without making transparent which of them is operational at any given time. It is thus able to serve as kind of opaque junction box or function machine that seems to be able to explain or account for a wide range of phenomena—but frequently it does so at the cost of obscuring the particular connections on which it is drawing at any given time. From this follows the importance of setting out a complementary narrative to Kornbluh's investigation of how literary 'form seeks out connections where there were none, charts dislocations where there were destinations, re-presents what has been all too present.'[18] Such a complementary narrative aspires to seek out and reveal these connections by accounting for the discrepancies and tensions in the configuration of the concept of form. In doing so it not only further complicates the explanatory work of form, but also strives to locate the correlate of the resulting complications in the actually existing heteronomy of the existing social relations.

One instance where it becomes possible to develop such a complementary narrative is Kornbluh's discussion of what she terms 'formal disruptions', the 'strange moments in which the text is conspicuously self-reflexive', such as result from 'an excessively meddlesome narrator's mediation of the affections between characters and readers' in *Middlemarch*.[19] Within these disruptions can be found an analogue or motivated connection between the work and its worlds:

> These moments formalize the self-reflexive pattern of financial 'interest,' money generating more of itself. As these recurrent, extra-diegetic moments break the frame of the narrative, they reverberate with ironic energy, accentuating the metaphoric contrivance of the sympathetic economy.[20]

This theorization of some of the diverse ways in which literary works think about, respond to, and engage with the changing world gestures toward an account of how we can learn from literature in making interventions into this world. It does so by means not primarily of an analysis of the content or plot represented within (in this case) *Middlemarch*, charting the novel's preoccupation with gifts, loans, debts, usury, and interest in its setting in the run-up to the Charter Act of the 1830s, but rather by attending closely to shifts in the deployment of key tropes and figures within the book. Kornbluh's particular attention is directed to the 'economy of sympathy', which develops from a reference to a scarcity of goods and comes to connote 'an expansive financial horizon', to the interventions of narrative voice (in particular through its recoding of '"sympathy" as "interest"'), and to those self-reflexive moments of excess where the narrator steps outside what appear as the formal constraints of the rôle or function.[21]

These analyses gesture toward ways in which the reading and theorization of literature can indicate potential points of intervention into the social form, in particular by means of the questioning and destabilization of the 'psychic economy' that 'crystallizes one of the pivotal ideologies of modernity'.[22] As such Kornbluh goes beyond the classical Marxist account of the revolutionary political potential of novelistic realism as encapsulated by Engels's praise of Balzac as a 'master of realism' for his 'truthful reproduction of typical characters under typical circumstances' or Marx's of the nineteenth-century English novelists 'whose graphic and eloquent pages have issued to the world more political and social truths than have been uttered by all the professional politicians, publicists and moralists put together'.[23] For her account of Victorian form goes beyond the literary expression of moral and political truths, identifying ways in which form can (help us) identify potential interventions into society. In this respect form opens up new ways of thinking the social world and the possibility of our intervening into it.

On the one hand, the argument I have sought to develop within this book shares Kornbluh's concern with the capacity of literary works to intervene into the world, with the resulting social and political implications of the study and theorization of these works, and with the emphasis on the manifestations of the artistic and literary technique by means of which they are made as well as on the worlds that are represented within them. On the other hand, the conception of form that is deployed within her account contains within itself a certain tension or flexibility that is revealed by close attention to its contrasting meanings at different points in its deployment within the explanation. For what is described as the formalization of the 'self-reflexive pattern of financial "interest"' seems to refer less to the codification or institutionalization of this pattern than to its incorporation into the literary work. Meanwhile, what characterizes form as such—and in particular the 'formal disruptions', the 'recurrent, extra-diegetic moments' that 'break the frame of the narrative'—is that it is itself 'conspicuously self-reflexive'.

This formalization is thus the shaping or transposition of a phenomenon in the world represented within the novel into a self-reflexive effect within a literary work. But what is significant about this phenomenon is that it is itself already described as a 'self-reflexive pattern', before the event of the formalization that is its transposition into the literary work—this formalization, that is to say, the artistic making of which form is the mark, is the making self-reflexive of something that is itself already self-reflexive. The concepts of formalization and form at work here thus contain within themselves a kind of doubling or fold, whereby two different kinds of self-reflexivity are brought together: the self-reflexivity of the phenomenon of interest (a manifestation of surplus or commodity-producing labor) is brought into connection with that of the literary device (a manifestation of literary technique). Form thus serves here as a nexus not only between the work and the world, but also between two kinds of activity and the complex and sometimes apparently supernatural ways in which their products take shape.

Form plays a somewhat different role in Kornbluh's consideration of questions raised in *Great Expectations* by the tension within Pip's apostrophized expression of remorse toward the absent Joe, and its contrast to the absence of any explicit apology:

> Why does Joe receive an apology in the *form* of narrative, but not *within* the narrative. Why might Joe be 'you who read this,' but never be he who hears it?[24]

Here the appeal to form foregrounds the difference between the narrative and the events that it describes. It draws attention to the agency of narrative technique by helping to isolate it, to distinguish it from Pip's actions, and thus to accentuate the tension between the sentiments of remorse and the absence of apology. Thus the narrative as a whole functions as 'an act of counteraction, of atonement' and therefore of equilibrium, but in such a way that it focuses 'our eye on the remaining disequilibrium, the unspoken apologies to Joe'.[25] Form is used to make the distinction between the two spheres or fields—that of the narrative, and that of the events depicted within it—in order not only to highlight the contrast between the resolution in one and the irresolution in the other, but also (and as a result) to combine them. Form thus brings together these different, even incompatible worlds of the work of literature without effacing their particularity. In doing so it opens up the possibility of crossing between them.

This account of the tension between equilibrium in one sphere of the novel and disequilibrium in the other, between the narrative remorse and the fact that it never finds its expression in the form of an apology to Joe on the part of Pip, is itself a recursive effect that results from the technique of first-person narrative from the perspective of a single character within the events described. This technique enables the possibility of a dissociation within the single figure of Pip between that of the protagonist who interacts with the other characters and that of the narrator who conveys and mediates these interactions to the novel's readers, and thus between the acts described by the narrative and the (frequently divergent or inconsistent) intentions conveyed within it. Kornbluh's discussion, which proceeds on the basis that Joe might become 'you who read this', thus admits the possibility that this dissociation can be overcome, that Joe can traverse the barrier from the world of the characters to the world within which the novel's narrative is read. Form thus represents not only a nexus at which different worlds meet, but a bridge or portal that enables crossings to be made between them.

Beyond the New Formalism

In her 2015 book, Levine explores some of the implications of this account of form for the possibility of interventions into the world, arguing that 'if a new formalism has one lesson to offer it is this: a close analysis of contending and colliding hierarchies invites us to rethink effective political action'.[26] The claim here is not simply that the approaches, techniques, and habits of literary analysis can in some (unidentified) way be applied or deployed in such a way as to inform any attempts to identify, challenge, and redress injustice. More specifically, she argues that the examination of literature can serve to prompt and enable us better to understand how to intervene into society. Her argument proceeds from the conviction that there is a strong connection between reading literature and analyzing society, whether because literature and society can be read in the same way, or because literature and society share an affinity that enables them to be thought together in such a way that a decisive intervention becomes more easily thinkable. This conviction, furthermore, assumes a framework according to which literature is representative of the world—in such a way not only that this representation is accurate, that the forms of literature accurately represent the social and political forms of the world in such a way that literature can model society and therefore the potential for effective political action and positive social change, but also that literature and its analysis have some kind of reciprocal connection back to the world they represent, the world in which and into which they are made and sent, whereby this change can be efficacious. The site of this connection is form—the form of literature, and the form of society.

However, in Levine's conception the forms of literature are primarily the social and political forms—here the 'contending and colliding hierarchies'—that are represented in literature. The connection she theorizes between literature and society is thus not between social and literary form, but rather between social form and its literary representation. This underlying relationship of representation, correspondence and more or less direct interconnection between literature and the world somewhat undermines her characterization of her approach, according to which it 'looks not for a fit between literary forms and social facts [. . .] but rather for the ways in which social forms bring their logics with them into the novel, working both with and against literary forms and producing unexpected political conclusions out of their encounters'.[27] Such a formulation is reminiscent of her conviction discussed in the introduction 'that we now need new ways of connecting large and small, social flows and artistic objects' and her 'belief that *form* is going to be the way to do it'.[28] However, the 'literary forms' in this account refer specifically to the forms represented within the content of Elizabeth Gaskell's *North and South*, the 'irreconcilable spatial forms Gaskell invites into her novel', in which 'two different Norths and two different Souths and two different national unities contend for formal dominance'.[29] On closer inspection it becomes clear that Levine's underlying conception of literature as a representative model with a connection to the world it represents remains intact.

This becomes clearer still in her discussion of what Julia Sun-Joo Lee identifies as an 'ontological distress', a distress that Levine argues is 'precisely formal'.[30] For the evidence Lee provides for the distress she identifies not only does not come from any formal features or properties, however construed, of *North and South*—it does not in fact come from the novel at all, but from a letter to Charles Eliot Norton in which Gaskell describes herself as 'thoroughly *puzzled by* what is now going on in America'.[31] Levine construes this distress as formal in the sense that it 'grows out of the impossibility of resolving multiple political forms into a single containing unity', but it only pertains to the manifestations of literary technique in the most tangential manner: 'although we regularly call the formal phenomenon of a novel's ending its closure, what the novel imagines in its conclusion is really not an enclosure at all, but a *beginning*—the launching of a series of social and political relationships (a marriage, a set of alliances, investments, and meetings between management and labor) that have significance as a model for the nation precisely *because* they will endure beyond the narrative's end'.[32] The formal phenomenon to which Levine refers pertains to the relationships represented within the novel—and not to any particular way in which they are arranged or shaped, but rather to the fact that they are to persist beyond the novel's close.

Form serves within Levine's argument to forge links between things of a great variety of kinds, gathering them together under a single term. In her discussion of *The Wire* its plot is taken, without further discussion, to be a 'formal element' of the series, and narrative is described as an 'ideal form'.[33] There is no consideration, that is, of what it means to consider plot and narrative as form rather than in opposition to form (as is the case, for example, in my discussion in the fourth chapter of the distinction between content and material according to which what happens in a work is understood as the former), or reflection on what thinking of plot, say, specifically as form reveals either about plot or about form. This is an argument, then, in which it is not such much the case that anything can be thought of as form, as that everything—not only within but also beyond the work under consideration—is form. If for Leighton form is the 'sense of nothing', for Levine form can be the sense of anything.[34] And yet when her discussion turns, for example, to the elements or properties of the televisual genre or medium that render *The Wire* so suitable for her analysis, the term is avoided altogether: 'unlike many novels, no obtrusive omniscient narrator intervenes to tell us why something has happened, and since, like the novel but unlike conventional film, it has hours and hours and hours to unfold relationships'.[35] Indeed, this reference to length is the only cursory reference to what might be thought of as the formal properties of *The Wire* in this sense of the manifestations of medium-specific televisual technique that make themselves visible in generic or conventional features: there is no discussion of such matters as episodic structure, camera work, pace, length of seasons, broadcast time, casting, advertising and the like.

Levine's concentration is rather on the interactions between the social forms that are represented in *The Wire*, which 'gives us a social world constantly unsettled by the bewildering and unexpected effects of clashes among [*sic*] wholes, rhythms, hierarchies, and networks'.[36] Indeed, she praises the series for the complexity with which these forms and the changing relationships between then are represented, arguing, in a formulation reminiscent of Engels's assertion that in the works of Balzac can be found 'a most wonderfully realistic history of French "Society"', that *The Wire* 'is truly exceptional in its attention to the ways that multiple social forms unfold in relation to one another, their encounters producing serious, painful, and occasionally promising effects'.[37] This attention, meanwhile, is frequently described as if the analysis is taking place not in Levine's work, but in the work to which she is attending, such as when she refers to 'the particular affordances of fiction that elude conventional sociological scholarship': here the work of the new formalist seems to be to compete with the sociologist or social theorist to elucidate the analysis of society that is performed by the (in this instance televisual) work under consideration.[38]

This becomes more explicit when Levine acknowledges that her 'reading departs from Jameson's interest in genre to come much closer to that of sociologists like [William Julius] Wilson', as her discussion of *The Wire* comes to view its object not only as a representation of the world, but as a conceptually and analytically sophisticated feat of imagining and understanding the workings of the world.[39] Similarly, she praises *The Wire's* 'capacity to represent multiple forms operating at once, providing a serious analytical alternative to the usual scholarly attention to one or two forms at a time'.[40] Here *The Wire* is credited not only with the work of representation (which must then be analyzed), but also that of analysis. Levine's analysis of *The Wire* is conflated with the uncovering of *The Wire's* own analysis or even theorization, as she seeks 'to turn to David Simon's series for a theory of social forms'.[41] What is presented as a formalist reading of *The Wire* in fact becomes an argument that *The Wire* itself constitutes or carries out 'a reading of the social that is nothing other than a canny formalism'.[42] What is characterized as a formalism becomes a way of claiming or asserting an affinity between the study and the works studied, as if these works themselves are carrying out the analytical, conceptual, and theoretical work.

This is not specific to her discussion of television. Levine's is a model according to which the literary and cultural works under discussion are frequently described as analyzing as much as if not more than as analyzed. She refers, for example, to the success of the nineteenth-century novel in 'analyzing the complexity and power of networked social experience', arguing that '*Bleak House* invites a careful analysis of the ways that the time-bound form of narrative collides with the overlaying of multiple networks' and that in doing so 'Dickens makes brilliant use of the affordances of narrative form to conceptualize the ways that networks unfold temporally'.[43] Again, this has strong affinities with Marx and Engels's accounts of the political potential of the realist novel. For Levine, what Dickens provides is not only truthful reproduction or even the political and social truths that Marx finds in the nineteenth-century English novel, but also analysis and conceptualization. This shares with the Marxist account of artistic realism the assumption that literature's political potential consists in the accuracy of its representation of society, and that conclusions about interventions in literature can be applied to the nonliterary world, but it simultaneously goes beyond this account by attributing to literature a capacity to analyze.

Conclusion

There are three distinct procedures or components of these new formalist arguments to which I should like to draw attention. The first is that according to which, for the new formalist, there seems to be no limit to what can be thought as (a) form. Form can be identified within (and beyond) the wholes, rhythms, hierarchies, and networks of Levine's title: whether within the work of literature or culture that is under discussion or outside that work, within the worlds that are represented in the work, and within the worlds in which the work is made; whether pertaining to the what or the how of the work, to that which it represents, or to the manifestations of the repertoire of techniques deployed within its making. The second is that the equation of the forms of the world and those represented in the literary and cultural work presumes or posits a thinking of a connection between the work and the worlds it represents, which are taken to be comparable with the worlds in which we live. The third is the way in which this hybrid analysis–intervention is attributed to or deferred into the work under discussion, as if it is that work itself that conducts the formalist analysis which is presented as the precondition or even the manifestation of emancipatory social practice.

However, there are multiple problems with the conception of form that is at work in these accounts. The sheer capaciousness of the concept of form means that it frequently brings together diverse phenomena without acknowledging or accounting for their difference. Moreover, the identification of form as a link between the world represented within the work and the world into which we might wish to intervene seems to involve two kinds of fetish: first, the connection between the work and the world; and second, the connection between analyzing the work and intervening into the world. (It also raises the questions of whether and how such a new formalism is equipped to respond to nonrepresentative works.) At the same time, when form is used in this capacious way it loses sight of the specifically poetic aspects of form—its character as the mark of artistic making or technique—that I have frequently suggested are central to any account of the transformative potential of form. While the strength of the new formalist concept of form is that it can bring together so many diverse phenomena, it all too frequently does so at the cost of effacing their difference. More particularly, it can identify sites of self-reciprocity, of the agency of the work, and even of ways in which the work calls into question the structures of domination that characterize our lived heteronomy—but it cannot account for them.

The account of form I have developed in dialogue with Adorno offers a tentative explanation for the fact that form not only appears to present a way of theorizing the relationship between artworks and social change, and therefore a way of drawing on artworks and their analysis in order to lay the ground for more effective emancipatory political action, but also makes it appear as if artworks are themselves carrying out this theorization and clearing the way for such a political praxis. Through the optic of form, works of art and literature seem not only to carry out their own analysis but also to begin to investigate the implications of this analysis for interventions into the world. Form is able to function as such an optic precisely because of the complex structure that both enables and is revealed by the constellation carried out within the first four chapters of this book, according to which it constitutes a dense nexus of conceptual connections that lie at the heart of an equally dense set of artistic and social practices—practices of making, of reception, of analysis. The multiple kinds of conceptual and analytical work that form is able to carry out derive from the fact that it reflects and brings together diverse, complex, and often opposing aspects of the history of these practices. Form thus not only stands at but also stands for the complexity of the enigmatic human relationships with works of art.

In doing so form is able both to combine and to distinguish, to refer at once to the singularity of an individual work and to features that persist across multiple works, at once to manifestations of literary technique, to events represented within the internal world of the work, and to phenomena within our empirical reality, and thus to bring about and conceptualize their unity. The account of form I have developed in this book by means of close examination of Adorno's writings on literature—an account that is not so much historical as temporal and processual—indicates how these diverse and apparently incompatible phenomena can nonetheless consistently be thought together, under the rubric of form, without being conflated, without the erasure of what is differentiated in each of them. This investigation of form sheds light on the ways in which we experience multiple aspects of artworks as simultaneously the same and different. This is most clearly the case in the account of the determinate unity of form and content—form's shaping itself to content while content is transported into the work—in the first chapter, but is just as germane to the relationship between the work and the world, and that between the work itself and the work of analyzing it: for this relocation of analytical and theoretical work into the work itself is also a kind of partial recognition of the way in which art, as discussed in the previous chapter, is tasked with the continuation of the critical project that philosophy is no longer able to carry out.

The investigation of the implications of the constellation of form against the concepts to which it is opposed thus reveals that form is not only what Jürgen Ritsert, in his discussion of Adorno's concept of the nonidentical, terms a 'problem-concept'—a concept, that is, which 'presents a summarizing expression for a complex plenitude of philosophical *and* sociological *problems*'.[44] Whereas for Ritsert Adorno's concept of the nonidentical 'draws together the subliminal normative strata of the Adornian critique of tendencies toward the desubjectification of subjects in the modern world', form as it emerges from this study is not an encapsulation or deposit of prior knowledge or critique in the form of a concept, however complex or difficult.[45] Form rather expresses and implies (and frequently conceals) a great many unacknowledged ways of thinking about artworks and the ways in which we relate to them—ways of thinking which are only (and frequently partially) revealed by the excavation of the different ways in which the term is deployed. And these ways of thinking encapsulate the artwork as the result of a specific kind of making that refuses to submit to the instrumental logic that permeates everyday life. In this respect, form as it emerges is in many respects not a concept at all, at least not in the sense of a singular and consistently analyzable constituent of thought.

I should like to suggest that form has in common with concepts that it is a way of thinking, but that it does not congeal into the unity of a single concept. Indeed, it is a way of thinking that resists the limitations of conceptual thought as set out within Adorno's account of conceptuality, according to which concepts efface the particularity of the objects that never go into them without leaving a remainder. The resources of form as it emerges from critical examination of Adorno's writings on literature, and the potential it seems to show in the new formalist accounts of the relationship between art and society, come about precisely because it is never hypostatized into a single concept (in this account, Heidegger's objection in 'The Origin of the Work of Art' as discussed in the first chapter can be seen precisely as an objection to such a hypostatization into a 'concept of the thing that is equally pertinent to things of nature and things of use' which offers 'a conceptual mechanism that nothing can resist').[46] Whereas the form to which Heidegger objects is one that reduces that which it considers to a preordained metaphysics, form as it has come to appear within this book is a way of thinking that escapes our best attempts to grasp ways of thinking—a way of thinking that learns from and comes to imitate the phenomena within which it appears (phenomena that are never fully comprehensible, and that are not only rational), the phenomena that characterize this strange institution called literature. Form is a way of thinking that learns from works of art, specifically in the respect that it preserves differentiation rather than seeking to resolve it into contradiction.

This investigation into Adorno's poetics of form has thus not only made a case for the importance of his writings on literature to his aesthetic theory—as became clear particularly in the discussion of the similarity to language of nonlinguistic artworks in the first chapter, his discussions of literary work also reveal certain truths about his aesthetics more generally, including the many tensions that it harbors. The prominence of language within poetic works also ensures that they cannot avoid confronting their relationship with conceptuality. In doing so, they necessitate reflection on the manner in which all artworks mean, and on their critical relationship to conceptuality. This is perhaps expressed most clearly in Adorno's discussion of the linguistic character of artworks in relation to the lyric 'I':

> Art's linguistic character leads to reflection on what might speak from art; it is this, and not the creator or the recipient, that is the subject of art. This subject is masked by the lyric I, which confessed itself for centuries and generated the semblance of the self-evidence of poetic subjectivity. (ÄT 249/AT 166-67)

Adorno argues that the I that conceals and is often taken to be the subject of the poem is in fact a creation of this subject, that 'the grammatical I is posited by the I which latently speaks through the work, the empirical function of the spiritual, and not the other way around' (ÄT 249/AT 167). This cognition, that is made by considering the distinction between the artistic subject and the grammatical subject within the artwork, reveals that art's resemblance to language consists in 'a selfhood that was not first excised from the interdependence of entities by identificatory thinking' (ÄT 171/AT 112). This is the sense in which 'new art strives to transform communicative language into mimetic language' (ÄT 171/AT 112). The consideration of linguistic artworks clarifies the understanding of the linguistic character of all artworks.

This clarification reveals that the linguistic character pertains not to the understanding of language as conceptual and predicative, as the knowing and knowable medium for the communication of a prior, given content. Form, rather, functions as a deposit for many of the ways in which literature thinks that are not reducible to predicative and communicative paradigms. It thus gestures toward the possibility of theorizing the ways in which artworks think—in order not only to provide an account of these nonlinguistic and not-only-linguistic kinds of thought, but also to come to inhabit them to reshape our world with them. In the terms of Adorno's programmatic claim discussed in the first chapter, the aim here is 'a synthesis of a different type, its self-reflection, critical of language, while language nonetheless retains synthesis' (NzL 476/NtL 2: 136): such a synthesis would be a mode of thinking in response to and in dialogue with the work, rather than the imposition onto it of concepts that are indifferent or even hostile to its particularity.

These ways of thinking that can be found within artworks bear the promise of a kind of thinking that operates according to procedures that it learns from its object—procedures that are learned as a result of a relationship not of classification or identity, but of affinity. Indeed, in his discussion of the essay as form, Adorno makes clear not only that it is such an affinity that is at stake, but also that this affinity follows exclusively from the essay's respect for the nonidentical:

> Consciousness of the nonidentity of presentation and subject-matter compels the presentation to unrestricted effort. In this alone does the essay resemble art. (NzL 26/NtL 1: 18)

This is what is at stake in Adorno's rejection of the uncritical 'philological procedure that imagines that it grasps the substantive content of the work as something secure by grasping its intention' (ÄT 226/AT 150), to which I referred in the introduction to this book. The corrective to this procedure—and the task ahead—is better to learn how works of literature think, to learn how to think with them, a thinking that involves developing affinities with its object, and in certain respects coming to resemble it.

In the discussion of the essay which concludes the third chapter I described how Adorno's account of the way in which concepts function in the essay displays strong affinities with Hölderlin's parataxis as discussed in the first chapter. The long opening paragraph of 'The Essay as Form' makes a related but perhaps more conjectural claim as to the status of concepts within the essay:

> Neither are its concepts derived from a first principle, nor do they fill out into a last. Its interpretations are not philologically hardened and judicious, but in principle over-interpretations, according to the automatized verdict of that vigilant understanding that hires itself out to stupidity as a bailiff to be deployed against the spirit. (NzL 10/NtL 1: 13)

Adorno's account of the essay makes room for a certain arbitrariness, and in doing so rejects the modes both of logical derivation from first principles and of measured and restrained philological interpretation. The personified 'vigilant understanding' (Nicholsen makes the personification more explicit and individualized by translating it as 'vigilant intellect') emphasizes that the division of intellectual labor is not a process that takes place independently of individual action, but one in which individual scholars and writers and thinkers are complicit in advancing and enforcing. That is, the features of the essay that can be denounced as arbitrary or criticized as over-interpretations are at the same time precisely those that admit into consideration those aspects which are often excised as irrelevant or inappropriate.

The examination of form that I have carried out within this book suggests two responses to this programmatic claim. The first is that form serves as a figure for precisely those aspects: it focuses attention on that which is apparently incidental, but which is in fact central to all the ways in which works of art say more than their words say. As a label for all these nonsignifying, paralinguistic, not obviously meaningful material aspects of artworks, form enables attention to be focused on ways in which these works think outside and beyond the constraints of linguistic, conceptual thought. And as the mark of a making that is not that of abstract labor, form testifies to the possibility that the power of the value form might be dismantled. The second response is that the complexities, tensions, and contradictions within form as it is revealed by the examination of its deployment reflect the complexity of the ways in which literature thinks, and the inability of conceptual thought fully to grasp them. This reflection is an indication of the extent to which form as it is deployed within Adorno's discussions of literature is consonant with the priority of the (aesthetic) object.

This investigation of form thus provides a prompt and a model for the development of new ways of thinking through close attention to literature and the apparently commonsense ways in which we think about it, ways which in turn have implications for the social and political significance of the study of literature, not in the instrumentalized sense according to which Hohendahl argues that it ought to 'attempt to provide the lower classes—under the conditions of a diffuse public sphere—with the opportunity of coming to terms with their own situation, one which they themselves did not create', but rather by developing new conceptualities, and challenging those which serve as restrictions on shared life in the world.[47] These conceptualities, these ways of thinking, come both from literature and from our experience of it: in this respect they can only come about as the result of an engagement with literary works that is characterized by an attunement to their requirements that is similar to the artist's attunement to the material, rather than by seeking to interpret them according to what can be revealed by means of previously existing concepts and theories.

Such a middle-voiced attunement holds the promise not only of a reconfiguration of the concepts of poetics, the conceptualities by means of which we analyze and engage with literature, according to which apparently linguistic features such as metaphor, tense, and mood might be rethought by means of reflection on encounters with literary artworks. But it also gestures toward ways in which we might, starting from this comportment of attunement, come to interrogate and reformulate the concepts with which we think more generally, the concepts that characterize and delineate our interactions with our worlds. These ways of thinking, developed in dialogue with our experience of works of art, have the potential to transform the ways in which we relate both to one another, and to the nonhuman worlds we inhabit, beyond the constraints of instrumental reason. That is to say, an attunement of the study of literature to the procedures of its object, the playful, nonobjectifying, noncoercive mode of affinity with its object that characterizes mimetic comportment, holds the promise of the expansion of that comportment beyond the worlds of the artwork.

Notes

Introduction

1. 'Introduction', in *The New Historicism*, ed. by H. Aram Veeser (London; New York: Routledge, 1989), pp. ix–xvi (p. xi).

2. Terry Eagleton, *Criticism and Ideology: A Study in Marxist Literary Theory* (London: Verso, 1978), p. 114.

3. Susan J. Wolfson, *Formal Charges: The Shaping of Poetry in British Romanticism* (Stanford, CA: Stanford University Press, 1997), p. 231.

4. Verena Theile, 'New Formalism(s): A Prologue', in *New Formalisms and Literary Theory*, ed. by Verena Theile and Linda Tredennick (Basingstoke, UK; New York: Palgrave Macmillan, 2013), pp. 3–26 (p. 18).

5. This designation established itself despite Wolfson's own hesitancy with respect to the term, as expressed in her insistence that 'reading for form does not imply advocacy of formal*ism*, in the traditional political, literary, and critical sense of an ideologically toned disciplinary commitment that prioritizes and privileges form in relation to other possible locations of value'. Susan J. Wolfson, 'Reading for Form', *MLQ: Modern Language Quarterly*, 61.1 (2000), 1–16 (p. 8), emphasis original.

6. Marjorie Levinson, 'What Is New Formalism?', *PMLA*, 122.2 (2007), 558–69 (p. 559).

7. Levinson, pp. 559, 560.

8. George Levine, 'Introduction: Reclaiming the Aesthetic', in *Aesthetics and Ideology*, ed. by George Levine (New Brunswick, NJ: Rutgers University Press, 1994), pp. 1–28 (pp. 1, 2).

9. Carolyn Lesjak, 'Reading Dialectically', in *Literary Materialisms*, ed. by Mathias Nilges and Emilio Sauri (New York: Palgrave Macmillan, 2013), pp. 17–47 (p. 32).

10. Stephen Cohen, 'Introduction', in *Shakespeare and Historical Formalism*, ed. by Stephen Cohen (Aldershot, UK; Burlington, VT: Ashgate Publishing, Ltd., 2007), pp. 1–27 (p. 3).

11. Cohen, p. 14.

12. Fredric V. Bogel, *New Formalist Criticism: Theory and Practice* (Basingstoke, UK; New York: Palgrave Macmillan, 2013), p. 3.

13. Anna Kornbluh, *Realizing Capital: Financial and Psychic Economies in Victorian Form* (New York: Fordham University Press, 2013), p. 14. It is striking that Bogel and Kornbluh both not only appeal to 'close reading' in order to characterize their versions of formalism to but also surround it in scare quotes. It is of note that these formulations coincide with Franco Moretti's criticism of close reading in all its incarnations as 'a theological exercise' that 'necessarily depends on an extremely small canon'; *Distant Reading* (London; New York: Verso, 2013), p. 48. It is equally striking that Moretti endorses Jonathan Arac's characterization of his work as a 'new formalism without close reading'; 'Anglo-Globalism?', *New Left Review*, 2002, 35–45 (p. 38); cf. Moretti, pp. 65, 118, 180; in his endorsements Moretti tends to drop the adjective 'new'.

14. W. J. T. Mitchell, 'The Commitment to Form; Or, Still Crazy after All These Years', *PMLA*, 118.2 (2003), 321–25 (p. 323).

15. Geoffrey Hartman, 'Beyond Formalism', *MLN*, 81.5 (1966), 542–56 (p. 542).

16. Caroline Levine, 'Strategic Formalism: Toward a New Method in Cultural Studies', *Victorian Studies*, 48.4 (2006), 625–57; *Forms: Whole, Rhythm, Hierarchy, Network* (Princeton, NJ; Oxford: Princeton University Press, 2015).

17. 'Strategic Formalism', p. 630; *Forms*, p. 3; 'Strategic Formalism', p. 626.

18. 'Strategic Formalism', p. 631, emphasis original.

19. 'Strategic Formalism', p. 631.

20. 'Scaled Up, Writ Small: A Response to Carolyn Dever and Herbert F. Tucker', *Victorian Studies*, 49.1 (2006), 100–105 (p. 105).

21. C. Levine, *Forms*, pp. 4–6.

22. C. Levine, *Forms*, p. 74.

23. Levinson, p. 561.

24. Simon Jarvis, 'Seconds Out', *TLS*, 13 January 2006, p. 23.

25. If Plato's *Republic* is taken as the moment of birth, it is perhaps appropriate to wonder how long it will take for the philosophy of literary form to begin to pass through further stages of development—it also offers a certain consolation that a second childishness seems some way off. Plato, 'Republic', in *The Collected Dialogues of Plato*, ed. by Edith Hamilton and Huntington Cairns, trans. by Paul Shorey (Princeton, NJ: Princeton University Press, 1963), pp. 575–844.

26. Angela Leighton, *On Form: Poetry, Aestheticism, and the Legacy of a Word* (Oxford: Oxford University Press, 2007), p. 263.

27. Levinson, p. 558; Theile, pp. 16, 17.

28. Theile, p. 17.

29. Ewan James Jones, *Coleridge and the Philosophy of Poetic Form* (Cambridge: Cambridge University Press, 2014), p. 4.

30. Levinson, p. 563; Ellen Rooney, 'Form and Contentment', *MLQ: Modern Language Quarterly*, 61.1 (2000), 17–40 (p. 27). Contra Wolfson's terminological distinction, Rooney uses 'the terms form and formalism more or less interchangeably' contending that 'resistance to the latter term by those who seem to concede the importance of form is symptomatic of a fundamental suspicion of form itself' (p. 19).

31. Simon Jarvis, 'What Is Historical Poetics?', in *Theory Aside*, ed. by Jason Potts and Daniel Stout (Durham, NC; London: Duke University Press, 2014), pp. 97–116 (p. 100).

32. Mitchell, p. 322. As formalisms go, this of course tends toward the 'old' with its privileging of the work of art and its radical distinction from everything that it is not. Moreover, in asserting that this fact 'is well known', Mitchell implicitly accepts that the potential contribution Adorno has to make to the theorization of form in particular and to literary studies in general is one with which we are already familiar.

33. Robert Kaufman, 'Negatively Capable Dialectics: Keats, Vendler, Adorno, and the Theory of the Avant-Garde', *Critical Inquiry*, 27.2 (2001), 354–84 (p. 363).

34. Levinson, p. 563, emphasis original.

35. Gillian Rose, *The Melancholy Science: An Introduction to the Thought of Theodor W. Adorno* (New York: Columbia University Press, 1978), pp. 111–12.

36. Rose, *The Melancholy Science*, p. 112.

37. Fredric Jameson, *Marxism and Form: Twentieth-Century Dialectical Theories of Literature* (Princeton, NJ: Princeton University Press, 1974), pp. 42, 4.

38. Max Hallé Paddison, 'Music and its Social Mediation: The Concepts of Form and Material in T. W. Adorno's Aesthetics of Music' (unpublished doctoral dissertation, University of Exeter, 1990).

39. Max Paddison, *Adorno's Aesthetics of Music* (Cambridge: Cambridge University Press, 1993), p. 149.

40. Paddison, *Adorno's Aesthetics of Music*, pp. 80, 81, emphasis original.

41. Gerald L. Bruns, 'On the Conundrum of Form and Material in Adorno's Aesthetic Theory', *The Journal of Aesthetics and Art Criticism*, 66.3 (2008), 225–35.

42. Examples of the first tendency include, to a greater or lesser extent, Susan Buck-Morss, *The Origin of Negative Dialectics: Theodor W. Adorno, Walter Benjamin, and the Frankfurt Institute* (New York; London: The Free Press, 1977); Martin Jay, *Adorno* (London: Fontana, 1984); Fredric Jameson, *Late Marxism: Adorno or the Persistence of the Dialectic* (London: Verso, 1990); Peter Uwe Hohendahl, *Prismatic Thought: Theodor W. Adorno* (Lincoln, NE; London: University of Nebraska Press, 1997); where Adorno's aesthetics is mentioned in these works, it tends to be in the context of debates within western Marxism, and more or less divorced from the German aesthetic tradition. The most striking example of the second is the near absence of discussion of *Aesthetic Theory* in Gillian Rose's *The Melancholy Science*, a book in which consideration of aesthetics is primarily restricted to discussion of

Adorno's (earlier) writings on music and study of Kierkegaard. Significant exceptions to this trend include Lambert Zuidervaart, *Adorno's Aesthetic Theory: The Redemption of Illusion* (Cambridge, MA; London: MIT Press, 1991); J. M. Bernstein, *The Fate of Art: Aesthetic Alienation from Kant to Derrida and Adorno* (Cambridge, UK: Polity, 1993). Examination of the implications of Adorno's aesthetics to his œuvre as a whole has also been something of a minority pursuit within the German-language reception of his thought; cf. Friedemann Grenz, 'Zur architektonischen Stellung der Ästhetik in der Philosophie Adornos', in *Theodor W. Adorno*, Text + Kritik Sonderband (Munich: Edition Text + Kritik, 1983), pp. 119–29.

43. Simon Jarvis, *Adorno: A Critical Introduction* (Cambridge, UK: Polity, 1998), p. 138.

44. Robert Kaufman, 'Adorno's Social Lyric, and Literary Criticism Today: Poetics, Aesthetics, Modernity', in *The Cambridge Companion to Adorno*, ed. by Tom Huhn (Cambridge: Cambridge University Press, 2004), pp. 354–75 (p. 354); 'Red Kant, or the Persistence of the Third "Critique" in Adorno and Jameson', *Critical Inquiry*, 26.4 (2000), 682–724 (p. 682).

45. Ulrich Plass, *Language and History in Theodor W. Adorno's 'Notes to Literature'* (London; New York: Routledge, 2006), p. xxxix; cf. Josh Robinson, 'Review of Ulrich Plass, *Language and History in Theodor W. Adorno's "Notes to Literature"*', *British Journal of Aesthetics*, 49.2 (2009), 194–96.

46. David Cunningham and Nigel Mapp, 'Introduction', in *Adorno and Literature*, ed. by David Cunningham and Nigel Mapp (London: Continuum, 2006), pp. 1–5 (p. 4), emphasis original.

47. David Nowell Smith, *Sounding/Silence: Martin Heidegger at the Limits of Poetics* (New York: Fordham University Press, 2013), p. 23.

48. Nowell Smith, pp. 9, 1, 195.

49. Nowell Smith, p. 4. I discuss the relationship between Heidegger's dismissal of the concept of form to Adorno's deployment of it, particularly with respect to Hölderlin's poetry, in the first chapter.

50. Immanuel Kant, *Kritik der Urteilskraft*, ed. by Wilhelm Weischedel, Werkausgabe in 12 Bänden, 10 (Frankfurt am Main: Suhrkamp, 1974), p. 139. As Theodore Edward Uehling observes, in the experience of beauty the central concern 'is not with any property of an object, but fundamentally with the disposition of the cognitive faculties of producer and perceiver'; *The Notion of Form in Kant's 'Critique of Aesthetic Judgment'* (The Hague; Paris: Mouton, 1971), p. 112.

51. Rodolphe Gasché, *The Idea of Form: Rethinking Kant's Aesthetics* (Stanford, CA: Stanford University Press, 2003), p. 7.

52. Gasché, p. 8.

53. Gasché, p. 82.

54. Günter Figal, *Erscheinungsdinge. Ästhetik als Phänomenologie* (Mohr Siebeck, 2010), pp. 61–62.

55. Miguel de Beistegui, *Aesthetics After Metaphysics: From Mimesis to Metaphor* (London; New York: Routledge, 2012), p. 5, emphasis original.
56. de Beistegui, p. 62.
57. de Beistegui, pp. 171, 1.
58. de Beistegui, p. 6.
59. de Beistegui, p. 7.
60. Charles Bambach, *Thinking the Poetic Measure of Justice: Hölderlin–Heidegger–Celan* (Albany: State University of New York Press, 2013), p. 4.
61. Bambach, pp. 44, 162.
62. Forest Pyle, *Art's Undoing: In the Wake of a Radical Aestheticism* (New York: Fordham University Press, 2013), p. 4.
63. Pyle, pp. 3, 14.
64. Vittorio Hösle, *Zur Geschichte der Ästhetik und Poetik* (Basel: Schwabe, 2013), p. 19.
65. Hösle, pp. 70, 101.
66. Josh Robinson, 'Poetics', *The Year's Work in Critical and Cultural Theory*, 22 (2014), 131–54 (p. 201); Josh Robinson, 'Poetics', *The Year's Work in Critical and Cultural Theory*, 23 (2015), 248–69.
67. Hösle, p. 10.
68. Nowell Smith, p. 2.
69. John Arthos, *Gadamer's Poetics: A Critique of Modern Aesthetics*, Bloomsbury Studies in Continental Philosophy (London: Bloomsbury, 2013), p. x.
70. Arthos, pp. 168–69.
71. Robinson, 'Poetics' (2014), p. 140.
72. Robinson, 'Poetics' (2014), pp. 134–35.
73. Gerald L. Bruns, *The Material of Poetry: Sketches for a Philosophical Poetics* (Athens: University of Georgia Press, 2005), p. 4.
74. Werner Hamacher, *95 Thesen zur Philologie* (Frankfurt am Main; Holderbank: Engeler, 2010), p. 15; Werner Hamacher, 'Für—die Philologie', in *Was ist eine philologische Frage? Beiträge zur Erkundung einer theoretischen Einstellung*, ed. by Jürgen Paul Schwindt (Frankfurt am Main: Suhrkamp, 2009), pp. 21–60 (p. 32); Werner Hamacher, *Minima Philologica* (New York: Fordham University Press, 2015), p. 109.
75. Hösle, p. 69.
76. Bogel, p. 21.
77. Dana Gioia, 'Notes on the New Formalism', *The Hudson Review*, 40.3 (1987), 395–408 (p. 408).
78. Charles Bernstein, 'Preface', in *The Politics of Poetic Form: Poetry and Public Policy*, ed. by Charles Bernstein (New York: Roof, 1990), pp. vii–viii (p. vii).
79. Charles Bernstein, 'Comedy and the Poetics of Political Form', in *The Politics of Poetic Form: Poetry and Public Policy*, ed. by Charles Bernstein (New York:

Roof, 1990), pp. 235–44 (p. 235); Bruce Andrews, 'Poetry as Explanation, Poetry as Praxis', in *The Politics of Poetic Form: Poetry and Public Policy*, ed. by Charles Bernstein (New York: Roof, 1990), pp. 23–43 (p. 26); Erica Hunt, 'Notes for an Oppositional Poetics', in *The Politics of Poetic Form*, ed. by Charles Bernstein (New York: Roof, 1990), pp. 197–212 (p. 198).

80. Rose, *The Melancholy Science*, p. 111.

81. Derek Attridge, *The Singularity of Literature* (London; New York: Routledge, 2004), p. 112.

82. Michael Wood, *Literature and the Taste of Knowledge* (Cambridge: Cambridge University Press, 2005), pp. 135–36.

83. Cf. Max Horkheimer, 'Traditionelle und kritische Theorie', in *Kritische Theorie. Eine Dokumentation*, ed. by Alfred Schmidt, 2 vols. (Frankfurt am Main: Fischer, 1968), II, pp. 137–91.

84. James I Porter, *Nietzsche and the Philology of the Future* (Stanford, CA: Stanford University Press, 2000), p. 224.

85. Peter Szondi, 'Über philologische Erkenntnis', in *Schriften*, 2 vols (Frankfurt am Main: Suhrkamp, 1978), I, 263–86 (pp. 263–64).

86. Hösle, p. 52.

87. Jameson, *Late Marxism*, p. 11.

88. Jameson, *Late Marxism*, p. 31; Steven Helmling, *Adorno's Poetics of Critique* (London; New York: Continuum, 2009), pp. 2, 179.

89. Hamacher, *Minima Philologica*, pp. 109, 110.

90. Hamacher, *Minima Philologica*, p. 110.

91. Kevin McLaughlin, *Poetic Force: Poetry after Kant* (Stanford, CA: Stanford University Press, 2014), p. xxi.

92. Walter Benjamin, 'Die Aufgabe des Übersetzers', in *Gesammelte Schriften*, ed. by Rolf Tiedemann (Frankfurt am Main: Suhrkamp, 1972), 4.1, 9–21 (p. 9).

93. Benjamin, 'Die Aufgabe des Übersetzers', p. 18.

94. Benjamin, 'Die Aufgabe des Übersetzers', p. 13.

95. Buck-Morss, pp. 90–91.

96. Walter Benjamin, *Das Passagen–Werk*, ed. by Rolf Tiedemann, Gesammelte Schriften, 5, 2 vols (Frankfurt am Main: Suhrkamp, 1982), I, p. 576.

97. Jameson, *Late Marxism*, p. 30.

98. Jameson, *Late Marxism*, p. 169.

99. Steven Helmling, 'Constellation and Critique: Adorno's Constellation, Benjamin's Dialectical Image', *Postmodern Culture*, 14.1 (2003) <https://doi.org/10.1353/pmc.2003.0036>.

Chapter 1

1. Friedrich Beißner, 'Einführung in Hölderlins Lyrik', in *Sämtliche Werke*, by Friedrich Hölderlin, ed. by Friedrich Beißner, 6 vols (Stuttgart: Kohlhammer/

Cottasche Buchhandlung, 1953), II, 499–511 (p. 506); cf. Gerhard van den Bergh, *Adornos philosophisches Deuten von Dichtung. Ästhetische Theorie und Praxis der Interpretation: Der Hölderlin-Essay als Modell* (Bonn: Bouvier, 1989), p. 170.

2. Martin Heidegger, 'Der Ursprung des Kunstwerkes', in *Holzwege* (Frankfurt am Main: Klostermann, 1994), pp. 1–74 (pp. 14–15).

3. Martin Heidegger, 'Der Ursprung des Kunstwerkes', in *Holzwege* (Frankfurt am Main: Klostermann, 1950), pp. 7–68 (pp. 7, 29). Adorno's personal copy is archived at NB Adorno 413 in the Nachlassbibliothek of the Theodor W. Adorno Archiv, Frankfurt am Main.

4. Immanuel Kant, *Kritik der reinen Vernunft*, ed. by Wilhelm Weischedel, Werkausgabe in 12 Bänden, 3, 2 vols (Frankfurt am Main: Suhrkamp, 1974), I, p. 69.

5. This nonsensuous aspect of artworks is central to their philosophical import. As Zuidervaart emphasizes, in this respect Adorno is in agreement with Hegel in seeing 'philosophy and art as forms of spirit that are dynamically interrelated' (Zuidervaart, p. 147). Raymond Guess sees in the 'nonempirical concept' of spirit the basis for a 'philosophically informed mode of understanding which is not a competitor to observation and empirical theorizing, but which places empirical social research in its proper context'; *Outside Ethics* (Princeton, NJ; Oxford: Princeton University Press, 2005). For a more detailed examination of the relationship of spirit to Adorno's aesthetics, see Espen Hammer, *Adorno's Modernism: Art, Experience, and Catastrophe* (Cambridge: Cambridge University Press, 2015), pp. 24–32; in particular, Hammer identifies in Adorno's lectures on history and freedom (NS 4.13) the recurring theme 'that while Hegel was wrong in ascribing to spirit an ontological primacy, it is not possible to theorize historical development philosophically without some account of spirit' (p. 24).

6. Heidegger, 'Der Ursprung des Kunstwerkes' (1994), p. 9.

7. Klaus Betzen, 'Bericht über die Jahresversammlung in Berlin, 7.–9. Juni 1963', *Hölderlin Jahrbuch*, 13 (1963–64), 172–84 (p. 178); W. Binder, 'Bericht über die Diskussion', *Hölderlin Jahrbuch*, 13 (1963–64), 185–86 (p. 185).

8. Betzen, p. 178.

9. Theodor W. Adorno to Peter Szondi, 3 December 1963, currently uncatalogued TS from the Theodor W. Adorno Archiv, Frankfurt am Main.

10. van den Bergh, p. 233.

11. Hermann Mörchen, *Adorno und Heidegger. Untersuchung einer philosophischen Kommunikationsverweigerung* (Stuttgart: Klett-Cotta, 1981), pp. 174–75. The wrestling which Mörchen mentions is presumably a reference to Adorno's discussion of the status of those words in Hölderlin which are neither names nor concepts, such as *Äther* [ether] and *See* [ocean]; cf. NzL 463–65/NtL 2: 123–25.

12. Cf. Albrecht Wellmer, *Zur Dialektik von Moderne und Postmoderne. Vernunftkritik nach Adorno* (Frankfurt am Main: Suhrkamp, 1985), p. 14.

13. Cf. Friedrich Hölderlin, 'Brod und Wein', in *Sämtliche Werke, Briefe und Dokumente*, ed. by D.E. Sattler, 12 vols (Munich: Luchterhand), IX, 240–48 (pp. 240–41).

14. Friedrich Hölderlin, *Sämtliche Werke*, ed. by Friedrich Beißner, 6 vols (Stuttgart: Kohlhammer/Cottasche Buchhandlung, 1953), II, p. 197, cited (with line-breaks replaced by slashes) NzL 469.

15. Friedrich Hölderlin, *Selected Poems and Fragments*, trans. by Michael Hamburger (London: Penguin, 1998), p. 253.

16. Cf. Friedrich Hölderlin, 'Andenken', in *Sämtliche Werke, Briefe und Dokumente*, ed. by D. E. Sattler, 12 vols (Munich: Luchterhand), XI, 121–123 (p. 123).

17. For Hegel, classical art consists in a 'reality of spirit in its substantial individuality', while in romantic art 'spirit comes to the consciousness of having its other, its *existence*, on and in itself as spirit' Georg Wilhelm Friedrich Hegel, *Vorlesungen über die Ästhetik*, ed. by Eva Moldenhauer and Karl Markus Michel, Werke in 20 Bänden, 14, 3 vols (Frankfurt am Main: Suhrkamp, 1986), II, pp. 127–28, emphasis original.

18. Adorno's theory of sedimentation thus offers a response to those critiques of aesthetics that are based on claims that the concept of art is arbitrary. The challenge made to the concept of art by Raymond Firth's argument against the conceptual separation of purposive from non-purposive artifacts, that 'historically, the line between art and craft is hard to draw', for example, finds a response in Adorno's schema insofar as it does not rely on such an arbitrary separation precisely because it proceeds from the presumption of a transition from one pole to the other; Raymond Firth, 'Art and Anthropology', in *Anthropology, Art and Aesthetics*, ed. by Jeremy Coote and Anthony Shelton (Oxford: Clarendon Press, 1992), pp. 15–39 (p. 17). Certainly, something akin to the transformation of content into form can be seen in Alfred Gell's account of the development of Trobriand canoe-boards, carved such that they induce mild optical disturbances in those who see them, 'their purpose being to induce the Kula partners of the Trobrianders to disgorge their best valuables, without holding any back, in the most expeditious fashion'; Alfred Gell, 'The Technology of Enchantment and the Enchantment of Technology', in *Anthropology, Art and Aesthetics*, ed. by Jeremy Coote and Anthony Shelton (Oxford: Clarendon Press, 1992), pp. 40–63 (pp. 44–46); Kula is the name given to the regional circuit of exchange. Or in the development of calligraphic arts by a process according to which 'a script is simply modulated to meet a number of practical purposes, one of which is the celebration of the Prophet's name', or as a result of the intensification of the documentary character of Chinese paintings 'ever since written texts came to be physically lined, either as inscriptions or as separate colophons, to the painting within the larger artifact of the scroll'; Oleg Grabar, *The Mediation of Ornament* (Princeton, NJ: Princeton University Press, 1992), p. 76; Jonathan Hay, 'The Functions of Chinese Painting: Toward a Unified Field Theory', in *Anthropologies of Art*, ed. by Mariët Westermann (Williamstown, MA: Sterling and Francine Clark Art Institute, 2005), pp. 111–123 (p. 112). Again, to inscribe these processes as a transition from content to form, or as the becoming-form of content,

presupposes to a certain extent a conceptual schema that only arises after the event, from the standpoint of a society in which such transitions have already taken place.

19. Kant, *Kritik der Urteilskraft*, p. 264. Robert S. Lehman has recently drawn attention to the distinction between the mere form of the subjective judgment of taste and the phenomenal form of its object in order to argue against the formalist claim that close attention to the details of the artwork (that is, to the details of its phenomenal form) results in our being 'somehow *closer* to the artwork; 'Formalism, Mere Form, and Judgment', *New Literary History*, 48.2 (2017), 245–63 (p. 255), emphasis original.

20. This understanding of artistic form as the resolution of contradiction resonates with the underlying motif in Adorno's thought that the form of the dialectic itself, as the 'ontology of the wrong state of things' (ND 22/Ashton 11), is itself a historically specific response to a society constituted on a conception of diversity and difference primarily as contradiction. At the heart of this aesthetics lies a profoundly normative claim (to which I return in the fifth chapter and in the coda): that artworks worthy of the name must necessarily bring together divergent moments in a way that nonetheless preserves their differentiation.

21. Cf. Kant, I, p. 98, and also J. M. Bernstein's discussion of Adorno's rewriting of Kant's relationship between concept and intuition 'as form and content, spirit and mimesis, form and expression', *The Fate of Art*, p. 199.

22. Hölderlin, *Sämtliche Werke*, II, p. 167, cited NzL 471–72.

23. Hölderlin, *Selected Poems and Fragments*, pp. 227–29.

24. Clive Scott, *The Poetics of French Verse: Studies in Reading* (Oxford: Clarendon Press, 1998), p. 82.

25. Martin Heidegger, *Der Satz vom Grund* (Pfullingen: Neske, 1957), p. 161.

26. Martin Heidegger, 'Der Weg zur Sprache', in *Unterwegs zur Sprache* (Pfullingen: Neske, 1959), pp. 239–268 (p. 255).

27. Cf. Derek Attridge, *The Rhythms of English Poetry* (London: Longman, 1982), p. 68; Horst Ruthrof, *The Body in Language* (London; New York: Cassel, 2000), p. 22–33, 98–116, and passim.

28. Friedrich Hölderlin, *Sämtliche Werke* (Leipzig: Insel, undated), p. 761, cited NzL 476.

29. *The Linguistic Turn: Recent Essays in Philosophical Method*, ed. by Richard Rorty (Chicago: University of Chicago Press, 1967).

30. Richard Rorty, 'Twenty-Five Years After', in *The Linguistic Turn: Recent Essays in Philosophical Method*, ed. by Richard Rorty (Chicago: University of Chicago Press, 1992), pp. 371–74 (p. 373).

31. This foregrounding of the problem of representation helps to clarify the extent to which Adorno's poetics of form to the 'speculative' thinking represented by the proponents of 'object-oriented' philosophy. For in their attempt to go beyond 'correlationism' (the persistence and ineluctability of 'the idea according to which

we only ever have access to the correlation between thinking and being, and never to either term considered apart from the other'), the proponents of the 'speculative turn' take up an avowedly post-critical and anti-representationalist position; Quentin Meillassoux, *After Finitude: An Essay on the Necessity of Contingency, with a Preface by Alain Badiou*, trans. by Ray Brassier (London; New York: Bloomsbury, 2008), p. 5; Levi R. Bryant, Nick Srnicek, and Graham Harman, 'Towards a Speculative Philosophy', in *The Speculative Turn: Continental Materialism and Realism*, ed. by Levi R. Bryant, Nick Srnicek, and Graham Harman (Melbourne: re.press, 2011), pp. 1–18 (p. 3). Graham Harman in particular seeks to liberate us from our imprisonment within 'an ever-tinier ghetto of solely human realities' by theorizing on the basis of the 'sensual encounter' with 'sensual objects', untouched by conceptual mediation; 'On Vicarious Causation', *Collapse: Philosophical Research and Development*, 2 (2007), 171–205 (pp. 174, 204). This encounter, to which he gives the name 'allure', is one of a deep attraction or affinity, in which the sensual object remains separate and free from its qualities; *Guerrilla Metaphysics: Phenomenology and the Carpentry of Things* (Chicago: Open Court, 2005), pp. 142–44; 'On Vicarious Causation', p. 199. At the heart of Harman's claim that 'aesthetics becomes first philosophy' there thus lies a conception of a relation between objects in their immediacy, without mediation through quality or conceptuality; Harman, 'On Vicarious Causation', p. 205. I share with some of the proponents of object-oriented philosophy a conviction that rational coherence and indeed rationality itself need to be rethought in the light of the aesthetic. In particular, my account of Adorno's poetics shares with Steven Shaviro an objection to the subordination of aesthetics to ethics and politics; *The Universe of Things: On Speculative Realism* (Minneapolis: University of Minnesota Press, 2014), p. 20. My objection is that the object-oriented philosophy of the 'speculative turn' does not take this rethinking far enough, in particular by leaving unexamined the categories of aesthetics, which are treated as if they are free from conceptual mediation. In its refusal to treat aesthetic experience or the concepts of aesthetics as beyond mediation, my account of Adorno's poetics of form thus gestures toward an alternative to the 'aestheticized account of ethics' that Shaviro, following Whitehead, founds on a 'spontaneous aesthetic *decision*' (pp. 24, 25, emphasis original). For in drawing attention to ways in which close attention to poetry might compel us to rethink what we think we know about language, Adorno's foregrounding of the problem of representation in his analysis of Hölderlin's verse also implies that a speculative philosophy worthy of the name would itself require a reconfiguration beyond these limits of conceptual language. For a fuller account of my critique of the 'speculative turn', cf. 'Speculation upon Speculation; or, a Contribution to the Critique of Philosophical Economy', in *Credo, Credit, Crisis: Speculations on Faith and Money*, ed. by Aidan Tynan, Laurent Milesi, and Christopher John Müller (Lanham, MD: Rowman and Littlefield, 2017), pp. 239–70.

32. Bernhard Lypp, 'Selbsterhaltung und ästhetische Erfahrung. Zur Geschichtsphilosophie und ästhetischen Theorie Adornos', in *Materialien zur ästhetischen*

Theorie. Theodor W. Adornos Konstruktion der Moderne, ed. by Burkhardt Lindner and W. Martin Lüdke (Frankfurt am Main: Suhrkamp, 1980), pp. 187–218 (p. 206).

33. Rainer Nägele, 'Ancient Sports and Modern Transports: Hölderlin's Tragic Bodies', in *The Solid Letter: Readings of Friedrich Hölderlin*, ed. by Arios Fioretos (Stanford, CA: Stanford University Press, 1999), pp. 247–67 (p. 252).

34. 'Fragment als Form und Zufall' radio discussion between Adorno and Peter von Haselberg, Norddeutcher Rundfunk, recorded February 2, 1967.

35. The term 'imprisonment in nature' [*Naturbefangenheit*] also appears in the essay on progress, in which Adorno equates the potential of the maturity of humanity with the possibility that 'the imprisonment in nature, in which progress itself is integrated, should not have the last word' (S 625/CM 150). Here even more than in 'Progress', the term alludes to Hegel's discussion of the end or purpose of art in the third section of the introduction to the *Lectures on Aesthetics* on the concept of art beauty. He argues that art is capable of offering liberation from sensuality within the sensual sphere. To the extent that art dissolves the raw wildness of the immediate unity of human and nature, it 'elevates humanity above the imprisonment in nature with its soft hands'; Georg Wilhelm Friedrich Hegel, *Vorlesungen über die Ästhetik*, ed. by Eva Moldenhauer and Karl Markus Michel, Werke in 20 Bänden, 13, 3 vols (Frankfurt am Main: Suhrkamp, 1986), I, pp. 74–75.

Chapter 2

1. Surti Singh, 'The Spiritualization of Art in Adorno's Aesthetic Theory', *Adorno Studies*, 1.1 (2017), 31–42 (p. 32).

2. Theodor W. Adorno, *Berg. Der Meister des kleinsten Übergangs*, Österreichische Komponisten des XX. Jahrhunderts, 15 (Vienna: Lafite / Österreichischer Bundesverlag, 1968), p. 36; cf. B 359–60/AB 29, ÄT 173/AT 371.

3. Kant, *Kritik der Urteilskraft*, pp. 141–42.

4. A tentative hypothesis is that the characteristics identified by Adorno (and others) as being particular to artworks of modernity might in fact be aspects of many or all successful artworks, of which modernism makes us aware. They might equally— and these possibilities are not mutually exclusive—be specific to understandings of art that develop with or in response to modernism. That such understandings can exert a substantial influence on aesthetic judgments is a phenomenon that has been documented, if not so thoroughly investigated. See for example Jonathan Culler's observation that '[t]hose of us who had been nurtured on the New Criticism and thought Donne and the moderns the supreme examples of poetic achievement were inclined to find Romantic poetry the aberration'; 'The Mirror Stage', in *High Romantic Argument: Essays for M. H. Abrams*, ed. by Lawrence Lipking (Ithaca, NY: Cornell University Press, 1981), pp. 149–63 (p. 149). Similarly, the observations on which many attempts to formulate an aesthetic theory are based tend themselves to

be historically contingent. Wolfson, for example, offers in *Formal Charges* a reading of the agency of poetic form based on a conception that differs radically from those both of the New Critics and of their most stringent detractors.

5. Like the rest of the 'Nineteen Contributions on New Music' collected in GS 18, this article was originally written for *Encyclopedia of the Arts*, ed. by Dagobert D. Runes and Harry G. Schrickel (New York: The Philosophical Library, 1946). Only the article on Jazz was ultimately published (in English translation) in the Encyclopedia, the remaining contributions remaining unpublished until 1984 (cf. GS 19: 641).

6. Walter Benjamin, 'Der Sürrealismus: Die letzte Momentaufnahme der europäischen Intelligenz', in *Gesammelte Schriften*, ed. by Rolf Tiedemann (Frankfurt am Main: Suhrkamp, 1972), 2.1, 295–310 (pp. 308–09).

7. André Breton, *Manifestes du surréalisme* (Paris: Gallimard, 1969), pp. 23–24.

8. Richard Wolin, 'Benjamin, Adorno, Surrealism', in *The Semblance of Subjectivity: Essays in Adorno's Aesthetic Theory*, ed. by Tom Huhn and Lambert Zuidervaart (Cambridge, MA; London: MIT Press, 1997), pp. 93–122 (p. 108), emphasis original.

9. Jameson, *Marxism and Form*, p. 96.

10. Benjamin, 'Der Sürrealismus, pp. 310, 306.

11. Wolin, p. 107; cf. Buck-Morss, pp. 124–31; Eugene Lunn, *Marxism and Modernism: An Historical Study of Lukács, Brencht, Benjamin, and Adorno* (Berkeley; Los Angeles; London: University of California Press, 1982), pp. 270–72; Jay, *Adorno*, pp. 129–30; Martin Jay, *Marxism and Totality: The Adventures of a Concept from Lukács to Habermas* (Berkeley; Los Angeles: University of California Press, 1984), pp. 288–90.

12. Wolin, p. 107.

13. At stake in this disagreement over the political potential of surrealism is what Adorno persistently presents as his more fundamental disagreement with Benjamin concerning mediation and the dialectical image. In their correspondence concerning Benjamin's draft outline for the Arcades project Adorno singles out a single Baudelaire sentence quoted by Benjamin, and locates in it the concentration of 'all the motifs of the theory of the dialectical image that underlie my critique— namely that it is *undialectical*'; 'Letter to Walter Benjamin, August 2, 1935', in *Briefe*, by Walter Benjamin, ed. by Gershom Sholem and Theodor W. Adorno, 2 vols (Frankfurt am Main: Suhrkamp, 1978), II, 671–83 (p. 672), emphasis original. Three years later, in a letter responding to a draft of the second section of Benjamin's study of Baudelaire, he accuses Benjamin of using 'metaphors in the place of binding statements', and failing adequately to account for the relation of his theoretical discussion to specific instances, asserting that 'the materialist determination of cultural characters is possible only if mediated through the *total process*'; 'Letter to Walter Benjamin, November 10, 1938', in *Briefe*, by Walter Benjamin, ed. by Gershom Sholem and Theodor W. Adorno, 2 vols (Frankfurt am Main:

Suhrkamp, 1978), II, 782–90 (p. 785), emphasis original. At two different points in his letter he draws together his objections in the form of pointed accusations: 'Unless I am very much mistaken, this dialectic is missing one thing: mediation' (p. 785); 'The "mediation" that I miss and find obscured by materialist-historiographical invocation is nothing other than the theory which your study omits' (p. 786). It is of significance here that almost two months previously Benjamin had written to Horkheimer (with whom Adorno had discussed his response before sending it) including a manuscript in which the theme of each section was marked 'in case a montage of shorter sections would be of interest to you editorially'; 'Letter to May Horkheimer, September 28, 1938', in *Briefe*, by Walter Benjamin, ed. by Gershom Sholem and Theodor W. Adorno, 2 vols (Frankfurt am Main: Suhrkamp, 1978), II, 772–76 (p. 775). It is worth observing that, in turning to the figure of constellation in order to avoid the subordinating logic of conceptual abstraction, Adorno himself develops a philosophical procedure—or in Wolin's terms 'incorporated an *aesthetic* dimension into philosophy' (p. 114, emphasis original) that in many respects starkly resembles that for which he criticizes Benjamin here.

14. Cf. Ernst Bloch, *Erbschaft dieser Zeit* (Frankfurt am Main: Suhrkamp, 1962); Ernst Bloch, *Geist der Utopie* (Frankfurt am Main: Suhrkamp, 1971); Georg Lukács, *Essays über Realismus* (Neuwied; Berlin: Luchterhand, 1971); Ernst Bloch and others, *Aesthetics and Politics*, ed. by Ronald Taylor (London: Verso, 1980).

15. Franz Kafka, *Das Schloss* (Munich: Wolff, 1926), p. 32.

16. *Marx & Engels on Literature and Art: A Selection of Writings*, ed. by Lee Baxandall and Stefan Morawski (St. Louis, MO: Telos, 1973), pp. 90–92; P. N. Medvedev and M. M. Bakhtin, *The Formal Method in Literary Scholarship: A Critical Introduction to Sociological Poetics*, trans. by Albert J. Wehrle (Baltimore, MD; London: Johns Hopkins University Press, 1978).

17. Cf. Leon Trotsky, 'The Formalist School of Poetry and Marxism', in *Literature and Revolution*, trans. by Rose Strumsky (Ann Arbor: University of Michigan Press, 1960), pp. 162–83.

18. Werner Hamacher, *Premises: Essays on Philosophy and Literature from Kant to Celan* (Stanford, CA: Stanford University Press, 1999), pp. 329–30.

19. The quotation in question is 'Auch sollten Sie überhaupt im Reden zurückhaltender sein, fast alles, was Sie vorhin gesagt haben, hätte man auch, wenn Sie nur ein paar Worte gesagt hätten, Ihrem Verhalten entnehmen können, außerdem war es nichts für Sie übermäßig Günstiges' ['You should also be more circumspect in general when you speak; almost everything that you said earlier could have been inferred from your behavior, even if you had only said a few words; besides, it was nothing that was overly beneficial to you.']; cf. Franz Kafka, *Der Prozeß*, ed. by Malcolm Pasley (Frankfurt am Main: Fischer, 2002), p. 22.

20. Rüdiger Bubner, 'Concerning the Central Idea of Adorno's Philosophy', in *The Semblance of Subjectivity: Essays in Adorno's Aesthetic Theory*, ed. by Tom Huhn and Lambert Zuidervaart, trans. by Cara Gendel Ryan (Cambridge, MA; London:

MIT Press, 1997), pp. 147–75 (p. 163); Karla L. Schultz, *Mimesis on the Move: Theodor W. Adorno's Concept of Imitation* (Berne; Frankfurt am Main; New York; Paris: Peter Lang, 1990), p. 15.

21. Richard Wolin, *The Terms of Cultural Criticism: The Frankfurt School, Existentialism, Poststructuralism* (New York: Columbia University Press, 1995), p. 75.

22. Martin Jay, 'Mimesis and Mimetology: Adorno and Lacoue-Labarthe', in *The Semblance of Subjectivity: Essays in Adorno's Aesthetic Theory*, ed. by Tom Huhn and Lambert Zuidervaart (Cambridge, MA; London: MIT Press, 1997), pp. 29–53 (p. 32).

23. Josef Früchtl, *Mimesis. Konstellation eines Zentralbegriffs bei Adorno* (Würzburg: Königshausen & Neumann, 1986).

24. Wellmer, p. 12.

25. Hohendahl, *Prismatic Thought*, p. 205.

26. J. M. Bernstein, *The Fate of Art*, p. 199.

27. J. M. Bernstein, *The Fate of Art*, p. 202.

28. J. M. Bernstein, *The Fate of Art*, p. 202.

29. Howard Caygill, *Art of Judgement* (Oxford: Blackwell, 1989); Kaufman, 'Red Kant, or the Persistence of the Third "Critique" in Adorno and Jameson'; Ross Wilson, *Subjective Universality in Kant's Aesthetics* (Oxford; New York: Peter Lang, 2007), pp. 203–06; Ross Wilson, 'Dialectical Aesthetics and the Kantian *Rettung*: On Adorno's *Aesthetic Theory*', *New German Critique*, 35.2 104 (2008), 55–69.

Chapter 3

1. Jameson, *Late Marxism*, p. 128, emphasis original.

2. Alastair Fowler, *Kinds of Literature* (Oxford: Oxford University Press, 1982), p. 278.

3. Fowler, p. v.

4. Gillian Rose, *Hegel Contra Sociology* (London: Athlone Press, 1981), p. 140.

5. Adorno's most extensive use of *sich verfransen* is within this talk, the text of which was published in *Ohne Leitbild* in 1967, which accounts for twelve of the seventeen occurrences of *verfransen* and its cognates within his œuvre. Four of the five other occurrences are later references to this text, while in the twelfth of the 'Marginalia to Theory and Praxis' he offers a critique of the 'happenings' staged by contemporary actionists which 'conflate [*verfransen*] aesthetic semblance and reality', a phrase which further develops his rejection of a 'theatre that mistakes itself for reality', a critique in comparison to which he praises Brecht's acknowledgment that 'if being honest with himself, he was fundamentally more interested in theatre than in changing the world' (S 778–79/CM 275); in a footnote to this claim Adorno provides a reference to Walter Benjamin, *Versuche über Brecht* (Frankfurt am Main: Suhrkamp, 1966), p. 118.

6. Michael McKeon, *The Origins of the English Novel, 1600–1740* (Baltimore, MD: Johns Hopkins University Press, 1987), pp. 52–64.

7. Walter Benjamin, 'Der Autor als Produzent', in *Gesammelte Schriften*, ed. by Rolf Tiedemann (Frankfurt am Main: Suhrkamp, 1972), 2.2, 683–701 (pp. 687, 694).

8. It is significant that Adorno's remarks are not derived from an attempt to investigate the consequences of his theory of the becoming-purposeless of purposive forms for the distinction between purposeful and purposeless—and thus to the dividing line between architecture and sculpture—but from observation of the tendency of 'quasi-architectonic formations' to intrude into sculpture (OL 432–33/COL 369). (Indeed, it is perhaps strictly speaking more accurate to talk of Adorno's being informed of this process than of his observation of it, since the source he offers for his remarks is a conversation with Austrian sculptor Fritz Wotruba, who had mentioned the influence on his own work of Berlin-based architect Hans Scharoun.) The question of whether the dissolution of the limits between the arts that Adorno sees in such tendencies is such a new phenomenon as he sees it is of little consequence to his argument, which rests not on a conception of the arts as static and unchanging until the mid-twentieth century, but rather on the claim that the limits between the arts as they currently appear are not rigidly fixed. Indeed, he recognizes that Schumann's claim that the aesthetics of one art is also the aesthetics of the others results from the romantic intention to ensure that the different structural elements of music should be animated and become poetic (OL 439/COL 374).

9. See, for example, Raymond Williams, 'Base and Superstructure in Marxist Cultural Theory', in *Culture and Materialism: Selected Essays* (London: Verso, 2005), pp. 31–49.

10. Theodor W. Adorno, 'Kapitelästhetik', 1968, p. TS203333, Theodor W. Adorno-Archiv, Frankfurt am Main. This quotation is from a list of additions to the fourth ('Nominalism') of the seven chapters of the 'Kapitelästhetik', described by Adorno as a draft of his book on aesthetics, dating probably from 1968. This draft consisted itself to a considerable extent in a substantial reworking of the 'Paragraphenästhetik', written between 1961 and 1966; cf. Rolf Tiedemann and Gretel Adorno's editorial afterword to *Aesthetic Theory* (ÄT 538–39/AT 362–63).

11. Gérard Genette, 'Genres, "Types", Modes', *Poétique*, 1977, 389–421 (p. 394).

12. Jameson, *Late Marxism*, p. 29.

13. Gillian Rose, 'From Speculative to Dialectical Thinking—Hegel and Adorno', in *Judaism and Modernity: Philosophical Essays* (Oxford; Cambridge, MA: Blackwell, 1993), pp. 53–63 (pp. 61–62).

14. For arguments that it is perhaps not, see Simon Jarvis, 'What Is Speculative Thinking?', *Revue Internationale de Philosophie*, 2004.1 (no. 227) (2004), 69–83; Josh Robinson, 'Dialektik und Spekulation. Über die Grenzen der spekulativen

Vernunft', in *Probleme der Dialektik heute*, ed. by Stefan Müller (Wiesbaden: VS Verlag für Sozialwissenschaften, 2009), pp. 229–46.

15. Hammer, p. 88.

16. Nicholas Brown, 'The Work of Art in the Age of its Real Subsumption under Capital', *Nonsite.Org*, 2012 <http://nonsite.org/editorial/the-work-of-art-in-the-age-of-its-real-subsumption-under-capital> [accessed 10 May 2015].

17. Heidegger, 'Der Ursprung des Kunstwerkes'.

18. Rose, *Hegel Contra Sociology*, p. 49, emphasis original.

19. Jameson, *Late Marxism*, p. 157.

20. Hegel, *Vorlesungen über die Ästhetik*, I, p. 151.

21. McKeon, pp. 91–105.

22. Ian Watt, *The Rise of the Novel: Studies in Defoe, Richardson and Fielding* (London: Chatto & Windus, 1963), p. 80.

23. McKeon, pp. 120–22.

24. This distinction is perhaps expressed most clearly in the 142nd aphorism of *Minima Moralia*, entitled 'Dem folgt deutscher Gesang', the title the (editorially disputed) final line of Hölderlin's *Patmos*, in which Adorno discusses the relationship between free verse and prose ('Patmos', in *Sämtliche Werke*, ed. by Friedrich Beißner, 6 vols [Stuttgart: Kohlhammer/Cottasche Buchhandlung, 1953], II, 172–80 [p. 180]). Adorno insists that the 'free rhythms' of free verse are not reducible to 'prose periods set below one another in an elevated tone', and that claims to the contrary (such as those of Stefan George) focus instances of free verse in decay at the expense of the potential realized by Goethe and Hölderlin's late hymns (MM 252/Jephcott 221). He polemically rejects claims that the category of 'worked prose', defined as 'a system of free rhythms, the attempt to align the magic spell of the absolute with the negation of its appearance, an effort of the mind to save the metaphysical violence of expression by means of its own secularization', can be seen as equivalent to or identical with poetry, insisting rather that 'prose's ascetic isolation from verse serves to invoke song' (MM 253/Jephcott 222).

25. McKeon, p. 20.

26. Watt, p. 13. For Watt this realism consists both in characterization and in the presentation of background, construed both spatially and temporally (pp. 17–18). As examples he offers the 'unprecedentedly detailed time-scheme' of *Clarissa* (p. 24), Defoe's 'treatment of movable objects in the physical world' such the linen and gold in *Moll Flanders*, or clothing and hardware on Crusoe's island (p. 26).

27. Watt, p. 32.

28. McKeon, p. 336.

29. I have chosen, here and elsewhere, to translate *das Moment* as 'moment' rather than the occasionally employed 'element' in order to preserve the sense of dynamism inherent in the concept, despite the ambiguity of the English word that does not exist in German, which distinguishes between *der Moment*, a moment or instant of time, and *das Moment*, a moment in the natural-scientific and mathematical sense of the tendency of a force to rotate or twist, a tendency that acts in combination

with others to constitute the static or dynamic state of a system. Perhaps the most significant example of Hegel's use of the term is found in his claim in the *Science of Logic* that being and nothing are the two moments of becoming. Discussing his use of the term *Aufheben* (which here as elsewhere I translate as 'suspend' in preference to the idiolectical 'sublate' more commonly used in English-language editions of Hegel), he argues that 'something is only suspended to the extent that it has entered into unity with its opposite; in this more precise definition as something reflected it can fittingly be termed a *moment*', and draws the parallel with the use of the term to refer to the physical effect of a force on a lever; *Wissenschaft der Logik*, ed. by Eva Moldenhauer and Karl Markus Michel, Werke in 20 Bänden, 5, 2 vols (Frankfurt am Main: Suhrkamp, 1986), I, p. 104, emphasis original.

30. He refers to the loss of experience in the 'Elements of Antisemitism' in *Dialectic of Enlightenment* (DA 233/DE 172), to its sickness in the essay 'On the Theory of Ghosts' in the appendix to *Dialectic of Enlightenment* (DA 243/DE 178), to necrosis in *Minima Moralia* (MM 44/Jephcott 40, MM 298), and to decay in *Minima Moralia* and *The Philosophy of New Music* (MM 269/Jephcott 235, PnM 177/PMM 194). For an account of the category of 'spiritual experience' in Adorno in opposition to this narrative of loss, see Roger Foster, *Adorno: The Recovery of Experience* (Albany: State University of New York Press, 2007).

31. 'A factory in which the workers were really and totally mere cogs in the machine, blindly executing the orders of management, would come to a stop in a quarter of an hour.' Cornelius Castoriadis, *The Imaginary Institution of Society*, trans. by Kathleen Blamey (Cambridge, UK: Polity, 1987), p. 16.

32. Here Adorno has an unacknowledged debt to Lukács, who argues that the novel's hero is the result of an alienation from a nature that is 'nothing other than the historico-philosophical objectivation of man's alienation from his own constructs'; Georg Lukács, *Theory of the Novel*, trans. by Anna Bostock (London: Merlin, 1978), p. 64.

33. René Descartes, *A Discourse on Method*, trans. by John Veitch (New York: Dutton, 1951), p. 15; Adorno cites the German edition, NzL 22/NtL 1: 14, 277.

34. There is a similar move in the discussion of the ontological need in the first section of *Negative Dialectics* on the relationship of the negative dialectic to ontology, in which Adorno asserts that '[t]he kitschy exoticism of arts-and-crafts worldviews (such as the astonishingly consumable Zen Buddhism) casts light on today's restorationist philosophies' (ND 76/Ashton 68). The context of the preceding (and indeed subsequent) discussion makes it clear that Heidegger is again the principal target.

Chapter 4

1. Bruce Andrews, 'Total Equals What: Poetics and Praxis', in *A Guide to Poetics Journal: Writing in the Expanded Field, 1982–1998*, ed. by Lyn Hejinian and

Barrett Watten (Middletown, CT: Wesleyan University Press, 2013), pp. 185–96 (p. 189), emphasis original.

2. Bruns, *The Material of Poetry*, p. 9.

3. Bruns, *The Material of Poetry*, p. 7.

4. Bruns, 'On the Conundrum of Form and Material in Adorno's Aesthetic Theory', p. 230.

5. Jameson, *Late Marxism*, p. 189.

6. Walter Benjamin, 'The Work of Art in the Age of its Technological Reproducibility', in *Selected Writings: 1938–1940*, ed. by Howard Eiland and Michael William Jennings, trans. by Edmund Jephcott and Harry Zohn, 4 vols (Cambridge, MA: Harvard University Press, 2003), III, 101–33 (p. 101).

7. Paddison, *Adorno's Aesthetics of Music*, p. 88.

8. Michael de la Fontaine, 'Künstlerische Erfahrung bei Arnold Schönberg. Zur Dialektik des musikalischen Materials', in *Materialien zur ästhetischen Theorie. Theodor W. Adornos Konstruktion der Moderne*, ed. by Burkhardt Lindner and W. Martin Lüdke (Frankfurt am Main: Suhrkamp, 1980), pp. 467–93 (p. 469).

9. Theodor W. Adorno to Peter Rühmkorf, 13 February 1964. Currently uncatalogued TS from the Theodor W. Adorno–Archiv, Frankfurt am Main.

10. Peter Bürger, 'Das Vermittlungsproblem in der Kunstsoziologie Adornos', in *Materialien zur ästhetischen Theorie. Theodor W. Adornos Konstruktion der Moderne*, ed. by Burkhardt Lindner and W. Martin Lüdke (Frankfurt am Main: Suhrkamp, 1980), pp. 169–84 (p. 175).

11. J. M. Bernstein, *Against Voluptuous Bodies: Late Modernism and the Meaning of Painting* (Stanford, CA: Stanford University Press, 2006), p. 15.

12. Bruns, 'On the Conundrum of Form and Material in Adorno's Aesthetic Theory', p. 228.

13. Benjamin, 'Der Autor als Produzent', pp. 694, 698.

14. The literary historian to whom Adorno refers is Wolfgang Kayser, who in *Das sprachliche Kunstwerk. Eine Einführung in die Literaturwissenschaft* (Berne; Munich: Francke, 1948) discusses the relationships between some of the different objects of literary studies. It should also be noted that 'poetry' and 'poems' are not entirely satisfactory translations of *Dichtung* and *Dichtungen*: both Thomas Mann and Frank Wedekind are described as *Dichter* (NzL 45/NtL 1: 34, NzL 629–30/NtL 2: 275-76), while in Adorno's discussion of committed works he claims that 'The residues in poems of meanings from outside are what is indispensably nonartistic in art. Art's law of form cannot be derived from poems, but from the dialectic of both moments' (NzL 411/NtL 2: 77-78). From the essay's discussion of Sartre's and Brecht's plays it is clear that he is not talking only about poetry in the narrow sense. The characteristics Adorno describes are not unique to poetry, but include other literary works subject to what he terms the formal law. I nonetheless favor the translation 'poetry' throughout, both in the absence of any more suitable English-language alternative, and out of conviction that central to what Adorno

refers to as *Dichtung* is what can in English only satisfactorily be termed 'poetic', regardless of whether the resulting work is in verse or prose.

15. J. M. Bernstein, *Against Voluptuous Bodies*, p. 211, emphasis original.
16. Nowell Smith, pp. 29–30.
17. Plass, p. 63; further references to this volume appear as parenthesized references within the text.
18. Shierry Weber Nicholsen, *Exact Imagination, Late Work: On Adorno's Aesthetics* (Cambridge, MA; London: MIT Press, 1997), pp. 59–60.
19. Nicholsen, p. 63.
20. Adorno and von Haselberg, 'Fragment als Form und Zufall'.
21. 'Fragment als Form und Zufall'.
22. 'Fragment als Form und Zufall'.
23. Heidegger, 'Der Ursprung des Kunstwerkes' (1994), p. 14.
24. Simon Jarvis, 'What Does Art Know?', in *Aesthetics and the Work of Art: Adorno, Kafka, Richter*, ed. by Peter de Bolla and Stefan H. Uhlig (Basingstoke, UK: Palgrave Macmillan, 2009), pp. 57–70 (p. 61).

Chapter 5

1. Karl Marx, *Januar 1859–Februar 1860*, Karl Marx, Friedrich Engels: Werke, 13 (Berlin: Dietz, 1961), p. 18.
2. Marx, *Januar 1859–Februar 1860*, p. 19.
3. In *Wage, Price, Profit* Marx provides perhaps the clearest illustration of how and to what extent commodity-producing labor is social: 'In order to produce a commodity, a particular amount of labor must be used on it or worked into it. In this process I do not say simply labor, but *social labor*. Whoever produces an article for his immediate use, in order to consume it himself, makes a *product*, but not a *commodity*. As a producer who is operating alone he has nothing to do with society. But in order to produce a *commodity*, the article that he produces must not only satisfy some *social* need or other, but his labor must itself form a component and fraction of the total sum of labor that is expended by society. His labor must be subsumed under the *division of labor within society*. It is nothing without the other parts of labor, and it is necessary that it in turn complements these other parts.' *September 1864–Juli 1870*, Karl Marx, Friedrich Engels: Werke, 16 (Berlin: Dietz, 1962), p. 123, emphasis original. Here it becomes clear that abstract, commodity-producing labor is not being equated with social labor *tout court*, that social labor does not necessarily exist in a commodity-producing form. Rather than being its only possible form, commodity production is one form of social labor; indeed, the commodity-producing character of capitalist labor depends on its social character. As Marx makes clear, what is produced can only become a commodity under the two conditions that there exists a demand for it on the part of somebody other than

its maker, and that this production for the sake of exchange not be an as it were incidental or contingent relationship between individuals, but rather function as a set of social relations whereby needs are widely and routinely satisfied by means of the exchange of goods produced on this basis.

4. Marx, *Januar 1859–Februar 1860*, pp. 20–21.

5. Marx, *Januar 1859–Februar 1860*, p. 21.

6. Castoriadis, p. 16; cf. the discussion of the novel in chapter 3 above.

7. Karl Marx, *Das Kapital. Kritik der politischen Ökonomie*, Karl Marx, Friedrich Engels: Werke, 23, 3 vols (Berlin: Dietz, 1962), I, pp. 120, 344.

8. Marx, *Das Kapital*, I, p. 344.

9. 'A proportion of the instruments of labor takes on this social character before the labor process itself does so.' Marx, *Das Kapital*, I, p. 344.

10. Castoriadis, p. 16, emphasis original.

11. Marx, *Das Kapital*, I, pp. 348–49.

12. Cf. Theodor W. Adorno and Alfred Sohn-Rethel, *Briefwechsel 1936–1939*, ed. by Christoph Gödde (Munich: Text + Kritik, 1991), pp. 150–51; Sohn-Rethel's claim is more thoroughly documented in Alfred Sohn-Rethel, *Geistige und körperliche Arbeit. Zur Theorie gesellschaftlicher Synthesis* (Frankfurt am Main: Suhrkamp, 1970), first published after Adorno's death.

13. In this respect Adorno does not share Moishe Postone's conception of Marx's mature critical theory, according to which 'Marx's analysis does not refer to labor as it is generally and transhistorically conceived—a goal-directed social activity that mediates between humans and nature, creating specific products in order to satisfy determinate human needs—but to a peculiar role that labor plays in capitalist society alone'; *Time, Labor, and Social Domination: A Reinterpretation of Marx's Critical Theory* (Cambridge; New York: Cambridge University Press, 2003), pp. 4–5. For Adorno it seems to makes sense to refer to social labor as a transhistorical conception, of which wage labor is a specific form that exists under particular relations of production. Moreover, the inalienably social labor to which he appeals exists alongside the abstract labor of the commodity form.

14. This becomes particularly clear in Michael Hardt and Antonio Negri's identification in the early part of the twenty-first century of the increasing importance to the production of surplus value of what they term 'intellectual, immaterial, and communicative labor power'; *Empire* (Cambridge, MA: Harvard University Press, 2001), p. 29. In their and Maurizio Lazzarato's accounts of 'immaterial labor' they not only identify the increased value-producing power of the 'new nature of productive activity' as a result of the emergence of 'a new "mass intellectuality"' that supposedly transforms the opposition of intellectual and manual labor, but also advance the claim that these changes harbor within them a latent capacity to result in emancipatory social change, a claim according to which 'immaterial labor thus seems to provide the potential for a kind of spontaneous and elementary communism'; Maurizio Lazzarato, 'Immaterial Labor', trans. by Paul Colilli and Ed Emory [*sic*], in

Radical Thought in Italy: A Potential Politics, ed. by Paolo Virno and Michael Hardt (Minneapolis: University of Minnesota Press, 1996), pp. 133–47; Hardt and Negri, p. 294. For in this account of the power of contemporary capitalist production they conflate the production of abstract value with that of social material wealth: they mistake what takes place on the level of the production of abstract value (that is to say, the increasing subsumption under capital of certain kinds of creative and intellectual labor) for that which happens in the production of material social wealth—the things and experiences that enrich life. In doing so they misrecognize the increasing mediation of intellectual and creative processes through the structures of the commodity form and the wage relation for a transformation in the nature of abstract labor such that it comes to represent a potential for emancipatory social change. That is to say, this misrecognition involves the failure to acknowledge the distinction between on the one hand surface similarity and resemblance, and on the other hand the fungibility that results from the subsumption of activities under the wage relation, regardless of any surface similarity (or lack thereof): what characterizes this fungibility is that it is indifferent to the particularity of the processes, and thus also to any similarities. The 'immateriality' of the immaterial labor discussed by Lazzarato and Hardt and Negri pertains solely to its surface qualities, and is as such indifferent to the (themselves no less material) economic and social conditions under which it takes place. Rather than being emancipatory, the phenomenon of 'immaterial labor' is an index of the increasing commodification, instrumentalization, and monetization—the increasing mediation through the value form—not only of leisure time and activities, but also of creative and intellectual activity, and thus the expansion of the working day, or rather the increasing permeability of its limits. In this respect my dissent from Hardt and Negri's account of the immaterial labor—that their analysis of its immateriality refers to its surface characteristics in such a way that it distracts from the material social and economic conditions which efface the distinction between 'material' and 'immaterial' labor, rendering them equivalent and reciprocally exchangeable—is not only terminological (which it is insofar as it sites materiality on the side of the surface activity rather than that of the structural relations within which it takes place), but also substantive in that their identification of a change in the constitution of labor is in fact evidence of the increasing fungibility of intellectual and creative activity as the result of its subsumption under capital; cf. Josh Robinson, "'Abject Self on Patrol": Immaterial Labour, Affect, and Subjectivity in Andrea Brady's "Cold Calling"', in *Complicities: British Poetry 1945–2007*, ed. by Robin Purves and Sam Ladkin (Prague: Litteraria Pragensia, 2007), pp. 253–70 (pp. 262–63). Hardt and Negri are right to see that the dichotomy between manual and intellectual labor has been broken down. And precisely because it has been broken down—because manual and intellectual labor are increasingly exchangeable—the surface change they observe in the labor process pales into insignificance when set against the background of the resulting increase in the activities that become exchangeable as a result. And this misrecognition becomes visible when one attends not to the materiality or immateriality of the product of labor, but rather to the material social and economic conditions under which labor takes place.

15. Alfred Sohn-Rethel, *Intellectual and Manual Labour: A Critique of Epistemology*, trans. by Martin Sohn-Rethel (Atlantic Highlands, NJ: Humanities Press, 1978), p. 20, emphasis original. When Jürgen Ritsert observes that Adorno's 'lines of the argument occasionally seem to be constructed as if comparing [*Vergleichen*], equating [*Gleichsetzen*], that is to say identifying [*Identifizieren*] a with b . . . n, meant the same as "equalizing" ["*Gleichmachen*"]', he is thus drawing attention to a tendency that is repudiated by Adorno's own distinction between surface similarity and the exchangeability of this real abstraction (which goes back to Marx's analysis of the separation of exchange value from use value in the analysis of the commodity in the first chapter of *Capital*). 'Das Nichtidentische bei Adorno—Substanz- oder Problembegriff?', *Zeitschrift für kritische Theorie*, 4 (1997), 29–51 (p. 44).

16. Kant, *Kritik der Urteilskraft*, pp. 119–22.

17. Ernst Lohoff, 'Die Kategorie der abstrakten Arbeit und ihre historische Entfaltung', *Marxistische Kritik*, 1 (1986), 49–69 (p. 51). Adorno's assertion thus calls into question the claim of abstract labor to be a transhistorical category, and to stand for all the historical and possible kinds of making (the claim advanced not only the classical political economists who retrospectively apply the categories of the capitalist economy to historical or [more usually] fictional or imagined non-capitalist situations in order to find the historical justification for the analysis of the factors of production, but also of those who misinterpret the Marxian labor theory of value as the claim that everything worthwhile in society is the result of labor, transhistorically understood, and who thus miss the implications of the critique of political economy, arguing for a fairer distribution of the surplus value that results from commodity-producing labor rather than for the end to the mediation of life through the oppressive category of abstract labor).

18. For a critical account of Adorno's appeal to the irreversibility of the historical relationships between art, society, capital, and (particularly) religion, see Simon Jarvis, 'Irreversibility', *Anglia—Zeitschrift für Englische Philologie*, 129.1–2 (2011), 41–57.

19. James Gordon Finlayson, 'The Artwork and the *Promesse du Bonheur* in Adorno', *European Journal of Philosophy*, 23.3 (2015), 392–419 (p. 410).

20. Hammer, p. 214. This of course illuminates the extent of the gap between Adorno's modernist aesthetics and the cynicism (whether resigned or avowedly reactionary) of a great many contemporary artworks. The normative force of Adorno's poetics of form is thus directed not only at the way in which the process of forming shapes the content, expression and material that is formed, but also (and to the same extent and for the same reasons) at the stance taken by art with respect to society and its critique. This is the force of Hammer's claim that art 'continues the project that philosophy, in its Kantian and post-Kantian shape, had articulated

but, with the exhaustion of this tradition (and especially its claims to totality), is no longer capable of adequately addressing' (p. 211): the achievements of artworks that are worthy of the name are never merely aesthetic.

21. This is made clearest in as his discussion of the dissonance in *The Philosophy of New Music*:

> Dissonances originated as the expression of tension, contradiction and pain. They have sedimented and have become 'material'. They are no longer media of subjective expression. But this does not mean that they deny their origin. They become characters of objective protest. It is the enigmatic happiness of these sounds that precisely because of their transformation into material they master the suffering that they made known by holding on to it. Their negativity holds faith in utopia; it confines the concealed consonance within itself. Thus new music's passionate sensitivity to everything that resembles consonance. (PnM 84–85/PMM 86)

This passage, from a book first published in 1949, Adorno's first to be published in Germany after the end of the National Socialist regime (PnM 207), brings together several of the elements of the conceptual constellation of form explored in the first four chapters of this book. Dissonances are conceived as subjective expression; in the account of their sedimentation into material can be seen a condensed version of that which is later expanded, as discussed in the first and fourth chapters in particular, of the sedimentation of content into form, and of form into the material repertoire for the composition of future artworks. What becomes clear here is the intimate relationship of dissonance to harmony. It is not simply the case that dissonance, defined in opposition to harmony, retains a reciprocal connection to its other by means of this conceptual distinction; it is rather the case that dissonance comes to contain harmony within itself as a result of this process of sedimentation. As the expression of suffering, dissonance comes to master the suffering that it expresses by preserving it for the sake of the utopian abolition of suffering—the aspiration which dissonance contains within itself is the cause of its aversion to consonance or harmony as the false proclamation of utopia's realization, which can in fact be nothing other than resigned accommodation to the administered world.

22. Finlayson, p. 411.

23. Walter Benjamin, 'Über Sprache überhaupt und über die Sprache des Menschen', in *Gesammelte Schriften*, ed. by Rolf Tiedemann (Frankfurt am Main: Suhrkamp, 1972), 2.1, 141–57 (p. 151).

24. Benjamin, 'Über Sprache überhaupt und über die Sprache des Menschen', p. 156.

25. The distinction of artworks from this instrumental human language gives the lie to any attempt to formulate a structuralist account of artworks as

meaning-producing within a semiotic system. For the formulation of such a system in order to analyze language involves removing the elements of particularity that defy systematization, and reducing language to those elements on the basis of which such a generalized account can be made (something of this reduction can be seen, for example, the designation as 'paralanguage' of the apparently incidental aspects of expression, and their discussion—as well as that of literature—under the rubric of communication). And it is important to acknowledge that such attempts are also more strongly encouraged than they might be by Benjamin and Adorno's potentially misleading use of the term 'language' to refer both to human language and to the silent and nameless language of things that has so little in common with our language of names. Indeed, Adorno's sense that the language proper to artworks, their proximity to the language of things, consists in the 'organization of their disparate moments' is in danger of falling prey to the same pitfall, of the conception of organization as an (albeit nonreferential) meaning-producing, relational system.

26. My argument here is in many respects analogous to Finlayson's reinterpretation of the promise of happiness presented by artworks away from a view founded on the contrast between 'the subject's aesthetic delight in the work' and 'the subject's disappointment at existing society', and toward its foundation on the artwork's revelation of 'the social world as one that is unworthy of affirmation'; Finlayson, pp. 403, 410. The happiness at stake here is not that of the culinary, the satisfaction of manufactured desires, but nonetheless includes physical as well as intellectual pleasure, 'visceral enjoyment, bliss, [. . .] sensuous, somatic satisfaction' or in Jarvis's terms 'the utopian wish for undeluded happiness, including bodily pleasure, the wish for an end to suffering'; Finlayson, p. 396; Simon Jarvis, 'Adorno, Marx, Materialism', in *The Cambridge Companion to Adorno*, ed. by Tom Huhn (Cambridge: Cambridge University Press, 2004), pp. 79–100 (p. 80).

27. This thinking finds its echo in Adorno's repeated the characterization of existing social relations in his postwar writings as those of a 'false society' (cf. DA 73/DE 43, DA 163/DE 112, DA 232/DE 170, MM 50/Jephcott 45, ND 293/Ashton 298, ÄT 35/AT 18, GS 8: 64, NzL 28/NtL 1: 19, NzL 553/NtL 2: 208).

28. Marx, *Januar 1859–Februar 1860*, p. 15; *Das Kapital*, I, p. 49.

29. Endnotes, 'The History of Subsumption', *Endnotes*, 2 (2010), 130–53 (p. 139).

30. The word that I have translated as intrapersonal, *innermenschlich*, can arguably refer to a quality that abides as much within the human as within the individual human being. It is not used here in opposition to *zwischenmenschlich*, interpersonal, but to refer to everything that is within the capacity of human thought in its current state.

31. Peter Osborne claims that '[g]enerally, although by no means always, Adorno writes of *kunstliche* [sic] *Erfahrung*, "artistic experience", rather than *Ästhetische* [sic] *Erfahrung*, "aesthetic experience", when it is the experience of the art work qua art work that is at issue' ('Art Beyond Aesthetics: Philosophical Criticism, Art

History and Contemporary Art', *Art History*, 27.4 [2004], 651–70 [p. 669n]). In *Aesthetic Theory* Adorno regularly uses *ästhetische Erfahrung* to refer to the experience of artworks as such (e.g. ÄT 95/AT 60, ÄT 141/AT 91, ÄT 159/AT 103, ÄT 185/AT 122). However, this is not to claim that he uses the two terms interchangeably: while *künstlerische Erfahrung* is restricted to the experience of artworks, *ästhetische Erfahrung* is on occasion used more broadly, whether to refer to the experience of natural beauty (e.g. ÄT 107/AT 68, ÄT 109/AT 69) or the potential relationships between aesthetic experience and society more generally, such as the need for 'genuine aesthetic experience to become philosophy it is to be anything' (ÄT 197/AT 131).

32. This is a strikingly similar position to that taken by Peter de Bolla, who, following late Heidegger and Lacoue-Labarthe, argues that what he terms art experiences, experiences of art as they occur to a perceiving subject, 'do not belong to that subject, nor are they made by the subject'; 'Toward the Materiality of Aesthetic Experience', *Diacritics*, 32.1 (2002), 19–37 (p. 34). In making this argument, however, de Bolla attributes what is in effect an Adornian position to Heidegger, who is discussing not aesthetic experience but the general experience of a something, 'be it a thing, a person, a god'; Martin Heidegger, 'Das Wesen der Sprache', in *Unterwegs zur Sprache* (Pfullingen: Neske, 1959), pp. 157–216. Adorno, in contrast, insists on the distinction, that the experience of artworks cannot be considered a particular case of experience in general, but rather calls into question what we think we know about experience, insisting on its falsity because of its conceptual mediation; cf. de Bolla, p. 34. For a fuller account of the affinities between Adorno's thought and that of Heidegger, see Mörchen.

33. This is arguably more strongly the case in the German-speaking world than elsewhere, where the *Naturfreunde* or 'Friends of Nature' was the name taken by the socialist organization, founded in Vienna in 1895, with the aim of organizing and providing leisure activities for trade unionists.

34. Brian O'Connor, *Adorno* (London; New York: Routledge, 2013), p. 73.

35. This implies that the concept of the subject is itself not, or not only, subjective, as is expressed most clearly in Adorno's insistence that 'subject is for its part object in a qualitatively different, more radical sense than object itself, because object simply is not known except through consciousness, is also subject' (S 746/CM 249). This is not a denial of or an attempt to efface the distinction between subject and object, less still an insistence on or assertion of their unarticulated unity: Adorno works with a clear demarcation between not their identities but their functions, according to which the subject is the how of the mediation of which object is that which is mediated (S 746/CM 249). It is rather the case that they are intertwined, that the hypostatization of the function of the how into a concept of the subject transforms this subjective function into something that is no longer wholly subjective. Moreover, the function is only subjective to the extent that it mediates a something: just as object is also subject because it is only consciousness that turns it into object, so too is subject also object because without this something mediated

there is no mediation. And not only through this mediation but also through its transformation from function into a concept with the object to which it refers, it is transformed into something objective: 'If subject is not something—and "something" denotes an irreducibly objective moment—it is not at all' (S 747/CM 250).

36. Rose, 'From Speculative to Dialectical Thinking—Hegel and Adorno', p. 61.

37. Jarvis, 'What Is Speculative Thinking?', p. 81. Jarvis is referring to the closing pages of the 'Meditations on Metaphysics' that conclude *Negative Dialectics*, but the same can certainly be said of the 'Dialectical Epilegomena' in *Keywords*, the second volume of *Critical Models*.

38. Kant, *Kritik der Urteilskraft*, p. 132.

39. Jameson, *Late Marxism*, p. 159.

Coda

1. This is not a claim that lyric is the origin of all literature, less still that it represents its highest form, but rather that the primacy of language within lyric reveals something that is the case, if less evidently, in all literature. In this respect it is not an endorsement of the Kantian claim that poetry occupies the highest rank among the arts (*Kritik der Urteilskraft*, pp. 265–67). Adorno's insistence on language as the site of this resemblance also distinguishes his claim from Heidegger's famous assertion that '*[a]ll art*, as the letting happen of the future of the truth at which is as such, is *in essence poetry*'; 'Der Ursprung des Kunstwerkes' (1994), p. 59, emphasis original.

2. Jonathan Culler, 'Why Lyric?', *PMLA*, 123.1 (2008), 201–06 (p. 203).

3. Immanuel Kant, *Kritik der praktischen Vernunft. Grundlegung zur Metaphysik der Sitten*, ed. by Wilhelm Weischedel, Werkausgabe in 12 Bänden, 7 (Frankfurt am Main: Suhrkamp, 1977), pp. 67–73.

4. Stewart Martin, 'The Absolute Artwork Meets the Absolute Commodity', *Radical Philosophy*, 146 (2007), 15–25 (p. 19).

5. This represents the culmination of the process identified by Marx in *Capital*, in which the use value of the money commodity is doubled as it takes on the additional use value of representing value; *Das Kapital*, I, pp. 104–05.

6. Cf. Sigmund Freud, *Abriss der Psychoanalyse. Das Unbehagen in der Kultur* (Frankfurt am Main: Fischer, 1987), p. 92.

7. Martin, p. 18.

8. Robert Kaufman, 'Lyric Commodity Critique, Benjamin Adorno Marx, Baudelaire Baudelaire Baudelaire', *PMLA*, 123.1 (2008), 207–15 (p. 211).

9. Howard Caygill, 'Lyric Poetry before Auschwitz', in *Adorno and Literature*, ed. by David Cunningham and Nigel Mapp (London: Continuum, 2006), pp. 69–83 (p. 73).

10. Kornbluh, p. 14.
11. Kornbluh, p. 13.
12. Kornbluh, p. 15.
13. Wolfson, 'Reading for Form', p. 8.
14. Kornbluh, p. 15.
15. My tentative hypothesis is that this commitment at once to close reading and to its wider implications (not only literary but also intellectual, political and social) is the motivation for Kornbluh and Bogel's use of scare quotes when referring to close reading; cf. Bogel, p. 3, and my discussion in the opening section of the introduction.
16. Kornbluh, pp. 15–16.
17. Kornbluh, p. 16; Wolfson, 'Reading for Form', p. 16; Kornbluh, p. 165.
18. Kornbluh, p. 16.
19. Kornbluh, pp. 70, 65.
20. Kornbluh, p. 70.
21. Kornbluh, p. 70.
22. Kornbluh, p. 20.
23. *Marx & Engels on Literature and Art*, pp. 114–15, 105.
24. Kornbluh, p. 57, emphasis original.
25. Kornbluh, p. 57.
26. C. Levine, *Forms*, p. 111.
27. C. Levine, *Forms*, p. 42.
28. C. Levine, 'Scaled Up, Writ Small', p. 105, emphasis original.
29. C. Levine, *Forms*, p. 42.
30. Julia Sun-Joo Lee, *The American Slave Narrative and the Victorian Novel* (New York: Oxford University Press, 2010), p. 111; C. Levine, *Forms*, p. 42.
31. Cited in Lee, p. 111, emphasis original.
32. C. Levine, *Forms*, pp. 42, 41, emphasis original.
33. C. Levine, *Forms*, pp. 134, 135.
34. Leighton, p. 263.
35. C. Levine, *Forms*, p. 135.
36. C. Levine, *Forms*, p. 149.
37. *Marx & Engels on Literature and Art*, p. 9; C. Levine, *Forms*, p. 137.
38. C. Levine, *Forms*, p. 134.
39. C. Levine, *Forms*, p. 135.
40. C. Levine, *Forms*, p. 134.
41. C. Levine, *Forms*, p. 136.
42. C. Levine, *Forms*, p. 150.
43. C. Levine, *Forms*, pp. 123, 122.
44. Ritsert, p. 30, emphasis original.
45. Ritsert, p. 46.

46. Heidegger, 'Der Ursprung des Kunstwerkes' (1994), pp. 11, 12.

47. Peter Uwe Hohendahl, 'The Use Value of Contemporary and Future Literary Criticism', trans. by David Bathrick, *New German Critique*, 7 (1976), 3–20 (p. 18). One model for such a rethinking is provided by Kornbluh's contention 'that realist form is an economically astute mode of thinking' and her examination of the ways in which form can contribute to the destabilizing and challenging of the trope of psychic economy, a trope which 'crystallizes one of the pivotal ideologies of modernity' (Kornbluh, p. 20).

Works Cited

Adorno, Theodor W., *Gesammelte Schriften*, ed. by Rolf Tiedemann et al., 20 vols (Frankfurt am Main: Suhrkamp, 1972–86)

———, *Nachgelassene Schriften*, ed. by Theodor W. Adorno Archiv (Frankfurt am Main: Suhrkamp, 1993–)

———, *Aesthetic Theory*, trans. by Robert Hullot-Kentor (London: Continuum, 1997)

———, *Against Epistemology: A Metacritique*, trans. by Willis Domingo (Cambridge, UK: Polity, 2013)

———, *Alban Berg: Master of the Smallest Link*, trans. by Christopher Hailey and Juliane Brand (Cambridge: Cambridge University Press, 1994)

———, *Beethoven: The Philosophy of Music*, trans. By Edmund Jephcott (Cambridge, UK: Polity, 2002)

———, *Berg. Der Meister des kleinsten Übergangs*, Österreichische Komponisten des XX. Jahrhunderts, 15 (Vienna: Lafite/Österreichischer Bundesverlag, 1968)

———, *Can One Live after Auschwitz? A Philosophical Reader*, ed. by Rolf Tiedemann, trans. by Rodney Livingstone et al. (Stanford, CA: Stanford University Press, 2003)

———, *Critical Models: Interventions and Catchwords*, trans. by Henry W. Pickford (New York: Columbia University Press, 2005)

———, *The Culture Industry: Selected Essays on Mass Culture*, ed. by J. M. Bernstein (London: Routledge, 1973)

———, *Essays on Music*, ed. by Richard Leppert, trans. by Susan H. Gillespie et al. (Berkeley; Los Angeles; London: University of California Press, 2002)

———, *Hegel: Three Studies*, trans. by Shierry Weber Nicholsen (Cambridge, MA; London: MIT Press, 1993)

———, *In Search of Wagner*, trans. by Rodney Livingstone (London: New Left Books, 1981)

———, *Introduction to the Sociology of Music*, trans. by E. B. Ashton (New York: Seabury, 1976)

———, 'Kapitelästhetik', 1968, Theodor W. Adorno–Archiv, Frankfurt am Main

―――, 'Letter to Walter Benjamin, August 2, 1935', in *Briefe*, by Walter Benjamin, ed. by Gershom Sholem and Theodor W. Adorno, 2 vols (Frankfurt am Main: Suhrkamp, 1978), II, 671–83

―――, 'Letter to Walter Benjamin, November 10, 1938', in *Briefe*, by Walter Benjamin, ed. by Gershom Sholem and Theodor W. Adorno, 2 vols (Frankfurt am Main: Suhrkamp, 1978), II, 782–90

―――, Letter to Peter Rühmkorf, 13 February 1964, currently uncatalogued TS from the Theodor W. Adorno–Archiv, Frankfurt am Main.

―――, Letter to Peter Szondi, 3 December 1963, currently uncatalogued TS from the Theodor W. Adorno–Archiv, Frankfurt am Main.

―――, *Mahler: A Musical Physiognomy*, trans. by Edmund Jephcott (Chicago; London: University of Chicago Press, 1992)

―――, *Minima Moralia: Reflections from Damaged Life*, trans. by E. F. N. Jephcott (London: Verso, 1978)

―――, *Negative Dialectics*, trans. by E. B. Ashton (London; New York: Routledge, 1973)

―――, *Night Music: Essays on Music, 1928–1962*, ed. by Rolf Tiedemann, trans. by Wieland Hoban (London; New York; Calcutta: Seagull, 2009)

―――, *Notes to Literature*, ed. by Rolf Tiedemann, trans. by Shierry Weber Nicholsen, 2 vols (New York; Chichester, UK: Columbia University Press, 1991)

―――, *Philosophy of Modern Music*, trans. by Anne G. Mitchell and Wesley V. Blomster (New York; London: Continuum: 2004)

―――, *Prisms*, trans. by Samuel and Shierry Weber [Samuel Weber and Shierry Weber Nicholsen] (Cambridge, MA: MIT Press, 1983)

―――, *Quasi una Fantasia: Essays on Modern Music*, trans. by Rodney Livingstone (London; New York: Verso, 1998)

Adorno, Theodor W., and Hans Eisler, *Composing for the Films* (London and New York: Continuum, 2005)'

Adorno, Theodor W., and Peter von Haselberg, 'Fragment als Form und Zufall', Norddeutscher Rundfunk, recorded February 2, 1967.

Adorno, Theodor W., and Alfred Sohn-Rethel, *Briefwechsel 1936–1939*, ed. by Christoph Gödde (Munich: Text + Kritik, 1991)

Andrews, Bruce, 'Poetry as Explanation, Poetry as Praxis', in *The Politics of Poetic Form: Poetry and Public Policy*, ed. by Charles Bernstein (New York: Roof, 1990), pp. 23–43

―――, 'Total Equals What: Poetics and Praxis', in *A Guide to Poetics Journal: Writing in the Expanded Field, 1982–1998*, ed. by Lyn Hejinian and Barrett Watten (Middletown, CT: Wesleyan University Press, 2013), pp. 185–96

Arac, Jonathan, 'Anglo-Globalism?', *New Left Review*, 2002, 35–45

Arthos, John, *Gadamer's Poetics: A Critique of Modern Aesthetics*, Bloomsbury Studies in Continental Philosophy (London: Bloomsbury, 2013)

Attridge, Derek, *The Rhythms of English Poetry* (London: Longman, 1982)

———, *The Singularity of Literature* (London; New York: Routledge, 2004)

Bambach, Charles, *Thinking the Poetic Measure of Justice: Hölderlin–Heidegger–Celan* (Albany: State University of New York Press, 2013)

Beißner, Friedrich, 'Einführung in Hölderlins Lyrik', in *Sämtliche Werke*, by Friedrich Hölderlin, ed. by Friedrich Beißner, 6 vols (Stuttgart: Kohlhammer/Cottasche Buchhandlung, 1953), II, 499–511

de Beistegui, Miguel, *Aesthetics After Metaphysics: From Mimesis to Metaphor* (London; New York: Routledge, 2012)

Benjamin, Walter, *Das Passagen–Werk*, ed. by Rolf Tiedemann, Gesammelte Schriften, 5, 2 vols (Frankfurt am Main: Suhrkamp, 1982)

———, 'Der Autor als Produzent', in *Gesammelte Schriften*, ed. by Rolf Tiedemann (Frankfurt am Main: Suhrkamp, 1972), 2.2, 683–701

———, 'Der Sürrealismus. Die letzte Momentaufnahme der europäischen Intelligenz', in *Gesammelte Schriften*, ed. by Rolf Tiedemann (Frankfurt am Main: Suhrkamp, 1972), 2.1, 295–310

———, 'Die Aufgabe des Übersetzers', in *Gesammelte Schriften*, ed. by Rolf Tiedemann (Frankfurt am Main: Suhrkamp, 1972), 4.1, 9–21

———, 'Letter to May Horkheimer, September 28, 1938', in *Briefe*, by Walter Benjamin, ed. by Gershom Sholem and Theodor W. Adorno, 2 vols (Frankfurt am Main: Suhrkamp, 1978), II, 772–76

———, 'The Work of Art in the Age of its Technological Reproducibility', in *Selected Writings: 1938–1940*, ed. by Howard Eiland and Michael William Jennings, trans. by Edmund Jephcott and Harry Zohn, 4 vols (Cambridge, MA: Harvard University Press, 2003), III, 101–33

———, 'Über Sprache überhaupt und über die Sprache des Menschen', in *Gesammelte Schriften*, ed. by Rolf Tiedemann (Frankfurt am Main: Suhrkamp, 1972), 2.1, 141–57

———, *Versuche über Brecht* (Frankfurt am Main: Suhrkamp, 1966)

van den Bergh, Gerhard, *Adornos philosophisches Deuten von Dichtung. Ästhetische Theorie und Praxis der Interpretation: Der Hölderlin-Essay als Modell* (Bonn: Bouvier, 1989)

Bernstein, Charles, 'Comedy and the Poetics of Political Form', in *The Politics of Poetic Form: Poetry and Public Policy*, ed. by Charles Bernstein (New York: Roof, 1990), pp. 235–44

———, 'Preface', in *The Politics of Poetic Form: Poetry and Public Policy*, ed. by Charles Bernstein (New York: Roof, 1990), pp. vii–viii

Bernstein, J. M., *Against Voluptuous Bodies: Late Modernism and the Meaning of Painting* (Stanford, CA: Stanford University Press, 2006)

———, *The Fate of Art: Aesthetic Alienation from Kant to Derrida and Adorno* (Cambridge, UK: Polity, 1993)

Betzen, Klaus, 'Bericht über die Jahresversammlung in Berlin, 7.–9. Juni 1963', *Hölderlin Jahrbuch*, 13 (1963–64), 172–84

Binder, W., 'Bericht über die Diskussion', *Hölderlin Jahrbuch*, 13 (1963–64), 185–86
Bloch, Ernst, *Erbschaft dieser Zeit* (Frankfurt am Main: Suhrkamp, 1962)
———, *Geist der Utopie* (Frankfurt am Main: Suhrkamp, 1971)
Bloch, Ernst, Walter Benjamin, Bertold Brecht, Georg Lukács, Theodor W Adorno, and Fredric Jameson, *Aesthetics and Politics*, ed. by Ronald Taylor (London: Verso, 1980)
Bogel, Fredric V., *New Formalist Criticism: Theory and Practice* (Basingstoke, UK; New York: Palgrave Macmillan, 2013)
de Bolla, Peter, 'Toward the Materiality of Aesthetic Experience', *Diacritics*, 32 (2002), 19–37
Breton, André, *Manifestes du surréalisme* (Paris: Gallimard, 1969)
Brown, Nicholas, 'The Work of Art in the Age of its Real Subsumption under Capital', *Nonsite.Org*, 2012 <http://nonsite.org/editorial/the-work-of-art-in-the-age-of-its-real-subsumption-under-capital> [accessed 10 May 2015]
Bruns, Gerald L., 'On the Conundrum of Form and Material in Adorno's Aesthetic Theory', *The Journal of Aesthetics and Art Criticism*, 66 (2008), 225–35
———, *The Material of Poetry: Sketches for a Philosophical Poetics* (Athens: University of Georgia Press, 2005)
Bryant, Levi R., Nick Srnicek, and Graham Harman, 'Towards a Speculative Philosophy', in *The Speculative Turn: Continental Materialism and Realism*, ed. by Levi R. Bryant, Nick Srnicek, and Graham Harman (Melbourne: re.press, 2011), pp. 1–18
Bubner, Rüdiger, 'Concerning the Central Idea of Adorno's Philosophy', in *The Semblance of Subjectivity: Essays in Adorno's Aesthetic Theory*, ed. by Tom Huhn and Lambert Zuidervaart, trans. by Cara Gendel Ryan (Cambridge, MA; London: MIT Press, 1997), pp. 147–75
Buck-Morss, Susan, *The Origin of Negative Dialectics: Theodor W. Adorno, Walter Benjamin, and the Frankfurt Institute* (New York; London: The Free Press, 1977)
Bürger, Peter, 'Das Vermittlungsproblem in der Kunstsoziologie Adornos', in *Materialien zur ästhetischen Theorie. Theodor W. Adornos Konstruktion der Moderne*, ed. by Burkhardt Lindner and W. Martin Lüdke (Frankfurt am Main: Suhrkamp, 1980), pp. 169–84
Castoriadis, Cornelius, *The Imaginary Institution of Society*, trans. by Kathleen Blamey (Cambridge, UK: Polity, 1987)
Caygill, Howard, *Art of Judgement* (Oxford: Blackwell, 1989)
———, 'Lyric Poetry before Auschwitz', in *Adorno and Literature*, ed. by David Cunningham and Nigel Mapp (London: Continuum, 2006), pp. 69–83
Cohen, Stephen, 'Introduction', in *Shakespeare and Historical Formalism*, ed. by Stephen Cohen (Aldershot, UK; Burlington, VT: Ashgate, 2007), pp. 1–27
Culler, Jonathan, 'The Mirror Stage', in *High Romantic Argument: Essays for M.H. Abrams*, ed. by Lawrence Lipking (Ithaca, NY: Cornell University Press, 1981), pp. 149–63

——, 'Why Lyric?', *PMLA*, 123 (2008), 201–06
Cunningham, David, and Nigel Mapp, 'Introduction', in *Adorno and Literature*, ed. by David Cunningham and Nigel Mapp (London: Continuum, 2006), pp. 1–5
Descartes, René, *A Discourse on Method*, trans. by John Veitch (New York: Dutton, 1951)
Eagleton, Terry, *Criticism and Ideology: A Study in Marxist Literary Theory* (London: Verso, 1978)
Endnotes, 'The History of Subsumption', *Endnotes*, 2 (2010), 130–53
Figal, Günter, *Erscheinungsdinge. Ästhetik als Phänomenologie* (Mohr Siebeck, 2010)
Finlayson, James Gordon, 'The Artwork and the *Promesse Du Bonheur* in Adorno', *European Journal of Philosophy*, 23 (2012), 392–419
Firth, Raymond, 'Art and Anthropology', in *Anthropology, Art and Aesthetics*, ed. by Jeremy Coote and Anthony Shelton (Oxford: Clarendon Press, 1992), pp. 15–39
de la Fontaine, Michael, 'Künstlerische Erfahrung bei Arnold Schönberg. Zur Dialektik des musikalischen Materials', in *Materialien zur ästhetischen Theorie. Theodor W. Adornos Konstruktion der Moderne*, ed. by Burkhardt Lindner and W. Martin Lüdke (Frankfurt am Main: Suhrkamp, 1980), pp. 467–93
Foster, Roger, *Adorno: The Recovery of Experience* (Albany: State University of New York Press, 2007)
Fowler, Alastair, *Kinds of Literature* (Oxford: Oxford University Press, 1982)
Freud, Sigmund, *Abriss der Psychoanalyse. Das Unbehagen in der Kultur* (Frankfurt am Main: Fischer, 1987)
Früchtl, Josef, *Mimesis. Konstellation eines Zentralbegriffs bei Adorno* (Würzburg: Königshausen & Neumann, 1986)
Gasché, Rodolphe, *The Idea of Form: Rethinking Kant's Aesthetics* (Stanford, CA: Stanford University Press, 2003)
Gell, Alfred, 'The Technology of Enchantment and the Enchantment of Technology', in *Anthropology, Art and Aesthetics*, ed. by Jeremy Coote and Anthony Shelton (Oxford: Clarendon Press, 1992), pp. 40–63
Genette, Gérard, 'Genres, "Types", Modes', *Poétique*, 1977, 389–421
Geuss, Raymond, *Outside Ethics* (Princeton, NJ; Oxford: Princeton University Press, 2005)
Gioia, Dana, 'Notes on the New Formalism', *The Hudson Review*, 40 (1987), 395–408
Grabar, Oleg, *The Mediation of Ornament* (Princeton, NJ: Princeton University Press, 1992)
Grenz, Friedemann, 'Zur architektonischen Stellung der Ästhetik in der Philosophie Adornos', in *Theodor W. Adorno*, Text + Kritik Sonderband (Munich: Edition Text + Kritik, 1983), pp. 119–29
Hamacher, Werner, *95 Thesen zur Philologie* (Frankfurt am Main; Holderbank: Engeler, 2010)

——, 'Für—die Philologie', in *Was ist eine philologische Frage? Beiträge zur Erkundung einer theoretischen Einstellung*, ed. by Jürgen Paul Schwindt (Frankfurt am Main: Suhrkamp, 2009), pp. 21–60
——, *Minima Philologica* (New York: Fordham University Press, 2015)
——, *Premises: Essays on Philosophy and Literature from Kant to Celan* (Stanford, CA: Stanford University Press, 1999)
Hammer, Espen, *Adorno's Modernism: Art, Experience, and Catastrophe* (Cambridge: Cambridge University Press, 2015)
Hardt, Michael, and Antonio Negri, *Empire* (Cambridge, MA: Harvard University Press, 2001)
Harman, Graham, *Guerrilla Metaphysics: Phenomenology and the Carpentry of Things* (Chicago: Open Court, 2005)
——, 'On Vicarious Causation', *Collapse: Philosophical Research and Development*, 2 (2007), 171–205
Hartman, Geoffrey, 'Beyond Formalism', *MLN*, 81 (1966), 542–56
Hay, Jonathan, 'The Functions of Chinese Painting: Toward a Unified Field Theory', in *Anthropologies of Art*, ed. by Mariët Westermann (Williamstown, MA: Sterling and Francine Clark Art Institute, 2005), pp. 111–23
Hegel, Georg Wilhelm Friedrich, *Vorlesungen über die Ästhetik*, ed. by Eva Moldenhauer and Karl Markus Michel, Werke in 20 Bänden, 13–15, 3 vols (Frankfurt am Main: Suhrkamp, 1986)
——, *Wissenschaft der Logik*, ed. by Eva Moldenhauer and Karl Markus Michel, Werke in 20 Bänden, 5–6, 2 vols (Frankfurt am Main: Suhrkamp, 1986)
Heidegger, Martin, 'Das Wesen der Sprache', in *Unterwegs zur Sprache* (Pfullingen: Neske, 1959), pp. 157–216
——, *Der Satz vom Grund* (Pfullingen: Neske, 1957)
——, 'Der Ursprung des Kunstwerkes', in *Holzwege* (Frankfurt am Main: Klostermann, 1994), pp. 1–74
——, 'Der Ursprung des Kunstwerkes', in *Holzwege* (Frankfurt am Main: Klostermann, 1950), pp. 7–68
——, 'Der Weg zur Sprache', in *Unterwegs zur Sprache* (Pfullingen: Neske, 1959), pp. 239–68
Helmling, Steven, *Adorno's Poetics of Critique* (London; New York: Continuum, 2009)
——, 'Constellation and Critique: Adorno's Constellation, Benjamin's Dialectical Image', *Postmodern Culture*, 14 (2003) <https://doi.org/10.1353/pmc.2003.0036>
Hohendahl, Peter Uwe, *Prismatic Thought: Theodor W. Adorno* (Lincoln, NE; London: University of Nebraska Press, 1997)
——, 'The Use Value of Contemporary and Future Literary Criticism', trans. by David Bathrick, *New German Critique*, 7 (1986), 3–20
Hölderlin, Friedrich, 'Andenken', in *Sämtliche Werke, Briefe und Dokumente*, ed. by D. E. Sattler, 12 vols (Munich: Luchterhand), xi, 121–23

———, 'Brod und Wein', in *Sämtliche Werke, Briefe und Dokumente*, ed. by D. E. Sattler, 12 vols (Munich: Luchterhand), IX, 240–48
———, 'Patmos', in *Sämtliche Werke*, ed. by Friedrich Beißner, 6 vols (Stuttgart: Kohlhammer/Cottasche Buchhandlung, 1953), II, 172–80
———, *Sämtliche Werke*, ed. by Friedrich Beißner, 6 vols (Stuttgart: Kohlhammer/ Cottasche Buchhandlung, 1953), II
———, *Sämtliche Werke* (Leipzig: Insel, undated)
———, *Selected Poems and Fragments*, trans. by Michael Hamburger (London: Penguin, 1998)
Horkheimer, Max, 'Traditionelle und kritische Theorie', in *Kritische Theorie. Eine Dokumentation*, ed. by Alfred Schmidt, 2 vols (Frankfurt am Main: Fischer, 1968), II, pp. 137–91
Horkheimer, Max, and Theodor W. Adorno, *Dialectic of Enlightenment: Philosophical Fragments*, ed. by Gunzelin Schmid Noerr, trans. by Edmund Jephcott (Stanford, CA: Stanford University Press, 2002)
Hösle, Vittorio, *Zur Geschichte der Ästhetik und Poetik* (Basel: Schwabe, 2013)
Hunt, Erica, 'Notes for an Oppositional Poetics', in *The Politics of Poetic Form*, ed. by Charles Bernstein (New York: Roof, 1990), pp. 197–212
Jameson, Fredric, *Late Marxism: Adorno or the Persistence of the Dialectic* (London: Verso, 1990)
———, *Marxism and Form: Twentieth-Century Dialectical Theories of Literature* (Princeton, NJ: Princeton University Press, 1974)
Jarvis, Simon, *Adorno: A Critical Introduction* (Cambridge, UK: Polity, 1998)
———, 'Adorno, Marx, Materialism', in *The Cambridge Companion to Adorno*, ed. by Tom Huhn (Cambridge: Cambridge University Press, 2004), pp. 79–100
———, 'Irreversibility', *Anglia—Zeitschrift für Englische Philologie*, 129 (2011), 41–57
———, 'Seconds Out', *TLS*, 13 January 2006, p. 23
———, 'What Does Art Know?', in *Aesthetics and the Work of Art: Adorno, Kafka, Richter*, ed. by Peter de Bolla and Stefan H. Uhlig (Basingstoke, UK: Palgrave Macmillan, 2009), pp. 57–70
———, 'What Is Historical Poetics?', in *Theory Aside*, ed. by Jason Potts and Daniel Stout (Durham; London: Duke University Press, 2014), pp. 97–116
———, 'What Is Speculative Thinking?', *Revue Internationale de Philosophie*, 2004 (2004), 69–83
Jay, Martin, *Adorno* (London: Fontana, 1984)
———, *Marxism and Totality: The Adventures of a Concept from Lukács to Habermas* (Berkeley; Los Angeles: University of California Press, 1984)
———, 'Mimesis and Mimetology: Adorno and Lacoue-Labarthe', in *The Semblance of Subjectivity: Essays in Adorno's Aesthetic Theory*, ed. by Tom Huhn and Lambert Zuidervaart (Cambridge, MA; London: MIT Press, 1997), pp. 29–53
Jones, Ewan James, *Coleridge and the Philosophy of Poetic Form* (Cambridge University Press, 2014)

Kafka, Franz, *Das Schloss* (Munich: Wolff, 1926)

———, *Der Prozeß*, ed. by Malcolm Pasley (Frankfurt am Main: Fischer, 2002)

Kant, Immanuel, *Kritik der praktischen Vernunft. Grundlegung zur Metaphysik der Sitten*, ed. by Wilhelm Weischedel, Werkausgabe in 12 Bänden, 7 (Frankfurt am Main: Suhrkamp, 1977)

———, *Kritik der reinen Vernunft*, ed. by Wilhelm Weischedel, Werkausgabe in 12 Bänden, 3-4, 2 vols (Frankfurt am Main: Suhrkamp, 1974)

———, *Kritik der Urteilskraft*, ed. by Wilhelm Weischedel, Werkausgabe in 12 Bänden, 10 (Frankfurt am Main: Suhrkamp, 1974)

Kaufman, Robert, 'Adorno's Social Lyric, and Literary Criticism Today: Poetics, Aesthetics, Modernity', in *The Cambridge Companion to Adorno*, ed. by Tom Huhn (Cambridge: Cambridge University Press, 2004), pp. 354–75

———, 'Lyric Commodity Critique, Benjamin Adorno Marx, Baudelaire Baudelaire Baudelaire', *PMLA*, 123 (2008), 207–15

———, 'Negatively Capable Dialectics: Keats, Vendler, Adorno, and the Theory of the Avant-Garde', *Critical Inquiry*, 27 (2001), 354–84

———, 'Red Kant, or the Persistence of the Third "Critique" in Adorno and Jameson', *Critical Inquiry*, 26 (2000), 682–724

Kayser, Wolfgang, *Das sprachliche Kunstwerk. Eine Einführung in die Literaturwissenschaft* (Berne; Munich: Francke, 1948)

Kornbluh, Anna, *Realizing Capital: Financial and Psychic Economies in Victorian Form* (New York: Fordham University Press, 2013)

Lazzarato, Maurizio, 'Immaterial Labor', trans. by Paul Colilli and Ed Emory [*sic*], in *Radical Thought in Italy: A Potential Politics*, ed. by Paolo Virno and Michael Hardt (Minneapolis: University of Minnesota Press, 1996), pp. 133–47

Lee, Julia Sun-Joo, *The American Slave Narrative and the Victorian Novel* (New York: Oxford University Press, 2010)

Lehman, Robert S., 'Formalism, Mere Form, and Judgment', *New Literary History*, 48 (2017), 245–63

Leighton, Angela, *On Form: Poetry, Aestheticism, and the Legacy of a Word* (Oxford: Oxford University Press, 2007)

Lesjak, Carolyn, 'Reading Dialectically', in *Literary Materialisms*, ed. by Mathias Nilges and Emilio Sauri (New York: Palgrave Macmillan, 2013), pp. 17–47

Levine, Caroline, *Forms: Whole, Rhythm, Hierarchy, Network* (Princeton, NJ; Oxford: Princeton University Press, 2015)

———, 'Scaled Up, Writ Small: A Response to Carolyn Dever and Herbert F. Tucker', *Victorian Studies*, 49 (2006), 100–05

———, 'Strategic Formalism: Toward a New Method in Cultural Studies', *Victorian Studies*, 48 (2006), 625–57

Levine, George, 'Introduction: Reclaiming the Aesthetic', in *Aesthetics and Ideology*, ed. by George Levine (New Brunswick, NJ: Rutgers University Press, 1994), pp. 1–28

Levinson, Marjorie, 'What Is New Formalism?', *PMLA*, 122 (2007), 558–69
Lohoff, Ernst, 'Die Kategorie der abstrakten Arbeit und ihre historische Entfaltung', *Marxistische Kritik*, 1986, 49–69
Lukács, Georg, *Essays über Realismus* (Neuwied; Berlin: Luchterhand, 1971)
——, *Theory of the Novel*, trans. by Anna Bostock (London: Merlin, 1978)
Lunn, Eugene, *Marxism and Modernism: An Historical Study of Lukács, Brencht, Benjamin, and Adorno* (Berkeley; Los Angeles; London: University of California Press, 1982)
Lypp, Bernhard, 'Selbsterhaltung und ästhetische Erfahrung. Zur Geschichtsphilosophie und ästhetischen Theorie Adornos', in *Materialien zur ästhetischen Theorie. Theodor W. Adornos Konstruktion der Moderne*, ed. by Burkhardt Lindner and W. Martin Lüdke (Frankfurt am Main: Suhrkamp, 1980), pp. 187–218
Martin, Stewart, 'The Absolute Artwork Meets the Absolute Commodity', *Radical Philosophy*, 146 (2007), 15–25
Marx, Karl, *Das Kapital: Kritik der politischen Ökonomie*, Karl Marx, Friedrich Engels: Werke, 23–25, 3 vols (Berlin: Dietz, 1962)
——, *Januar 1859–Februar 1860*, Karl Marx, Friedrich Engels: Werke, 13 (Berlin: Dietz, 1961)
——, *September 1864–Juli 1870*, Karl Marx, Friedrich Engels: Werke, 16 (Berlin: Dietz, 1962)
Marx, Karl, and Friedrich Engels, *Marx & Engels on Literature and Art: A Selection of Writings*, ed. by Lee Baxandall and Stefan Morawski (St. Louis, MO: Telos, 1973)
McKeon, Michael, *The Origins of the English Novel, 1600–1740* (Baltimore, MD: Johns Hopkins University Press, 1987)
McLaughlin, Kevin, *Poetic Force: Poetry after Kant* (Stanford, CA: Stanford University Press, 2014)
Medvedev, P. N., and M. M. Bakhtin, *The Formal Method in Literary Scholarship: A Critical Introduction to Sociological Poetics*, trans. by Albert J. Wehrle (Baltimore, MD; London: Johns Hopkins University Press, 1978)
Meillassoux, Quentin, *After Finitude: An Essay on the Necessity of Contingency, with a Preface by Alain Badiou*, trans. by Ray Brassier (London; New York: Bloomsbury, 2008)
Mitchell, W. J. T., 'The Commitment to Form; Or, Still Crazy after All These Years', *PMLA*, 118 (2003), 321–25
Mörchen, Hermann, *Adorno und Heidegger. Untersuchung einer philosophischen Kommunikationsverweigerung* (Stuttgart: Klett-Cotta, 1981)
Moretti, Franco, *Distant Reading* (London; New York: Verso, 2013)
Nägele, Rainer, 'Ancient Sports and Modern Transports: Hölderlin's Tragic Bodies', in *The Solid Letter: Readings of Friedrich Hölderlin*, ed. by Arios Fioretos (Stanford, CA: Stanford University Press, 1999), pp. 247–67

Nicholsen, Shierry Weber, *Exact Imagination, Late Work: On Adorno's Aesthetics* (Cambridge, MA; London: MIT Press, 1997)

Nowell Smith, David, *Sounding/Silence: Martin Heidegger at the Limits of Poetics* (New York: Fordham University Press, 2013)

O'Connor, Brian, *Adorno* (London; New York: Routledge, 2013)

Osborne, Peter, 'Art Beyond Aesthetics: Philosophical Criticism, Art History and Contemporary Art', *Art History*, 27 (2004), 651–70

Paddison, Max, *Adorno's Aesthetics of Music* (Cambridge: Cambridge University Press, 1993)

Paddison, Max Hallé, 'Music and its Social Mediation: The Concepts of Form and Material in T. W. Adorno's Aesthetics of Music' (unpublished doctoral dissertation, University of Exeter, 1990)

Plass, Ulrich, *Language and History in Theodor W. Adorno's 'Notes to Literature'* (London; New York: Routledge, 2006)

Plato, 'Republic', in *The Collected Dialogues of Plato*, ed. by Edith Hamilton and Huntington Cairns, trans. by Paul Shorey (Princeton, NJ: Princeton University Press), pp. 575–844

Porter, James I, *Nietzsche and the Philology of the Future* (Stanford, CA: Stanford University Press, 2000)

Postone, Moishe, *Time, Labor, and Social Domination: A Reinterpretation of Marx's Critical Theory* (Cambridge, MA; New York: Cambridge University Press, 2003)

Pyle, Forest, *Art's Undoing: In the Wake of a Radical Aestheticism* (New York: Fordham University Press, 2013)

Ritsert, Jürgen, 'Das Nichtidentische bei Adorno—Substanz- oder Problembegriff?', *Zeitschrift für kritische Theorie*, 4 (1997), 29–51

Robinson, Josh, '"Abject Self on Patrol": Immaterial Labour, Affect, and Subjectivity in Andrea Brady's "Cold Calling"', in *Complicities: British Poetry 1945–2007*, ed. by Robin Purves and Sam Ladkin (Prague: Litteraria Pragensia, 2007), pp. 253–70

———, 'Dialektik und Spekulation. Über die Grenzen der spekulativen Vernunft', in *Probleme der Dialektik heute*, ed. by Stefan Müller (Wiesbaden: VS Verlag für Sozialwissenschaften, 2009), pp. 229–46

———, 'Poetics', *The Year's Work in Critical and Cultural Theory*, 22 (2014), 131–54

———, 'Poetics', *The Year's Work in Critical and Cultural Theory*, 23 (2015), 248–69

———, 'Review of Ulrich Plass, *Language and History in Theodor W. Adorno's "Notes to Literature"'*, *British Journal of Aesthetics*, 49 (2009), 194–96

———, 'Speculation upon Speculation; or, a Contribution to the Critique of Philosophical Economy', in *Credo, Credit, Crisis: Speculations on Faith and Money*, ed. by Aidan Tynan, Laurent Milesi, and Christopher John Müller (Lanham, MD: Rowman and Littlefield, 2017) pp. 239-70

Rooney, Ellen, 'Form and Contentment', *MLQ: Modern Language Quarterly*, 61 (2000), 17–40

Rorty, Richard, ed., *The Linguistic Turn: Recent Essays in Philosophical Method* (Chicago: University Of Chicago Press, 1967)

———, 'Twenty-Five Years After', in *The Linguistic Turn: Recent Essays in Philosophical Method*, ed. by Richard Rorty (Chicago: University of Chicago Press, 1992), pp. 371–74

Rose, Gillian, 'From Speculative to Dialectical Thinking—Hegel and Adorno', in *Judaism and Modernity: Philosophical Essays* (Oxford; Cambridge, MA: Blackwell, 1993), pp. 53–63

———, *Hegel Contra Sociology* (London: Athlone Press, 1981)

———, *The Melancholy Science: An Introduction to the Thought of Theodor W. Adorno* (New York: Columbia University Press, 1978)

Runes, Dagobert D., and Harry G. Schrickel, eds, *Encyclopedia of the Arts* (New York: The Philosophical Library, 1946)

Ruthrof, Horst, *The Body in Language* (London; New York: Cassel, 2000)

Schultz, Karla L., *Mimesis on the Move: Theodor W. Adorno's Concept of Imitation* (Berne; Frankfurt am Main; New York; Paris: Peter Lang, 1990)

Scott, Clive, *The Poetics of French Verse: Studies in Reading* (Oxford: Clarendon Press, 1998)

Shaviro, Steven, *The Universe of Things: On Speculative Realism* (Minneapolis: University of Minnesota Press, 2014)

Singh, Surti, 'The Spiritualization of Art in Adorno's Aesthetic Theory', *Adorno Studies*, 1 (2017), 31–42

Sohn-Rethel, Alfred, *Geistige und körperliche Arbeit. Zur Theorie gesellschaftlicher Synthesis* (Frankfurt am Main: Suhrkamp, 1970)

———, *Intellectual and Manual Labour: A Critique of Epistemology*, trans. by Martin Sohn-Rethel (Atlantic Highlands, NJ: Humanities Press, 1978)

Szondi, Peter, 'Über philologische Erkenntnis', in *Schriften*, 2 vols (Frankfurt am Main: Suhrkamp, 1978), I, 263–86

Theile, Verena, 'New Formalism(s): A Prologue', in *New Formalisms and Literary Theory*, ed. by Verena Theile and Linda Tredennick (Basingstoke, UK; New York: Palgrave Macmillan, 2013), pp. 3–26

Trotsky, Leon, 'The Formalist School of Poetry and Marxism', in *Literature and Revolution*, trans. by Rose Strumsky (Ann Arbor: University of Michigan Press, 1960), pp. 162–83

Uehling, Theodore Edward, *The Notion of Form in Kant's 'Critique of Aesthetic Judgment'* (The Hague; Paris: Mouton, 1971)

Veeser, H. Aram, ed., *The New Historicism* (London; New York: Routledge, 1989)

Watt, Ian, *The Rise of the Novel: Studies in Defoe, Richardson and Fielding* (London: Chatto & Windus, 1963)

Wellmer, Albrecht, *Zur Dialektik von Moderne und Postmoderne. Vernunftkritik nach Adorno* (Frankfurt am Main: Suhrkamp, 1985)
Williams, Raymond, 'Base and Superstructure in Marxist Cultural Theory', in *Culture and Materialism: Selected Essays* (London: Verso, 2005), pp. 31–49
Wilson, Ross, 'Dialectical Aesthetics and the Kantian *Rettung*: On Adorno's *Aesthetic Theory*', *New German Critique*, 35 (2008), 55–69
——, *Subjective Universality in Kant's Aesthetics* (Oxford; New York: Peter Lang, 2007)
Wolfson, Susan J., *Formal Charges: The Shaping of Poetry in British Romanticism* (Stanford, CA: Stanford University Press, 1997)
——, 'Reading for Form', *MLQ: Modern Language Quarterly*, 61 (2000), 1–16
Wolin, Richard, *The Terms of Cultural Criticism: The Frankfurt School, Existentialism, Poststructuralism* (New York: Columbia University Press, 1995)
——, 'Benjamin, Adorno, Surrealism', in *The Semblance of Subjectivity: Essays in Adorno's Aesthetic Theory*, ed. by Tom Huhn and Lambert Zuidervaart (Cambridge, MA; London: MIT Press, 1997), pp. 93–122
Wood, Michael, *Literature and the Taste of Knowledge* (Cambridge: Cambridge University Press, 2005)
Zuidervaart, Lambert, *Adorno's Aesthetic Theory: The Redemption of Illusion* (Cambridge, MA; London: MIT Press, 1991)

Index

abstract labor, 166–70, 172–5, 177, 191, 221
abstract value, 188
abstraction, and exchange, 170–5
Adorno, Theodor W.: aesthetic theory of, 14 (regarding music, 9–10); critique of metaphysics, 194–5; on the form of the thing, 28–33; planned monograph on Beethoven, 69; rejection of method, 30; talk on lyric and society, 201–2; translations of, 22; writings of (*Aesthetic Theory*, 10, 13, 16, 19, 21, 25, 28, 30, 31–2, 40, 44, 46, 54, 63, 64, 67, 68, 72, 83, 84, 86, 93, 99, 101, 102, 107, 108, 110, 113, 115, 116, 117, 119, 125, 127, 131, 135, 142, 144, 146, 147, 149, 153, 165, 170–1, 187, 203, 204, 206; 'Arnold Schönberg,' 68; 'Art and the Arts,' 30, 97, 136; 'Aspects,' 169; 'Bach Defended from his Admirers,' 69; 'Bloch's *Spuren*,' 71; 'Bibliographical Sketches,' 19; 'Commitment,' 164, 170–1, 202; *Composing for Film*, 68, 118; *Dialectic of Enlightenment*, 19, 23, 71, 93, 115, 116, 167, 193; *Introduction to the Sociology of Music*, 143, 169; 'Looking Back on Surrealism,' 76; *Metacritique of Epistemology*, 51; *Minima Moralia*, 72, 81, 146; 'Musical Expressionism,' 73; *Negative Dialectics*, 13, 19, 24, 79, 93, 108, 110, 169, 173, 186–7, 194; 'Notes on Kafka,' 81, 83, 84; 'Notes on Wagner,' 68; *Notes to Literature*, 11, 70, 135, 155; on form, 7, 8–12; on literary expressionism, 70; on lyric, 26; on music, 25, 135; 'On Subject and Object,' 82, 184; 'On the Classicism of Goethe's *Iphigenie*,' 158; 'Paralipomena' to *Aesthetic Theory*, 80; 'Parataxis: on Hölderlin's Late Lyric,' 25, 28, 33, 112, 122, 131, 156, 157, 202; 'Presuppositions,' 71; 'Punctuation Marks,' 52; 'Reaction and Progress,' 139; 'The Essay as Form,' 29, 127, 129, 131, 221; 'The History of Style in Schönberg's Work,' 68; *The Faithful Chorus-Master*, 118; *The Philosophy of New Music*, 43, 73, 104, 139; 'The Position of the

Adorno, Theodor W. *(continued)*
  Narrator in the Contemporary Novel,' 121; 'Theories on the Origin of Art,' 30–1, 85, 149; 'Vers une musique informelle,' 21, 87; 'Why Still Philosophy?,' 20
aesthetic comportment, 191
aestheticism, radical, 15
aesthetics, 16; concept of, 10, 13; definition of, 12
agency, of makers, 198
Akademie der Künste, Berlin, 33
alienation: naming of, 124–5; use of term, 206 *see also* self-alienation
Althusser, Louis, 9
Andrews, Bruce, 18, 133
Anschauung, translation of, 32
antagonism, social, 201; contingency of, 186
anti-nominalism, 112, 114
anti-realism, 125
art: and non-art, 206; artifactual moment of, 178; as objective form of spirit, 43–4; connection with nature, 197; hostile to concept, 110; in present conditions of production, 134; inclusional definition of, 150; interaction with social reality, 131; language-like character of, 181–2; not identified with nature, 190; paradoxical task of, 78; possibility of, 1; pseudomorphosis into nature, 193; relapses into fetishism, 204; relation to empirical world, 44; relation to politics, 164; relation to reality, 178; relation to society, 26, 162, 219; resistant to domination of capital, 124, 142; resistant to domination of exchange, 110; resistant to social domination, 126 *see also* bourgeois art
art beauty, 189–94
Arthos, John, 16–17, 21
artistic, concept of, 95, 135
artistic freedom, 146
artistic *métier*, 189, 197
artistic making, 178, 190, 191, 192, 197, 207, 217, 218; relation to abstract labor, 172–3
artworks: abrogation of claim to direct effect, 180; absolute, 203; as conceptual slippages, 198; as container for emotions, 67, 68; as logical and inexplicable, 197; as longing for future society, 187; as monads, 192; as nexus of interrelating modalities, 186; as organic whole, 128; as phenomenon of capitalist society, 176–7; as products, 147 (of social labor, 166, 169, 174–5, 205); as totality, 106; as vector of power, 198; as writing of history, 191, 192; aspiration to reality, 186; criteria for judgment of, 145; dependent on fetishism, 204–5; distinct from documents, 109; do not belong to authers, 159; dual character of, 191; elude concept, 198; enigmatic character of, 94, 101; expression of, 64; formal specificities of, 47; hostile to their subordinating concepts, 111; integral, 158; language-like nature of, 11, 54, 55, 89, 101, 153; magical origins of, 46; make promise of happiness, 176; materiality of, 134; multiple aspects of, 218; not commodities, 174; not separate

from commodity, 170; opposed
 to commodity, 170, 177; opposed
 to exchangeability, 171, 174, 175;
 origin of, 31; relation to social
 change, 217; relation to society, 46;
 resistant to being-for-another, 110;
 resistant to domination, 165, 184,
 192; result of domination, 192;
 self-alienation of, 162; subjective
 paradox of, 86, 87; success of, 103,
 137; testify to sociality, 175; the
 how of, 87; thinking ways of, 220;
 turn away from praxis, 46; within
 capitalist society, 203
Attridge, Derek, 19
attuned comportment, 189, 207, 222
aufheben, translation of, 23
aufreihen, 115
Ausdruck, 64

de Balzac, Honoré, 83, 210, 215
Bambach, Charles, 15
Baudelaire, Charles, 203, 204
beautiful, the, 46, 49, 101
beauty: affinity with death, 64–5; in
 art, 166; natural, 119–20, 166,
 196–7; perfect, 66; pertaining to
 form, 13 *see also* art beauty *and*
 natural beauty
Beckett, Samuel, 118, 125; *Endgame*,
 78–9, 153
becoming-purposeless, 99
Beethoven, Ludwig van, 45–6, 69, 96,
 113, 139, 145; Fantasia for piano
 op. 77, 113
Beißner, Friedrich, 27, 43
Benjamin, Walter, 22, 36, 66, 74, 76,
 109, 134, 146, 184; *Arcades Project*,
 24; 'On Language as Such and on
 the Language of Humans,' 182–3;
 on translation, 23; *Trauerspiel*, 24
Benn, Gottfried, 160
Berg, Alban, 64, 100; *Lulu*, 78
sich bergen, 169
Bernstein, J. M., 18, 87, 89, 143, 151
de Beistegui, Miguel, 14
biography, 123
Bloch, Ernst, 80
Bogel, Fredric V., 3, 18
Borchardt, Rudolf, 25, 71, 135,
 156–8; *Bacchic Epiphany*, 156
bourgeois art, 115–21
Brecht, Bertolt, 82; with Hans Eisler,
 Die Maßnahme, 146
Brown, Nicholas, 109
Bruns, Gerald L., 10, 17, 25, 134,
 145
brushwork, in painting, 147
Buck-Morss, Susan, 24
Bunyan, John, 117
Bürger, Peter, 141
Bussotti, Sylvano, 136

Cage, John, 136
canon of what is disallowed, 139
Cardew, Cornelius, 136
Castoriadis, Cornelius, 124, 167, 168
cave paintings, 85–6
Caygill, Howard, 205
Charter Acts (1830s), 210
chords: new, impossibility of, 140; pre-
 existence of, 140
chromatization, 68
civilization, and barbarism, dialectic
 of, 161
Clark, T. J., 9
close reading, 3, 207, 208, 217–18,
 222

closeness to, or distance from, material, 158
Cohen, Stephen, 3
collectively honed aesthetic forms, 165
color, 65, 70, 136
commodities, distribution of, 188
commodity, 194, 197, 203; absolute, 204
commodity form, 163–99; emancipation from, 188; use of term, 166
communication, 180–4, 205, 220; different meanings of, 185; nonconceptual nonobjective, 185
Communist Manifesto, 76
composing, distinct from pre-forming, 149
compositional, concept of, 135
concept, 24, 150, 185, 221; art's hostility to, 110; indispensable to language, 151; problem-concepts, 218; treatment of in essay form, 129; use of term, 85
conceptuality, 218–19; erasure of, 155
constellation, 21, 24–6, 130, 198, 217, 218
constitution of works, 178
content: and material, 135–42; as 'mere content,' 40; broad understanding of, 45; concept of, 136; form and, 27–61; propositional, 25, 55, 58, 136, 185; relation to material, 214; seeks linguistic form, 51; separate from form, 49; substantive, 25, 58, 59, 136, 185; unthinkable without form, 48
continuity, relationship with specificity, 180–1

craft, relation to technique, 148
craft production, pre-capitalist, 148
critical social consciousness, 186–7
critique, necessity of, 201
Culler, Jonathan, 202
culture industry, critique of, 115–21
Cunningham, David, with Nigel Mapp, *Adorno and Literature*, 11

Dada, 71
decomposed material, 148–9
deconstruction, 208
Defoe, Daniel, 117, 121
dequalifying, concept of, 68
diatonic scale, 138
Dichtung, use of term, 206
das Dichterische, see das spezifisch Dichterische
Dickens, Charles: *Bleak House*, 215; *Great Expectations*, 211
diesmal, 51–2, 53
differentiation, preservation of, 219
diminished seventh, 139, 141, 145
disenchantment, 180, 184, 193
disinterested delight, 174
dissonance, 152
distance, aesthetic, 126
division of intellectual labor, 221
dominant ninth in second inversion, 140
domination, 191; freedom from, 191
Don Quixote, 123
Duchamp, Marcel, *Fountain*, 179

Eagleton, Terry, 2
Eichendorff, Joseph Freiherr von 153–5, 161
eidos, 30
Eisler, Rudolf, 19

Eliot, George, *Middlemarch*, 209–10
Empson, William, 19
Engels, Friedrich, 83, 210, 215, 216
Enlightenment, 80, 153
equilibrium and disequilibrium in novel, 212
equivocation, 129, 130
erfüllen, 69
essay, 97, 221; as form, 128 (critical, 131); as hybrid product, 127; as sister of poetry, 129; respect for the nonidentical, 220; theory of, 127–31
ether, 100
exchange, 173, 197; abstraction and, 170–5
exchange value, 204
exchangeability, 170–1, 176
exegesis, non-necessity of, 36–7
experience, loss, sickness, necrosis or decay of, 123
experimentalism, 165
expression: failure of, 150; mediation with form, 67–70; objective, physiognomy of, 79; relation to form, 63–94; relation to mimesis, 89–94; relation to semblance, 91–2
Expression, 64
expressionism, 70; and surrealism, 74–81; literary, 70–4; musical, 70–4, 77
expressive, 64

false whole, 111
fascism, 146
fetish, 204–5, 217
Figal, Günter, 14
film, 118
Finlayson, James Gordon, 176, 181
de la Fontaine, Michel, 139

forces of production, 100, 143–4, 188; artist's embodiment of, 189; concept of, 134
foreign words, use of, 155–6, 160
form, 1–8, 201–22; adaptability of, 164; aesthetics of, 1; and content, 27–61; and expression, contradiction between, 87; and genre, 95–131; and material, 133–62 (literary manifestation of, 155–9); artistic (and commodity form, 163–99; emancipation of, 141); as deposit for complexity, 67; as dialectical concept, 206; as genre, 96; as imposition on expression, 65; as manifestation of technique, 192; as mark of domination, 191; as nexus of conceptual connections, 217; as opaque junction box, 209; as sedimentation of content, 22, 25, 28, 43–9, 95, 104, 105, 137, 178, 179, 198; as site of connection to world, 213; as the sense of nothing, 7, 214; complexities, tensions and contradictions of, 221–2; concept of, 1, 163–4, 179, 190, 198, 207, 208–9, 210 (ambiguity of, 9; capaciousness of, 216; necessity of, 111); distinct from accident, 160; distinct from content, 44; emerging from content, 164; emerging from social practice, 165; encapsulating artistic and social processes, 26; engagement of, 207–12; expansion of category of, 7; formation of, 6; grammatical, 41–2, 54; in literature, 1–2; in relation to expression, 25; independent of content, 48; Kantian view of, 65; law of, 36, 206 (in the

form *(continued)*
   novel, 121); linguistic, 51; mediation and, 175–80; mediation with expression, 67–70; musical, 45–6; no limit to, 216; not a concept, 218; of what is formed, 133; opens possibility of intervention in social world, 210; originates in content, 65; poetic, fundamental nature of, 41; priority over content, 50–1, 54, 55; pure, concept of, 122; readings of, 25; relation to expression, 63–94; relation to material, 25, 164; relation to particular works, 19; relation to processes of forming, 2; relation to subjectivity, 91; resists limits of conceptual thought, 218; synonyms for, 6; that of what is formed, 134; the wish of, 126; theory of, 160–2; unity with content, 43; varieties of, 5; wields a conceptual agency, 208 *see also* commodity form, hybrid forms *and* linguistic form
Form, 60, 64, 161
formal disruptions, 209
formalism, 1, 47, 162, 207, 208, 215; activist and normative, 2; strategic, 4 *see also* New Formalism
forming: act of, 146 (poetic, 153; subjective, 159, 161); relation to form, 60
Formprinzip, 59
forms: canon of, 94; genesis of, 102–11; literary, 115
Fowler, Alastair, 96
fragment, 160; nature of, 60
fragmentation, of individual œuvres, 106
fragments, titled as such, 160
freedom of the artist, 163
freedom of the will, 57, 194
Freud, Sigmund, 205
Früchtl, Josef, 85
fugue, 102–3, 104

Gadamer, Hans-Georg, 16
Gasché, Rodolphe, 13
Gaskell, Elizabeth, *North and South*, 213
das Gedichtete, 29, 34
Gehaüse, 67–8
Gehalt, substantive content, 22, 40, 43, 48, 58
geistig, 63; translation of, 32
generic categories, destabilization of, 98
Genette, Gérard, 105
genius, category of, 145
genre, 25, 215; and form, 95–131; subverting of, 109; unity of, 101
George, Stefan, 203
Gesamtkunstwerk, 100, 143
Gestalt, 59, 60
Gestaltqualität, 206
gesture, 84
Glockner, Hermann, 19
Goethe, Johann Wolfgang von: *Faust*, 69, *Iphigenie*, 158, 161
Goia, Dana, 18
grammatical form *see* form, grammatical

Hamacher, Werner, 17, 21, 84
Hamm, character in *Endgame*, 153
Hammer, Espen, 109, 178
Harkness, Margaret, 83
harmonies, previously unheard, 140
Hartman, Geoffrey, 4
von Haselberg, Peter, 60, 160

Index

Hegel, G. W. F., 19, 28, 43–4, 59, 96, 108, 109, 112, 114, 135; aesthetics of content, 48
Hegelianism, 10, 104, 122
Heidegger, Martin, 16, 19, 20, 27, 30, 33–8, 39, 53, 58, 111, 130, 151, 152; account of the artwork, 30–1; dismissal of aesthetics, 12–13; on the form of the thing, 28–33; rejection of the concept of form, 28, 29–30, 31, 160, 219; 'The Origin of the Work of Art,' 29–30, 219
Heimatkunst, 123
Helmling, Steven, 26
hiatus, 27, 40
von Hoffmannsthal, Hugo, 157
Hohendahl, Peter U., 86, 222
Hölderlin, Friedrich, 15, 25, 28, 33–8, 56–61, 69, 72, 112, 120, 130, 152, 153, 157, 158, 221; ordering technique of, 156; poetry of, relation to philosophy, 36; rhythm in, 47; writings of ('Andenken,' 39, 40; 'Brod und Wein,' 39, 40; 'Der Einzige,' 49–56; 'Hälfte des Lebens,' 42; 'Heimkunft,' 39; late hymns, 27, 59; 'Patmos,' 157)
Hölderlin Society, 33
Horace, 129
Horkheimer, Max, 115, 167
Hösle, Vittorio, 15–16, 17, 21
Hullor-Kentor, Robert, 115
Hunt, Erica, 18
hybrid forms, 165
hyle, 30

idealism, German, 10, 35
identity, 179, 190, 193; principle of, 51, 57
image, 152; as sign, 153
imitation: classes of, 105; theory of, 186
immediacy, 195
informal techniques, 98
Inhalt, 22, 40, 43, 47, 48 see also content, propositional
instrumental logic *see* reason, instrumental
intentio obliqua, 195
intentio recta, 194
intention, 57, 58, 61
interconnections, 129
interest, 210; self-reflexive pattern of, 209, 211
interpretative reason, 37
intersubjectivity, 94
intervention into society, 210, 212, 217
irony, as mode of critical inquiry, 207

Jameson, Fredric, 9, 23, 24, 76, 95, 106, 112, 134, 198, 215
Jarvis, Simon, 6, 11, 160, 195
Jephcott, Edmund, 23
Jones, Ewan James, 7

Kafka, Franz, 25, 66, 80, 81–5, 118; *The Castle*, 82; *The Trial*, 82, 84
Kant, Immanuel, 19, 28, 32, 49, 57, 105, 128, 166, 169, 174, 180, 196, 203; *Critique of Judgment*, 13, 47; on form, 46–7; theory of the sublime, 117
Kantianism, 11, 14, 46, 88, 89, 90, 93
Kaufman, Robert, 8, 11, 205
kingdom of ends, 203
Klee, Paul, 100, 101

knowledge, implicit, in artworks, 207
Konstruktion, 161
Kornbluh, Anna, 3, 207–12
Kraus, Karl, 70, 71

l'art pour l'art, 110
labor *see* abstract labor *and* social labor
language, 11, 127, 180–4; and poetry, 149–55; artwork as, 101; as poetic material, 185; as pure metonymy, 154; as purely acoustic phenomenon, 155; autonomy from logic or meaning, 207; becomes subject-like, 52–3; capacity to communicate, 158; conceptual, 184, 205; conceptual classificatory pole of, 151; division of, 153; dual character of, 57–8; function of, 42; in terms other than meaning, 134; literary, 205–6; mediation of, 150; music-like nature of, 49; musical, 152–3; non-linguistic, 182; of artworks, 185 (thingly, 185); of communication, 205–6; of nonlinguistic artworks, 219; of poetry, 72, 179, 219 (lyric, 201, 202–3); of things, 183; sign character of, 137, 152, 202 (in lyric, 205); signifying, 182, 185; 'soundless voice' of, 53; stands for itself, 203; transformation of, 153; unity of, 41 *see also* artworks, resemblance to language *and* form, linguistic
language-like character of art, 181–2
Lee, Julia Sun-Joo, 213
Leighton, Angela, 7, 214
Lesjak, Carolyn, 2
Levine, Caroline, *Forms*, 4–5, 7, 212–16

Levine, George, 2
Levinson, Marjorie, 2, 6, 7, 9
life, should imitate art, 186, 188, 199
Ligeti, György Sándor, 140; *Atmosphères*, 102
lightheartedness in art, 99
linguistic form, 39–43; relation to poetic form, 28
linguistic sign, arbitrariness of, 154
linguistic turn, 57–8
literalness, 23
literature: affinity with society, 212; intervenes into the world, 210; representative of the world, 212–13; thinking ways of, 221; value judgments of, 11
Livingstone, Rodney, 22, 23
Lohoff, Ernst, 175
longing, 186, 187
Lukács, György, 80, 127, 129
Lypp, Bernhard, 58
lyric, 201–22; as dramatic monologue, 202; as expression of social antagonism, 201
lyric 'I,' 219–20

Macherey, Pierre, 9
Mahler, Gustav, 68
making *see* artistic making
Mann, Thomas, 19
Martin, Stewart, 204, 205
Marx, Karl, 167, 168, 194, 210, 216; *Capital*, 167, 194; *Toward a Critique of Political Economy*, 166
Marxian critical aesthetics, 8–9
Marxism, 9, 10, 11, 80, 83, 100, 210
mass culture, 117, 118
material, 164, 188, 198, 207; anarchic resistance of, 145; and content,

135–42; concept of, 137–8; form and, 133–62; making choices of, 137; mastery of, 190; responsiveness to, 189; working of, 189, 197 *see also* decomposed material
McKeon, Michael, 117–18, 120–1
McLaughlin, Kevin, 22
means, distinct from technique, 147
means of production, 168; concentration of, 167
mediation, 77–8, 90, 94, 100, 107, 108, 112, 135, 141, 144, 178, 186, 187, 195, 205, 206, 208, 212; and form, 175–80; by narrator, 209; of art and nature, 166; of form and expression, 67–70; of language, 150, 202; of range of available material, 137–8; of society, through commodity exchange, 171
metaphor, 14
metaphysical passivity, 60
metaphysics, immanent critique of, 194–5, 197
meter, poetic, 15, 137, 147; as social rhythm, 5–6
métier, artistic *see* artistic *métier*
microtonal tunings, 140
middle-voiced attunement, 199, 222; of the artist, 197, 199
mimesis, 55, 67, 85–9, 193, 194, 220; relation to expression, 89–94; relation to technique, 192
minor ninth, 140
Mitchell, W. J. T., 4, 8
Modern Language Quarterly, 'Reading for Form,' 2
modernism, 74, 109, 151, 178
modes of production, 148
money, 209–10

montage, 75, 76–7, 139
Mörchen, Hermann, 34
Morgenstern, Christian, 136
Mörike, Eduard, 'Mousetrap Rhyme,' 153
Morphogenesis, 140
music, 9, 11, 25, 43, 45–6, 67–8, 73, 98, 113, 135–6, 137, 138–41, 143, 148, 156, 157; aesthetics of, 9–10; as sedimented spirit, 104; in language, 49, 152–3; manifesto for, 87; new, 118
musique informelle, use of term, 87

narration: impossibility of, 122; of war stories, 123
narrative, 216; first-person, 212
narrative technique, agency of, 211
narrator, 209, 214; position of, 122, 125
natural beauty, 189–94
nature: experience of, 196; incorporation of, into language, 154; separation of subject from, 57
naturhaft, use of term, 139
Naturwüchsigkeit, 193
necessity, 187; relation to contingency, 97
New Criticism, 1
New Formalism, 2–3, 4, 6, 7, 18, 207, 216–17; competing with social theorists, 215; moving beyond, 212–16
New Historicism, 1, 2, 3, 9
Nicholsen, Shierry Weber, 154, 155
nominalism, 25, 97, 111–15
nonidentical, 220; concept of, 218
non-signification, 183
Norton, Charles Eliot, 213

Novalis (Georg Philipp Friedrich Freiherr von Hardenberg), 160
novel, 97, 98, 114, 116, 117–18, 147, 165, 210, 212; analyzing complexity of social experience, 215; as form, 121–7; capitulation of, 126; claim to historicity, 118, 121; closure of, a beginning, 214; disintegration of, as form, 124; formlessness of, 121; genesis of, 122–3; paradoxical form, 127; realist, 208, 216; similar to reportage, 125; specificity of, 120
Nowell Smith, David, 12–13, 16, 151, 152

object: priority of, 194–9; relation to subject, 194–5
objectivity, 84, 92, 93, 123, 190, 191, 193, 201, 203
objects, category of, falsity of, 198
O'Connor, Brian, 194
oder, 40
Odysseus, 19, 23
ontological distress, 213
orchestration, 147
order, destruction of, 149
organic composition of capital, 167
organic wholeness of artworks, 181
outdated material, 139

Paddison, Max, 9–10, 25, 138
painting, 122
parataxis, 39–43, 49–56, 57, 58, 101, 130, 136, 221; use of term, 131
particularity: of artworks, 172, 173, 174, 176, 182, 203; sensuous, 187, 188
periods, logical position of, 56–7
perspective, in painting, 142

philia, 22
philology, 19–23; critical, 20
philosophical and philological knowledge, distinct, 34
philosophical communication, avoidance of, 34
philosophy, 127; necessity of, 35; task of, in relation to literature, 37–8
photography, 122
Pindar, 156
Plass, Ulrich, 11, 154, 155
poems, autonomous discursive elements of, 109
poetic form, relation to content, 27–61
poetic material, intertwined with apparatus of domination, 133
poetic transformation of language, 72
poetics, 12–19, 29; definition of, 18; objective, 17; of the wrong state of things, 26; use of term, 16, 17 *see also* form, poetic
poetry, 163, 179, 185, 217; absolute, 158; affinity with speculative thinking, 96; and language, 149–55; and reconciliation, 184–9; as philology, 17; as pragmatics, 52; contamination of, with thought, 158; materiality of, 134
political action, 212
Pollock, Jackson, *Full Fathom Five*, 151
polyphony, 102, 142
Porter, James I., 20
pre-artistic material, 136
pre-forming, 149, 190; of poetic material, 134
pre-ordained schemata, 96
productivity, social, 168
prose, 96
prose character of modern art, 105

prose character of the novel, 118–20
Proust, Marcel, 15, 109, 118, 125, 165
punctuation, 52–3, 54, 56–7, 136
purposelessness, 105, 180, 181
purposiveness, 101, 180–4; without purpose, 46, 49, 105, 166, 181, 182
Pyle, Forest, 15, 17

rationality, 86, 92, 143, 165; subjective, 161
Rauschen, 154–5
real abstraction, 173
realism, 79–80, 83, 85, 210; novelistic, 125
reality, 205; empirical, 186 (rejection of, 180); of artworks, 187; to come, 180
reason, instrumental, 177, 181, 186, 197, 218, 222; stepping outside of, 180
received tradition, negation of, 138
reconciliation, 80, 126, 192; poetry and, 184–9
reframing, 179
reification, 32, 76, 118, 124, 203
Reihen, translation of, 61
relations of production, 144; critique of, 189
representation, problem of, 58
responsiveness to material, 189
restorationist, use of term, 130
rhythm, 152
Rilke, Rainer Maria, 153
Ritsert, Jürgen, 218
Romanticism, 171, 203
Rorty, Richard, 58
Rose, Gillian, 18, 108, 111, 195

satire, as mode of critical inquiry, 207

de Saussure, Ferdinand, 154
Schein, 23
Schlegel, Karl Wilhelm Friedrich, 160
Schönberg, Arnold, 43, 64, 67–8, 73, 74, 118; *Die glückliche Hand*, 75; *Moses und Aron*, 142; piano pieces op 11, 146; 'Verklärte Nacht,' 140
Schumann, Robert, settings of Eichendorff texts, 161
Schwitters, Kurt, 136
Scott, Clive, 52
scream, 74
sculpture, 98
secularization, 180, 184
sedimentation, concept of, 104
self-alienation, 162
self-instantiation, 15
self-reflexive pattern, 211
semblance, 23, 38, 117, 145, 187, 190, 195, 205; relation to expression, 91–2
sense, 57; primacy of, 158
sensible, relation to supersensible, 14
seriousness in art, 99
sign, dominance over image, 58
signification, 72, 84, 152, 153, 182 *see also* non-signification
Simon, David, 215
Singh, Surti, 64
singing voices, sacrality of, 204
sitting down with a good book, 123
social labor, 166–70, 176; artwork as, 205; not identical with commodity-producing labor, 168, 169
socialist realism, 79
sociality, 185; embodied in artworks, 177; in the commodity form, 167; of art, 192
society, 201–22

Sohn-Rethel, Alfred, 169, 173
sonata, 137, 165; use of term, 72
sounds, 136; previously unheard combinations of, 140
specificity, relationship with continuity, 180–1
das spezifisch Dichterische, 29
spirit, 43, 63, 89, 99, 104, 112, 114, 169, 186, 221; absolute, 60; as opposed to nature, 193; capacity for reconciliation, 192–3; condition of, 138; evil, 50, 51; identity with itself, 51; igniting of, 193; objective, theory of, 44
spiritualization, 63–4
Sprachgefälle, 154
Sprachkunstwerk, 150, 151
Staiger, Emil, 34
standardization and ever-sameness, 123
Stifter, Adalbert, 123
Strauss, Richard, 146; *Heldenleben*, 146
structure, of artwork, distinct from form, 38
stuttered sound, 71
style, 93, 94
style galant, 10
subject, ceases to be wholly subject, 155
subjective, and objective, relation between, 18
subjective intention, irrelevance of, 37
subjective paradox of art, 86, 87
subjective power to form, 90
subjective will, 88
subjectivism, 80
subjectivity, 159, 162, 163, 189–90, 191, 193, 196, 201, 202, 219; absolute, 81; constitutive, spell of, 108; estranged, 81; related to form, 91

sublimation, 188, 205
subsumption, formal and real, 188
success of artwork *see* artwork, success of
superstructure, cultural, 100
surplus, production of, 167
surrealism, 66, 139; and expressionism, 74–81; anti-organic nature of, 75; tendency to fragmentation, 75–6
Swinburne, Algernon Charles, 153
symbol, 110
sympathy, economy of, 210
synthesis, 51; relation to language, 56
system totality, 181
Szondi, Peter, 20, 33

τέχνη, 142
technique, 119, 142, 143–6, 172; as category, 145; as impulse to expression, 159; as interface between material and expression, 156; as means of working material, 148; as part of repertoire of material, 157; as something transferable, 157; concept of, 66; definition of, 143; historicity of, 149; in industrial production, 181; in relation to form, 98; literary, 149, 155; relation to material and form, 157; relation to mimesis, 192 *see also* informal techniques
technology, 144, 188; in industrial production, 148; relation of art to, 173
Theile, Verena, 2; and Linda Tredennick, *New Formalisms and Literary Theory*, 7
thing-character of the work, 33
thingness of the thing, 30
Thomistic theology, 111

timbre, 140
Tom Jones, 124
tonality, elimination of, 138
tools, relationship to, 172
totality of beings, 30
tragedy, 105, 165
tragic, decay of, 99
Trakl, Georg, 72–3, 152, 206
transcendental subject, Kantian, 79
translation, as form, 22
transposing, 179
Tredennick, Linda, 2
triad, 138
truth, 152; of art, 19, 55 (begins to waver, 205); of poetry, 37–8, 59; relation to form, 60
twelve-tone composition, 64, 68, 118, 138–9, 148–9

ugly, the, 101
uniqueness in artworks, 95
unity, 193; of artworks, 180; of form, 113 (and content, 122, 218; and material, 147); of political forms, 214; of sign and image, 155; of the word, 130; organic, of artworks, 181
universal, 93–4, 112; relation to particular, 25, 106, 107–11, 113
universality, 182
use value, demise of, 204
utopia, depiction of, 185

Valéry, Paul, 25, 135, 155, 158, 159
value *see* abstract value, exchange value, literature, value judgments of, *and* use value

value, critique of, 175
value form: dismantling the power of, 221; use of term, 166
van den Bergh, Gerhard, 27, 34
Varèse, Edgard, *Ionisation*, 102
Vendler, Helen, 8
sich verfransen, 97, 108
Vergeistigung, translation of, 63
vertreten, 23
vigilant understanding, 221
voice, distinct from meaning, 54

Wagner, Richard, 32, 67, 68, 100, 113, 140; *Tristan und Isolde*, 69
Was bleibet, 40
Watt, Ian, 117, 121
Weber, Carl Maria von, *Der Freischütz*, 141
Webern, Anton, 147
weichlich, 69
'what is form,' 7
will, subjective *see* subjective will
Wilson, William Julius, 215
Wire, The, 214–15
Wolf, Christian, 136
Wolfson, Susan, 207, 208; *Formal Charges*, 2–3
Wolin, Richard, 76, 85
Wolken, 153–4
Wood, Michael, 19
workplace, of artworks, 172
Wortgefälle, 154
writing, not open to decoding, 101
wrong state of things, 26, 187, 206

Zola, Émile, 83

www.ingramcontent.com/pod-product-compliance
Lightning Source LLC
Chambersburg PA
CBHW020641230426
43665CB00008B/270